Theodicy and Eschatology

Edited by Bruce Barber and David Neville

The Task of Theology Today Series is a publication of the Australian Theological Forum. Each volume is a collection of essays emanating from a colloquium organised by the Forum. The essays address a particular theological theme and draw upon the expertise of various branches of theology in this endeavour, including biblical scholars, systematic and philosophical theologians.

Series Editor: Hilary D Regan

ATF Press
Adelaide

Task of Theology Today Series

1. *The Task of Theology Today: Dogmas and Doctrines*, edited by Victor C Pfitzner and Hilary D Regan (Adelaide: ATF, 1998)
2. *Starting with the Spirit*, edited by Stephen Pickard and Gordon Preece (Adelaide: ATF, 2001)
3. *Sin and Salvation*, edited by Duncan Reid and Mark Worthing (Adelaide: ATF, 2003).

Theodicy and Eschatology

edited by Bruce Barber and David Neville

ATF Press
Adelaide

First published 2005

National Library of Australia
Cataloguing-in-Publication data

Theodicy and Eschatology
Includes index
ISBN 1 920691 48 0

1. Theodicy. 2. Eschatology. I. Barber, Bruce L.
II. Neville, David, 1958- .

214

Published by
ATF Press
An imprint of the Australian Theological Forum
P O Box 504
Hindmarsh
SA 5007
ABN 68 314 074 034
www.atfpress.com

Cover design and printed by Openbook Print, Adelaide, Australia

Contents

Abbreviations

General Abbreviations

ANE	Ancient near east(ern)
BCE	Before the Common Era (= BC)
CE	Common Era (= AD)
c	*circa* (about, approximately)
cf	*confer* (compare)
chap(s)	chapter(s)
ed(s)	edition; editor(s)
eg	*exempli gratia* (for example)
esp	especially
ET	English Translation
n	note
nd	no date
NRSV	New Revised Standard Version
NT	New Testament
OT	Old Testament
P	Papyrus
p or pp	page or pages
par(s)	parallel(s) in one or both of the other synoptic gospels
rev	revised
RSV	Revised Standard Version
trans.	translator or translated by
vol(s)	volume(s)
vs	versus
WCC	World Council of Churches

Books of the Bible

Gen	Genesis
Exod	Exodus
Lev	Leviticus
Num	Numbers
Deut	Deuteronomy
1–2 Sam	1–2 Samuel
1–2 Chr	1–2 Chronicles

1-2 Kgs	1-2 Kings
Prov	Proverbs
Qoh	Qoheleth (Ecclesiastes)
Isa	Isaiah
Jer	Jeremiah
Ezek	Ezekiel
Dan	Daniel
Hos	Hosea
Mic	Micah
Hab	Habakkuk
Zech	Zechariah
Mal	Malachi
1–2 Macc	1–2 Maccabees
Matt	Matthew
Rom	Romans
1–2 Cor	1–2 Corinthians
Gal	Galatians
Eph	Ephesians
Phil	Philippians
Col	Colossians
1–2 Thess	1–2 Thessalonians
1–2 Tim	1–2 Timothy
Heb	Hebrews
Jas	James
1–2 Pet	1–2 Peter
Rev	Revelation

Periodicals, Reference Works and Series

AB	Anchor Bible
ABD	David Noel Freedman (ed), *Anchor Bible Dictionary*, 6 vols (New York: Doubleday, 1992).
ABRL	Anchor Bible Reference Library
AH	Iraneus, *Against Heresies*
BETL	Bibliotheca Ephemeridum Theologicarum Lovaniensium
CD	Karl Barth, *Church Dogmatics* (1956–1975).
CTNS/VO	Center for Theology and the Natural Sciences/Vatican Observatory series
IRT	Issues in Religion and Theology
JBL	*Journal of Biblical Literature*

JSNT	*Journal for the Study of the New Testament*
JTS	*Journal of Theological Studies*
MQR	*Mennonite Quarterly Review*
NHL	*Nag Hammadi Library*
OBO	Orbis Biblicus et Orientalis
OTL	Old Testament Library
SJT	*Scottish Journal of Theology*
TTT	Task of Theology Today
WBC	Word Biblical Commentary

Other Abbreviations

ATF	Australian Theological Forum
CTNS	Center for Theology and the Natural Sciences

Introduction

Bruce Barber and David Neville

The essays in this volume were first presented and discussed at the fourth Task of Theology Today colloquium organised and hosted by the Australian Theological Forum in Melbourne early in May 2003.[1] The theme, 'Theodicy and Eschatology', was addressed from a variety of perspectives, including biblical, historical, theological and scientific viewpoints.

Neither 'theodicy' nor 'eschatology' belongs among the traditional theological *loci* of the Christian tradition. Leibniz seems to have coined the term 'theodicy' in the title of his 1710 work, *Essais de théodicée sur la bonté de Dieu, la liberté de l'homme, et l'origine du mal*.[2] As for the term 'eschatology', it was probably introduced into theological discourse by Philipp Heinrich Friedlieb in his 1644 *Dogmatics*.[3] Yet each term names a topic of concern reaching back to the Hebraic and classical Greek traditions.

What is the perceived problem that the term 'theodicy' names? Briefly stated, the problem arises from belief in God coupled with the shared experience of suffering and evil; if this world is God's creation, what explains both the reality of evil and the common experience of

---

1.   Three previous colloquia were held: in Brisbane (July 1997), Canberra (Easter 1999) and Adelaide (September 2001). The volumes from these gatherings have been published as *The Task of Theology Today: Dogmas and Doctrines*, edited by Victor C Pfitzner and Hilary D Regan (Adelaide/Edinburgh/Grand Rapids: ATF/T&T Clark/Eerdmans, 1998/199); *Starting with the Spirit*, edited by Stephen Pickard and Gordon Preece (Adelaide: ATF, 2001); *Sin and Salvation*, edited by Duncan Reid and Mark Worthing (Adelaide: ATF, 2003).

2.   Gottfried Wilhelm Leibniz, *Theodicy: Essays on the Goodness of God, the Freedom of Man and the Origin of Evil*, translated by EM Huggard (London: Routledge & Kegan Paul, 1952).

3.   See Gerhard Sauter, *Eschatological Rationality: Theological Issues in Focus* (Grand Rapids: Baker Books, 1996), 136. For a recent assessment of the significance of eschatology for the church's faith and theology, see Carl E Braaten and Robert W Jenson (eds), *The Last Things: Biblical and Theological Perspectives on Eschatology* (Grand Rapids: Eerdmans, 2002).

suffering? Taken alone, neither evil nor the experience of suffering is philosophically problematic. For non-theists, evil and suffering make life miserable but do not entail an intellectual conundrum. For theists, however, the experiences of suffering and evil call into question either the goodness or omnipotence of God.[4] Indeed, it is this disturbing dimension of human existence that post-enlightenment persons regard as the most significant obstacle to belief and trust in God.

While it is not so difficult to identify the problem of theodicy, it is much more challenging to provide an adequate survey of the various solutions to this problem. This task cannot be undertaken here, but it is perhaps worth noting that four influential types of theodicies are the Augustinian, Irenaean, free-will defence and process varieties. Equally important is the view advocated by various post-liberal theologians that theodicy has no legitimate place within *theological* discourse.[5]

'Eschatology' refers to 'last things' and is associated with concepts such as God's promised future, hope and the end (both *terminus* and *telos*) of history. Yet 'eschatology' is a perturbing topic because it is

---

4.   While not every theistic position conceives of its god(s) as necessarily good or all-powerful, traditional Jewish, Christian and Islamic theologies posit one god who is both good and omnicompetent.

5.   For various perspectives on theodicy, see Marilyn Adams and Robert Adams (eds), *The Problem of Evil* (Oxford: Oxford University Press, 1990); Marilyn McCord Adams, *Horrendous Evils and the Goodness of God* (Ithaca, NY: Cornell University Press; Melbourne: Melbourne University Press, 1999); Robert Farrar Capon, *The Third Peacock: The Problem of God and Evil*, rev ed (San Francisco: Harper & Row, 1986); James L Crenshaw (ed), *Theodicy in the Old Testament* (London: SPCK; Philadelphia: Fortress Press, 1983); Stephen T Davis (ed), *Encountering Evil: Live Options in Theodicy* (Atlanta: John Knox Press, 1981); Stanley Hauerwas, *Naming the Silences: God, Medicine, and the Problem of Suffering* (Grand Rapids: Eerdmans, 1990); John Hick, *Evil and the God of Love*, 2nd ed (New York: Harper and Row, 1978); Tyron L Inbody, *The Transforming God: An Interpretation of Suffering and Evil* (Louisville: Westminster John Knox Press, 1997); Alvin Plantinga, *God, Freedom, and Evil* (New York: Harper and Row, 1974); Hans Schwarz, *Evil: A Historical and Theological Perspective* (Minneapolis: Augsburg Fortress, 1995); Kenneth Surin, *Theology and the Problem of Evil* (Oxford: Basil Blackwell, 1986); Terrence W Tilley, *The Evils of Theodicy* (Washington, DC: Georgetown University Press, 1991); John E Thiel, *God, Evil, and Innocent Suffering: A Theological Reflection* (New York: Crossroad, 2002); and Barry L Whitney, *What are They Saying About God and Evil?* (New York/Mahwah, NJ: Paulist Press, 1989).

both speculative and ambiguous; it consists of speculation about what lies outside (or ahead of) human experience, and it signifies such different things to different people. However, eschatology of one kind or another is indispensable to most types of theodicy. For example, in *Jubilate: Theology in Praise*, Daniel Hardy and David Ford articulate a traditional theological stance on the relation between theodicy and eschatology. After expressing agreement with those who defend God's goodness in the face of evil and suffering on the basis of God's respect for human freedom (the traditional free-will defence), they write:

> We also agree with the mainstream tradition in seeing theodicy inseparable from eschatology: that is, that it is conceivable for God to be able to bring out of even the horrors of our history a quality of life, a salvation, that makes it all worthwhile even to those who have suffered most.[6]

In a number of ways, this volume is closely related to the previous volume in this series, *Sin and Salvation*.[7] Any Christian theodicy must address the concept of sin, and the theological concepts of eschatology and salvation overlap considerably. In *Sin and Salvation*, 'Evil and the Evil One' is the title of the first essay by Hans Schwarz, and the theme of eschatology features in a number of essays. There are also material connections between these two books. For example, both interrelate theological and scientific perspectives. Indeed, Bob Russell's essay in this book is part of a larger research project, an earlier part of which appeared in the previous volume. There are also points of contact between Brendan Byrne's paper on Paul in the earlier collection and Heather Thomson's reflections on atonement in this book. In short, these two volumes complement each other.

With respect to the biblical studies in this collection, one participant at the conference observed that to address the topic of theodicy and eschatology without examining the contribution of the apostle Paul

---

6.   Daniel W Hardy and David F Ford, *Jubilate: Theology in Praise* (London: Darton, Longman and Todd, 1984). In the USA this book was published as *Praising and Knowing God* (Philadelphia: Westminster Press, 1985).

7.   Duncan Reid and Mark Worthing (eds), *Sin and Salvation*, TTT III (Adelaide: ATF Press, 2003).

was an oversight. This was an understandable comment,[8] but perhaps it is worth noting that the only NT study in *Sin and Salvation* dealt with a Pauline theme. Furthermore, in a number of respects, not least in relation to how God deals with evil, Mark's Gospel is close to Paul (especially in his Corinthian correspondence).[9]

Knowing how best to organise the various essays in this collection proved to be difficult, so it was eventually decided to adopt a broadly historical sequence. In his survey of OT resources for reflecting on the theme of theodicy and eschatology Dominican Friar, Mark O'Brien, draws attention to the diversity of viewpoints within the Bible and its open-ended nature, thereby emphasising that one cannot go to the Bible for *the* answer to the problems of evil and suffering. He then discusses two scholarly perspectives on ancient Hebrew explanations for evil and suffering: (1) that God rewards goodness and punishes evil (reward/retribution); and (2) that actions have built-in consequences (act-consequence). Neither view captures the complexity of thought found in the Hebrew Bible, however, especially in Job and Qoheleth (Ecclesiastes), both of which have 'theodicy' as a central concern. O'Brien offers suggestive observations on these perplexing writings and notes the importance of creation for both their respective theological constructions. This in turn leads him to explore the relevance of the creation-history nexus in OT traditions. In brief, despite the presence of evil, creation reveals God's purpose; history allows for the divine purpose to be realised; and eschatological hope permits the present, however distressing, to be interpreted as a mean-ingful step towards the realisation of God's purpose.

---

8.   Cf Lisa Sowle Cahill, 'Kingdom and Cross: Christian Moral Community and the Problem of Suffering', *Interpretation* 50/2 (April 1996): 162: 'A theology of suffering, of God's compassion, and of salvation—not only from but also in and through—suffering could obviously take its point of departure in the passion narratives and resurrection accounts of the Gospels. But it is in the letters of Paul that the paradox of cross and resurrection is used most directly to focus the accountability of Christian faith to the limit experiences of grief, sorrow, and travail.'

9.   See C Clifton Black, 'Christ Crucified in Paul and in Mark: Reflections on an Intracanonical Conversation', in Eugene H Lovering, Jr, and Jerry L Sumney (eds), *Theology and Ethics in Paul and His Interpreters* (Nashville: Abingdon Press, 1996), 184–206.

In the first of two NT studies focusing on particular gospels, David Neville probes Mark's crucifixion narrative for insights into how early Christians maintained faith in the goodness and power of God despite their continued experience of evil and suffering decades after the death and resurrection of Jesus. He suggests that Mark's response to the brutality that overwhelmed Jesus was to reinterpret the presence and power of God in light of Jesus' suffering and death. This entailed both christological innovation (reversing traditional ideas of messiahship) and the creative use of Jewish scripture (intertextuality). While Mark's 'theodicy' may not be philosophically satisfying, it does offer insights for those prepared either to begin or to continue along the rough road of discipleship.

Dorothy Lee's discussion of theodicy and eschatology in the Gospel of John focuses on theological implications of what the fourth gospel has to say about sin and evil, especially from the perspective of John's distinctive eschatology. After exploring the symbolism of darkness and light, the principal characterisation of evil and goodness within the fourth gospel, Lee expounds the Johannine understanding of sin and evil. She then considers John's eschatology, which she terms 'an eschatology of presence', arguing that within this narrative 'the signs of sin and evil are transformed eschatologically to become symbols of life'. She also wrestles with three passages that would seem to imply a Johannine theodicy of sorts, but contends that even in these passages theodicy is subservient to eschatology. 'Evil and suffering', she writes, 'are interpreted from the perspective of their final defeat in Christ.'

The essay by Kim Power, 'Making Excuses for God: Theodicy and Eschatology in the Patristic Era', provides a bridge between the biblical and systematic theological essays. She begins by situating Christianity in the context of its religious and pagan dialogue partners. After summarising Gnostic thought, she engages in a sustained examination of responses to Gnosticism by Irenaeus and Augustine, the latter especially in dialogue with Manicheism. In her view, the primacy of grace, predestination and eschatology set the context for considering the contribution of the patristic traditions for both formulating and resolving the theodicy question.

Christiaan Mostert's wide-ranging essay begins with observations on the hazardous nature of any discussion concerning evil, suffering and theodicy. He then takes soundings of the major points in the discussion of the problem among philosophers and philosophical

Augustine thought it might be evil to discuss evil itself.

theologians but concludes that a Christian theodicy is different because it is embodied in a narrative. Mostert explores the main features of this Christian narrative in its christological and trinitarian character, before developing in more detail the eschatological nature of this narrative alluded to in this rehearsal. His essay ends by noting the importance of two continuing conversations: 'the need to bring this narrative about the cosmos and human existence into connection with cosmological thinking about the likely future of the universe and the need to enter into dialogue with the pervasive mood about universal narratives and final endings'.

The competence required to participate intelligently, intelligibly and (perhaps most demanding) amicably in the 'theology and science' debate is of the highest order. Robert Russell has been at the forefront of this conversation for over two decades, especially since founding the Center for Theology and the Natural Sciences (CTNS) in 1981. Despite the history of frequent hostility between theology and science, especially since the publication of *The Origin of Species* by Charles Darwin in 1859, Russell is committed to a stance of 'creative mutual interaction' between theologians and scientists.

For Russell, one major concern is the problem of 'eschatology and cosmology'. In short, if big-bang cosmology is correct, the long-term future of the universe, and thus life as we know it, is destined for annihilation either by 'freezing' (more likely) or 'frying' (less likely). These scenarios pose significant, perhaps insurmountable, challenges to Christian eschatology, which envisages God's preservation and/or transformation of the created order. In this volume, Russell tackles a related concern: How should theology confront the problem of 'natural theodicy' posed by evolutionary biology, in which suffering, death and ` extinction are integral to the evolutionary process? As Russell asks, 'How can we believe in the goodness and power of the God who creates life through the very processes of evolution that constitutively involve natural evil?'

Russell confronts these challenges by proposing a development or refinement of Christian eschatology: 'My overall argument is that diverse areas in contemporary theology drive us to construct an eschatology that entails the transformation of the universe into a "new creation" and addresses the challenges of both natural evil and big-bang cosmology.' Taking as his starting point a theistic evolutionary stance, Russell recommends a model of divine action that is both noninterventionist and objective. As a result, however, the problem of theodicy is even more pressing because such a model of divine action is unable to sidestep the difficulty of explaining how God's goodness is compatible with an evolutionary model of creation. In short, Russell grapples seriously and creatively with one of the most existentially difficult questions imaginable. Along the way, he retrieves and interweaves insights from several influential figures in the Christian tradition (Irenaeus, Augustine, Schleiermacher, Reinhold Niebuhr and John Hick) as well as more recent conversation partners in theology and science. Important features of Russell's movement towards an evolutionary natural theodicy are the theological concept of *kenosis* and an eschatology of new creation modelled on the bodily resurrection of Jesus. In addition, he dares to hope that his theological proposals may open up new perspectives or insights in science.

Heather Thomson begins her essay, '"(I Can't Get No) Satisfaction": Eschatology, Theodicy and Our Sacred Power', by noting that God is often the scapegoat for our failure to use sacred power responsibly. From the perspective of theological anthropology, she probes the Christian doctrine of atonement to evaluate the picture of God that emerges. For Thomson, a Christian response to the theodicy question is inextricably linked to soteriology, in particular the question whether salvation is achieved by satisfying God's demand for vengeance. As she writes, 'The interpretation of Jesus' violent death is crucial to our understanding of God and the questions theodicy raises.'

An aspect of Thomson's concern is to explore social and ethical dimensions of atonement theories, which she does by bringing Barth's doctrine of atonement into conversation with the work of Robert Hamerton-Kelly, whose interpretation of Jesus' death on the cross is indebted to the hermeneutical theory of René Girard. Discussion of the three Girardian themes of the nature of desire, social causes of violence and the relation of violence to religion leads Thomson to reflect on the key Pauline statement in Rom 8:32 and the related interpretation of the cross as sacrifice. Following Hamerton-Kelly, she contends that Paul reversed the scapegoat image of redemption to demonstrate that the primary saving effect of the cross is the disclosure and deconstruction of religious violence, not a sacrificial transaction to appease divine wrath. She concludes by defending Girard against George Hunsinger's critique that Girard offers a 'Pelagian' solution to an 'Augustinian' problem; rather, she contends that even Augustine did not view the righteousness of God as requiring violence and vengeance. As a result, Barth's doctrine of atonement needs correcting along the lines of Girard and Augustine.

In 'Creation and Eschatology', Roland Chia sketches a framework within which reflection on the relationship between creation and eschatology might be undertaken. The first requirement, he contends, is to expound the meaning and purpose of creation, not as established by empirical observation of the world but as an article of faith, with its distinctive feature of *creatio ex nihilo*. This leads Chia to consider the relationship between the fall and creation, specifically whether the world as we know it is the world God intended. To answer this question in the negative requires reflection on the connection between creation, redemption and eschatology. Chia proceeds primarily by employing the thought of one ancient theologian, Irenaeus, and one modern theologian, Karl Barth. He concludes by reflecting on the continuities and discontinuities between this world and the world to come, where his focus is on the relationship between time and eternity and the bodily resurrection of the dead. His conclusion is that neither scientific cosmologies nor evolutionary science, but only a theological reading, can adequately explicate the relationship between creation and eschatology.

To those formed by Western philosophical, religious and cultural presuppositions, Archbishop Stylianos offers a divergent, even discomforting, perspective on the matter of theodicy. For Orthodoxy, all thinking about God, humanity and the nature of evil must pass through the theological prism of who God has shown Godself to be in creation and redemption. This 'thinking God's thoughts after God' throws a different light on the anthropocentric status of the form of the problem presumed in much Western thought. For example, his quotation of the statement, 'In the twentieth century, cancer has sent many people to heaven', was met by considerable mystification and even offence by some conference participants. For this reason, a close reading of his paper is salutary.

This volume concludes with a brief Afterword by Bruce Barber in which he explores a consideration of theodicy identified above but not taken up in the essays that follow, namely, that of theodicy from a post-liberal perspective.

In the Western world, terrorist attacks have forced us to reassess our thinking on evil and suffering.[10] But elsewhere in the world, and even in the West, suffering caused by poverty, hunger, injustice and violence is often part-and-parcel of everyday life. The fact that the Western world is considered responsible for at least some of this suffering and could certainly do more to alleviate it should sharpen our resolve not only to think carefully about the problem(s) of theodicy but to live and behave in ways that demonstrate solidarity with those who do suffer and contribute to the reduction of human misery.

---

10. So, too, has the devastation and massive loss of life caused by the tsunami that ravaged parts of South-East Asia on 26 December 2004, as this book was going to press.

Theodicy and Eschatology:
Old Testament Considerations

Mark O'Brien OP

1. Introduction

To speak about the Bible, whether it is Old Testament or New Testament, is to speak about faith. There is the faith of those who produced the Bible; there is the faith of those who believe in the Bible. The faith of believers can have a powerful effect on others—for good but also, at times, for ill. One can become so absorbed in this 'world' of faith as to assume that those outside it have no faith at all. This would be an unfortunate mistake. To an outsider, a practitioner of this faith can give the impression that it is secret business, for initiates only. This would be a great pity.

As a countermeasure, it is good to remind oneself that faith is a basic component of human life, as are hope and love. Without them it is difficult to see how human beings can form what we call 'relationships'. We are social animals; relationships are essential to our humanity. Faith, hope and love help to forge a bond with others that can hold firm even in the darkest times. As Paul says in 1 Corinthians 13:13 'faith, hope, and love abide, these three, and the greatest of these is love'. It is not a question of *whether* I have faith but *what kind* of faith do I have? Even an atheist is a believer, because God's non-existence can no more be proved than God's existence. An atheist believes there is no God. Whether it is atheistic or theistic, faith is a response to human experience, an interpretation of it. Normally, it will find verbal expression in a 'confession of faith', which may take the form of a story, a song, or a manifesto. For most people in history, their interpretation of experience has led to some form of theism; for others it has led to a variety of non-theistic faiths.

Evil, suffering and death are the areas where human beings feel most powerless and needy. When confronted by these unwelcome intruders, a theist will instinctively turn to his or her God for help. When one does not experience help, when one's prayer seems to go unanswered, the challenge to maintain faith in the goodness of God becomes particularly acute. Given the monotheistic faith that permeates the OT, Israelites probably felt the challenge more acutely than most. Unlike polytheistic faiths, there was no other god to associate with the experience of evil. Although the OT never employs an equivalent term to theodicy, it has plenty to say about the relationship between the notion of the one God YHWH and the threatening presence of evil.

Like their modern counterparts, OT believers drew on their experience and their tradition, the record of past generations doing the same. This is indicated by the considerable variety, even disagreement, among OT texts that deal with the question of good and evil. It would be nice to be able to chart the historical course of this theological journey but contemporary critical scholarship is all too aware of the difficulty of doing so and the hypothetical nature of any reconstruction. It is likely that the catastrophe of the Babylonian exile of Judah and the earlier exile of the northern kingdom (Israel) by Assyria were among the more powerful catalysts for reflection and debate about evil, suffering and death. It seems clear that Israel and Judah were in frequent contact with their neighbours. The relationships were not always cordial but they were there and the exchange of ideas was presumably an important element in the articulation of faith. Ancient Israelites do not appear to have been self-absorbed. Because they lived on the crossroads between the superpowers of Egypt and Mesopotamia, they probably had little opportunity for such a preoccupation. However one understands these and other factors that influenced the production of the OT, it has bequeathed to its readers a rich and varied theological heritage. It has also left a number of things unresolved. The diverse and open-ended nature of the Bible needs to be taken into account by believers. There are implications here for how one understands its normative status.

2. Reward and retribution or act-consequence?

Until recently, a common scholarly opinion held that Israel's theologians accounted for evil via the schema or doctrine of reward and retribution. God rewards the good and punishes the wicked —albeit as a good God, according to a just norm. Proverbs 3:33, for example, states: 'The Lord's curse is on the house of the wicked, but he blesses the abode of the righteous'. The book of Deuteronomy proclaims God's blessing and curse in a similar vein (cf chapter 28). The pre-exilic prophets continually threaten God's wrath for a wayward Israel. As understood by scholars, the doctrine offered a rationale for the presence of good and evil and provided some firm ground for faith—one knows where one stands and God is in charge. It may look simplistic to a modern reader and indeed, not only to modern readers, as Job 21:29–30 shows. Nevertheless, it has built-in flexibility that enables it to respond to some challenges. If it could not do this, it would not have lasted long in the vigorous theological world of the OT. Within the faith context of OT society, one could appeal to divine authority to identify and justify the evil that brings retribution, or the good that brings blessing. A delay with either reward or retribution could be attributed to God's wise plan or purpose (Hebrew *ʿesâ*). All will take place in God's good time—a promise that aims to alleviate or exacerbate believers' anxiety, depending on whether it is a question of reward or punishment.

The doctrine is primarily concerned with moral evil but is able to embrace a range of evil experiences, as long as the context holds within which the explanation is made. For example, Judges 3 argues that God left warlike foreign nations in Israel in order to test the obedience of the people and that they might 'know war'—that is, how to fight. Natural disasters could be accounted for as punishment for national sin. Defeat at the hands of an enemy, which may look like a religious evil—that is, the power of one's God is weak—can be explained as the result of the people's moral failure. God is not weak; rather an all-powerful God hands the people over to defeat. The pre-exilic prophets used this rationale in relation to both the Assyrian and Babylonian invasions.

The reward–retribution schema faces two difficulties. One lies in the attempt to give a rational explanation for experiences. Because of the deeply personal nature of painful experiences in particular, some will find the explanation offered inadequate and even offensive. Such is Job's reply to his friends. The other difficulty concerns the foundations of the particular faith. These may give way under the burden of evil and suffering. People are no longer able to believe in the God portrayed in the theology, can no longer accept that their suffering is punishment for sin. Jeremiah 44 tells of a group of women who turned from YHWH to worship the queen of heaven under the strain of the exile. The book of Deuteronomy continually urges the people to hold fast to YHWH and reject foreign gods. The OT is not worried about whether Israelites will or will not remain believers, but which God—or which idea of God—will they believe in.

There is a certain parallel between the OT world and aspects of modern secular society. We place enormous faith in science and accept scientific explanations for any number of mysterious evils. Deep disagreement between scientific theories may cause people to take sides but it does not seem to shake their basic faith in science as such. Mutatis mutandis, the same may be said for economics. Whether in the OT or contemporary society, people make sense of their experiences in a variety of ways, but always within a faith context.

In 1955, Klaus Koch challenged the prevailing view of OT theodicy, triggering a vigorous debate that is still very much alive. He argued that the OT does not proclaim a doctrine of divine retribution for evil actions according to some previously established norm.[1] Rather, it operates on the principle that there is a built-in connection between an action and its consequences. Good actions have beneficial consequences while evil actions have bad consequences. Koch finds numerous examples of what he calls an 'action-consequences-construct' in the book of Proverbs. Thus, 26:27 states that 'Whoever digs a pit will fall into it, and a stone will come back on the one who starts it rolling' (cf also 24:30–34; 28:10, 18, 26; 29:23). Koch finds support for his thesis in studies of relevant Hebrew terminology. The term *ra'* means both 'ethically depraved' and 'bringing misfortune', while the word commonly translated as sin, *ḥaṭṭa't,* covers both 'sin' and 'disaster'.[2]

According to Koch, God's role in this theological construct is to ensure that the order God has created—the act-consequence-construct —operates effectively. One may say that God 'intervenes' in the arena of human activity but it is by way of 'facilitating the completion of something which previous human action has already set in motion' (cf Prov 25:21–22). It is not to punish someone according to an external norm. In fact, Hebrew has no word for punishment.

---

1.   K Koch, 'Is There a Doctrine of Retribution in the Old Testament?' in *Theodicy in the Old Testament*, edited by James L Crenshaw, Issues in Religion and Theology 4 (Philadelphia: Fortress Press, 1983), 57–87. German original 1955.

2.   Koch, 'Retribution', 75.

This act-consequence theology seems to be in conflict with OT covenant theology and the prophets who preach God's wrath against Israel's infidelity and corruption. Not so, argues Koch. Even though prophetic texts like Hosea 8:5 speak of God's anger burning against Israel because of evil, this is not a question of divine punishment as in the reward-retribution schema. Rather, such passages need to be understood in the sense of Hosea 12:15 (NRSV 12:14) where God 'turns/brings back' Ephraim (Hebrew *yašib*, cf Prov 24:12), that is, ensures that Ephraim (Israel) experiences the consequences of his evil actions.[3] One can explain the relationship (covenant) between God and Israel in a similar vein. God purges evil from the relationship by bringing the consequences of wicked actions to their completion. Despite Koch's arguments, one may ask whether the notion of God 'completing' the consequences of an act is retribution by another name.

Koch's study is important, not only because it challenges the reward-retribution explanation and provides considerable textual backup, but also because it points to a closer relationship between Wisdom, Torah and Prophecy than had hitherto been acknowledged. The tendency by some to see Wisdom as a foreign intrusion into the genuine Israelite theology of covenant and sacred history is not warranted.[4] The act-consequence-construct seems equally at home in the Israelite mind as it apparently was in the ANE mind.

The act-consequence hypothesis offers a rationale for the presence of evil that spares the divinity. God does not punish people and this is of some comfort to those troubled by the image of the 'avenging' God of the OT. Within the construct, evil begins and ends with the human beings who perpetrate it. All God does is see to it that they do not escape the 'natural' consequences of their actions—so, a righteous God. The prophetic proclamation 'I (the Lord) will bring evil upon him/them' is to be understood in this way. Natural disasters can be the result of a nation's sin, as the famous text in Hosea 4:1–3 proclaims. This passage has an uncanny resemblance to the kinds of statements made by contemporary ecologists. Even foreign invasions can be seen

---

3.   Koch, 'Retribution', 65.

4.   Cf for example, H Gese, *Lehre und Wirklichkeit in der alten Weisheit. Studien zu den Sprüchen Salomos und zu dem Buche Hiob.* (Tübingen: JCB Mohr, 1958, and more recently, H–D Preuss, *Einführung in die alttestamentliche Weisheitsliteratur* (Stuttgart: Kohlhammer, 1987).

in terms of the act-consequence-construct. A corrupt nation no longer has the strength and purpose to defend itself and so falls prey. Isaiah 1:5–9 can be read in this way.

Nevertheless, a number of scholars have problems with Koch's hypothesis, not because of their own theological stance but because of the variety and complexity of the OT textual evidence. They point to numerous passages that emphasise divine freedom, a notion that is central to OT thinking. The hypothesis appears to restrict divine freedom to the terms of the act-consequence-construct. They also point to texts that focus on the personal relationship between God and Israel, between God and the individual believer. The God of the construct hypothesis creates the impression of a rather distant and impersonal deity.[5]

The desire for faith in a personal God can be very deep. To meet such a deeply felt need or desire, believers are willing to accept pain at the hands of the divinity, and to take the blame for it (I must have done something wrong). Punishment is a kind of personal attention: some find it acceptable when applied to God, especially when placed in the context of an overall benign divine purpose; others, as indicated by the book of Job, find it intolerable.

Another area of OT theology that is difficult to mesh with the act-consequence-construct is salvation—God's deliverance of Israel from oppresssion. Deutero-Isaiah prophesies that God will deliver Israel, not because of any good deed Israel has done but because of God's love (cf Isa 43:4; see also Deut 7:8). There is no prior requirement for Israel to repent, to do a good deed so as to receive a good consequence.

---

5. See the criticisms by RE Murphy, 'Wisdom Theses', in *Wisdom and Knowledge* (J Papin Festschrift); edited by J Armenti (Villanova PA: Villanova UP, 1976) 2:187–200; more recently 'Recent Research on Proverbs and Qoheleth', *Currents in Research: Biblical Studies* 1 (1993): 119–40; W McKane, *Proverbs: A New Approach* (OTL; Philadelphia: Westminster, 1970), 420. A more nuanced view is taken by JL Crenshaw, *Urgent Advice and Probing Questions. Collected Writings on Old Testament Wisdom* (Mercer, 1995). On page 88, n. 66 he comments that 'One can posit the importance of order in the ancient sapiential worldview without deifying the concept. In Israel, Yahweh had the final word'.

3. Old Testament critique of theodicy

The doctrine of reward and retribution and the act-consequence-construct can both appeal to solid textual support in the OT. As in many areas of biblical thought, we find complexity and difference. Some texts could no doubt be explained either way, but not all. The difference suggests two things. One is awareness by OT theologians that they were constructing theologies, ways of explaining reality. There are different ways. A second is an awareness of the limitations of each theology and the value of a variety of theologies. A fundamentalist does not normally tolerate, let alone welcome, a competing theology. Awareness and acceptance of limitation is evident in texts that deny or challenge the claims and arguments made by OT theodicies, whether formulated as reward-retribution or act-consequence. No doubt this kind of thing went on throughout Israel's history. A vivid example is the diametrically opposed views of the following two psalms. Psalm 37:25 claims:

> I have been young, and now am old,
> yet I have not seen the righteous forsaken
> or their children begging bread.

This makes a massive claim that must, for most, fail the test of experience. Psalm 88 can be read as an outraged rejoinder: 'Wretched and close to death from my youth up, I suffer your terrors; I am desperate'. Another example is the so-called 'confessions' of Jeremiah which protest against Israel's suffering but in doing so appear to undermine the claims of chapters 2–6 that all are wicked and deserve punishment.

Texts of this kind show that OT theologising was not simply an intellectual exercise; it was an intense, at times desperate, search for meaning.

4. Job and Ecclesiastes (Qoheleth)

At a certain stage in Israel's history, most likely during the Persian period, the debate about theodicy reached a unique level of systematisation and sophistication in the books of Job and Ecclesiastes (Qoheleth). It is reasonable to think that the impact of the Babylonian exile and Judah's straitened circumstances thereafter stimulated the kind of thinking that characterises these books. Both are recognised as carefully constructed discourses on theodicy, although this does not make them any easier to decipher. Job in particular is a book that leaves most readers profoundly moved and just as profoundly perplexed.

The arrangement of the book looks something like the upstairs-downstairs scenes in a play. In the first scene, mainly chapters 1–2, God and the 'prosecutor' (Satan) debate about Job.[6] God sees Job as blameless, whereas Satan accuses him of acting from self-interest. The book then switches to a 'downstairs' scene where Job and his friends debate about God. The arrangement adds an ironic touch: the friends defend God as blameless and just, while Job appears to play the role of the prosecutor, accusing God of being unjust. Unlike the reader, Job and his friends are unaware of the debate taking place 'upstairs'. A further irony occurs in 42:7 when God 'descends the stairs' to proclaim the accuser right and the defenders wrong.

If, as many do, we take Job as representing 'anyone', the upstairs scene portrays a God who trusts the human being completely —expressed in God's word or 'evaluation' of Job. Satan takes the opposite view.[7] The debaters agree that the only way to resolve the matter is to put Job to the test. Satan proposes it; God permits it. From one point of view, this is an odd scenario. Given that God knows Job only as God can, what need is there for a test or trial to settle the matter? Even more perplexing, Job is unaware of the test. And lest one think this is completely out of left field, the OT runs the test theme again in Genesis 22!

What relevance can such a scenario have for a reader, ancient or modern? One possible way forward is to note that the affliction of Job does provide a 'fitting' setting for the dramatic debate with his friends. The test, or something like it, is required by the storyline. The author could not attribute the affliction of a blameless Job directly to the one

---

6.   This is the translation of 'Satan' preferred by EM Good in *In Turns of Tempest: A Reading of Job with a Translation* (Stanford: Stanford University Press, 1990).

7.   Good (*In Turns of Tempest*, 194–95) argues that Satan's reply in 1:11 is in effect a self-curse ('or else I will be cursed') and that this is the thrust of the debate with God, not a wager or a test. His exclusion of the alternatives is surprising, given his deconstructionist approach and acknowledgment of the ambiguity and complexity of the book.

good God, and attributing it to another god is out of the question for a monotheist. Hence, a compromise; God is portrayed permitting Satan to do evil for a greater good, the validation of the divine word about Job. For a believer, this would be the greatest good. Hence, chapters 1–2 present a God who exalts the human being but lets it suffer so that God's word concerning it may be verified—by the testimony of the human being. Is this overall benign divine purpose sufficient to protect God from the accusation of acting immorally towards Job?

Another angle on this perplexing scene is that it offers a reflection on the human condition and its role vis-à-vis God. Within the human arena, the authenticity and integrity of one's theology, one's portrait of God, depends on the authenticity and integrity of human beings—not only their words but also their whole lives. Even a theology that proclaims it is all in God's hands and we are merely God's instruments is still a case of human beings making what they believe to be an authentic claim about God. The vicissitudes of life are such that faith will be put to the test; at its most acute, this will take the form of afflictions that seem to contradict everything one believes (has proclaimed) about God. The belief that one is precious in God's sight and trusted completely, as the book of Job proclaims, can provide a powerful motivation to live through terrible affliction. One sees examples of human beings doing so for the sake of others time and time again.

How does the book portray Job's response to his afflictions? According to 1:22 and 2:10 Job 'did not sin' by accusing or cursing God. God's evaluation of Job was right and Satan's wrong. But, once the story sets the scene with his friends, Job launches into an intense and at times bitter debate with them about God's justice in the face of human suffering. Here, Job plays the role of the accuser, the friends the role of God's defender. In 42:7, God 'descends the stairs' to commend Job for having spoken thus. How might one relate these seemingly contradictory portraits of Job? Is the book implying that it is one thing not to sin but another, and better thing, to speak honestly about God and to God from one's experience?

Despite these questions, there are a number of points that one can make in the wake of 42:7. There is the claim that Job's criticism of his friends' theology—the traditional viewpoint—is valid. If this is phrased in terms of reward and retribution, suffering like Job's is not God's punishment for sin. If it is phrased in terms of act-consequence,

Job's suffering is not the normal consequence of sinful actions. Nevertheless, the book does not dismiss the traditional view out of hand; too much space is given to it for that. As well, the story ends with God 'rewarding' Job or 'restoring' in kind what he has lost. Perhaps the aim of the book is to expose the limitations of the traditional view and to make important distinctions that it believes are overlooked, distinctions such as the difference between innocent suffering and punishment. A second point is that the book promotes the integrity of a theology that is true to experience, even when this flies in the face of the 'received' wisdom. Job, who gave voice to his experience no matter how painful and offensive to his friends, embodies this view of authentic theology—of faith seeking understanding. The third point is related to this. While the book champions this view of authentic theology, it also cautions that one needs to recognise the limited ability of human experience to explain reality, whether it be the accumulated experience of the tradition or one's own experience. This is implied in the climactic speeches by God in chapters 38:1 – 40:2 and 40:6 – 41:34 and Job's replies in 40:3–5 and 42:1–6.

In the speeches, God proclaims that, despite Job's personal experience of chaos, creation is in as perfect order as it ever has been. Job, the human being, cannot know creation as God its creator knows it. He cannot judge it and, a fortiori, neither can he judge its maker. Moreover, God relates to and cares for his creature Job as God cares for all creation. This does not alleviate Job's present pain but it does affirm that there is a relationship with God within the reality of suffering —the one suffering evil is not abandoned. Indeed, as the reader who can view both upstairs and downstairs is aware, God is particularly focused on this suffering 'servant'.

The divine speeches do not explain the reason for Job's suffering. Is this because the theology of the time judged there was no satisfactory explanation or because the storyline ruled it out—could the author have God inform Job that it was all about settling a dispute with the prosecutor? The so-called 'suffering servant' passages in Deutero-Isaiah see a salvific role in suffering. But, unlike Job, the servant takes on the affliction of others (cf. Isa 52:13 – 53:12).

Job replies to God's speeches in 40:3–5 and 42:1–6. Presumably these are included in the approval of 42:7. The dispute between God and Satan is whether Job would fear God for nothing (1:9). Satan does his worst but in another of the many ironic turns in this book, it may be God's speeches that provide the ultimate test for Job—namely, to keep faith beyond any explanation of his suffering. Is this the most painful thing about being afflicted by evil—not knowing the reason why? Does the assertion of God's presence as creator provide a satisfactory substitute? Job seems to accept this, or at least recognise that human attempts to explain are in the end inadequate (cf 42:3). As well, even though he has only heard God's words, Job says 'now my eye sees you' (42:5). Is this expressive of a new insight? If so, is it the relationship of God to creation and Job's place in it, as proclaimed in God's speeches? The text is not explicit and the reader is left to ponder.

The book of Job seeks to make sense of the human condition and the goodness of God by a series of 'rational' debates but, in the speeches of chapters 38–41, invites the reader to look at creation from God's perspective. From this lofty eyrie one 'sees' that God works for the good of creation and nothing escapes God's attention and care. Nevertheless, a reader may feel that this is more about defending God than providing comfort for a suffering humanity. It is an OT form of the argument from authority.

The book of Ecclesiastes does not take this step. Qoheleth pursues the question of the human condition relentlessly from 'below', by research and reflection. The argument may be formulated as follows: One can presume (in faith) that the work of God's hands is good and a work of order. The human being's role is to avail of this created order in a way that fosters human wellbeing. The human being should be able to achieve this, to do good and avoid evil, by tuning in to the order of creation. Qoheleth's research leads him to conclude that this cannot be done. The best attempts to establish guidelines for human wellbeing end up as 'vanity'. The book does not go so far as to say that there is no order, for this would be to impugn God. Rather, Qoheleth concludes from his 'research', his experience, that the human being cannot perceive this order. The challenge of Qoheleth's position is that the order of things in God's creation should be accessible to human beings and should reveal God's purpose to them. If not, what is the point of creation for humanity?

Qoheleth does not seem so concerned about one's personal relationship with God as about making a life within God's creation. A common opinion is that Qoheleth's theology portrays a rather distant and impersonal divinity. As 5:2 puts it: 'for God is in heaven, and you upon earth'. In contrast, the book of Job is seen to be primarily concerned about Job's relationship with God. Despite these differences, the two do agree on the importance of creation for constructing theology. It is evident throughout the book of Qoheleth: in Job it comes to the fore in the climactic speech of God in chapters 38–41. This interest is not confined to Job and Qoheleth; it is in the book of Proverbs, in particular the poem on Lady Wisdom (chapter 8).

5. Creation and history

For a considerable time, creation theology was seen by modern scholarship as the preserve of wisdom literature. In contrast, Torah and Prophecy portrayed YHWH as the God who chose Israel, delivered her from oppression and gave her a history—a place and a purpose among the nations. The theologies of creation and history, or creation and election, were almost separate entities. Matters have changed considerably in recent years: a reassessment of the role of creation theology in Torah and Prophecy has taken place; due partly to the impact of the environment crisis, partly to the work of scholars like HH Schmid. In a 1973 study, Schmid argued that far from being on the periphery of OT thought—that is, in wisdom literature—creation theology is of central importance and forms 'the broad horizon of biblical theology'.[8] Law, nature and politics are all aspects of one comprehensive order of creation. This is why, according to Schmid, in Israel and ANE thinking in general, 'an offense in the legal realm obviously has effects in the realm of nature (drought, famine) or in the political sphere (threat of the enemy)'.[9] Doing right therefore means acting in accord with the order created by God: good consequences will follow as an integral part of this order. The righteous God created a righteous, that is, properly ordered world. Righteousness (*sĕdāqâ*) should not be understood in a narrow legal sense but as universal world order. To act in accord with this is, for Israel, what Schmid calls

---

8.   HH Schmid, 'Creation, Righteousness, and Salvation: 'Creation Theology' as the Broad Horizon of Biblical Theology', in *Creation in the Old Testament*, edited by BW Anderson; Issues in Religion and Theology 6 (Philadelphia: Fortress Press, 1984), 102–17.

9.   Schmid, 'Creation', 105.

'comprehensive salvation'—a blessed consequence.[10] Israel's vocation and purpose in history is to mediate this way of living to the nations.

Similar objections have been raised against Schmid as are raised against Koch. The notion of righteousness as world order overlooks the importance of righteousness as a key ingredient in Israel's personal, covenant relationship with God.[11] But, given that God's care for order in creation touches every aspect of it and every creature in it, the righteous relationship between God and Israel can be taken as an example, albeit a special one from the OT point of view, of God's universal world order.

Creation, as God's handiwork, is part of God's purpose or will. Time (change), being integral to creation, is also part of God's purpose. Creation thus has a history that unfolds the purpose of creation and in doing so manifests God's purpose.[12] As Schmid puts it, history is understood as 'the actualization of the order of creation'.[13] An integral component of creation history is human history and an integral component of human history is, in turn, the history of Israel. The history or story of Israel is an interpretation made in faith—the OT proclaims that Israel was chosen by God out of all the nations on the earth. The presentation of Israel's story is therefore a theology, employing the literary forms and modes of thinking of the culture. It is not history in the modern critical sense of the term. For believers, Israel's history is 'the sign and pledge that God supports the world order and intends to bring it into realization'.[14]

According to this theology, or may one call it a theodicy writ large, a key reason for Israel's election is that human history runs contrary to the order of creation and God's purpose in creation. The story of human rebellion and evil is told in Genesis 1 – 11. As the story unfolds, a number of themes emerge that prepare for the call of Israel. God

---

10.   Schmid, 'Creation', 107. Schmid accepts Koch's act-consequence-construct.

11.   See for example, J Krasovec, *La Justice (SDQ) de Dieu dans la Bible hébräique et l'interprétation juive et chrétienne*. OBO 76 (Göttingen: Vandenhoeck & Ruprecht, 1988), 14–17.

12.   For this and much of what follows, I am indebted to RP Knierim, *The Task of Old Testament Theology. Substance, Method and Cases* (Grand Rapids: Eerdmans, 1995), 171–224.

13.   Schmid, 'Creation', 108.

14.   Schmid, 'Creation', 110.

creates by bringing order out of chaos and the ordered creation
established by God is pronounced good in all aspects. Genesis 1:1 –
2:4a paints a picture of an ideal creation. Human beings disturb
creation by acting contrary to God's commands, commands that are
meant to enable them to live and work as stewards of creation. When
they fail to 'keep/guard' God's commands about the garden (2:15–17),
they are expelled and a new guardian installed—the cherub with the
flaming sword (3:24). The story of the flood tells how God countered
unbridled human evil and then, in an astonishing move, has God
swear that he will never again curse the ground even though the
inclination of the human heart is 'evil from youth' (8:21). Humanity
has not changed but God has. The oath is God's commitment to a less
than perfect creation, a humanity prone to evil.[15] It provides an
assurance for faith that evil will not overwhelm or annihilate creation.
In providing this assurance, it also fuels hope that the divine purpose
for creation will be realised. Armed with this faith and hope, human
beings can accept the presence of evil and incorporate it into an overall
positive worldview.

This faith and hope are central to Israel's perception of her identity
and vocation. Israel is called by God to bring blessing to 'all the
families of the earth' (Gen 12:3)—to mediate the realisation of God's
purpose to a troubled humanity and creation. God's commitment is
enshrined in the covenant and Torah. God delivers Israel from the
oppresssion of evil human beings in order to show her how she is to
establish a righteous society that is in harmony with the righteousness
of creation (universal world order). This will take place in the land that
God has chosen for Israel. The justification for this lies in the claim that
it comes from God. What God plans and proclaims is, by definition,
righteous. By living a righteous life in the land, Israel will be blessed
and enjoy the kind of life that God intends for all humanity. Deuteronomy 26:5–11 provides instructions as to how this blessed life is to be
celebrated. Here, vision and legislation become one—the mark of a
supremely confident faith. In short, the Pentateuch begins and ends
with the theme of creation. Genesis 1:1 – 2:4a presents the ideal of
creation: the book of Deuteronomy shows how the ideal is to be
realised by Israel in the land.

---

15.   Cf JD Levenson, *Creation and the Persistence of Evil. The Jewish Drama of
      Divine Omnipotence* (San Francisco: Harper & Row, 1988), 48.

This understanding of the Torah does not mean that creation is central and history peripheral. Both are integral and inseparable components. History is the arena in which the meaning of creation is revealed and its purpose realised. By the same token, there would be no human history without creation. From the point of view of theodicy, the Torah (and Prophets) thus understood is able to incorporate evil within a larger perspective of the purpose of creation, of God bringing about universal world order or righteousness. The act-consequence-construct and the reward-retribution schema would both seem able to find a place within its broad embrace. In fact, there is a case for seeing them in this context as two ways of speaking about the same reality. The reward and retribution that God decrees are righteous because they are from God. But this also means that they are in accord with the right order of creation. In terms of the construct terminology, actions will reap their appropriate consequences.[16] Similarly, when Israel judges cases according to the Torah, she will, like God, act righteously because the laws of the Torah come from God.

The advantage of the creation-history nexus is that it offers a reassuring view of creation and humanity's destiny within creation. But how does such a sweeping theology touch the personal experience (history) of human beings? As if in answer to this question, the 'Former Prophets' offers an interpretation of Israel's life in the land according to the deuteronomic version of Torah theology. It is a magnificent but flawed project—like the book of Job it testifies to the limitations of the theological endeavour. Two examples will help to point this out. The 'history' struggles to explain why Solomon, who is branded an apostate in his old age, escaped retribution. According to the text, God made an exception in his case for 'the sake of your father David' (1 Kgs 11:12). It struggles even more to explain the violent death of the good king Josiah at the hands of Pharaoh Neco. According to the text, Josiah's death is a reward for loyalty. It will spare him the sight of Judah's demise (2 Kgs 22:20). The explanation looks lame and was recognised as such by the Chronicler who abandoned it in favour of the other arm of the reward-retribution schema. This author claims

---

16.   Schmid sees no contradiction between consequence and God as executor 'so long as the inner force of the order of creation and the action of the creator god are not differentiated' ('Creation', 106).

that Josiah failed to heed a word from God via Neco. His death can thus appear as retribution for disobedience (2 Chr 35:20–24).

6. Theodicy and eschatology

Eschatology can be seen as a logical development, in response to the experience of evil, of the notion of creation's destiny or purpose. The present, however trying, can be understood as a step on the way to the realisation of God's purpose. Even a catastrophe like the Babylonian exile can be explained within this framework. God punishes Israel for its corruption—or ensures it experiences the consequences of its corruption—by handing it over to foreign domination. The exile is not a sign of God's weakness but of God's power as Lord of all history. God, who hands sinful Israel over to foreigners, is equally able to rescue her from foreigners, as at the exodus. When this new exodus happens the nations will accept YHWH as God. Universal peace and righteousness will ensue and the nations will worship YHWH on Zion (cf Isa 2:1–4).

One can also see in the development of eschatological theology the close relationship between faith, hope and love that I argued earlier is foundational for human life. Hope for a better future helps to shore up faith when present turbulent experiences buffet it. Hope can rekindle love and commitment in relationships that are crumbling under extreme pressure.

Eschatological theology is of course found principally in the prophetic corpus. The prophets appear to have drawn on and transformed liturgical themes that are preserved in the psalms. Messianic expectation provides an illustration. Psalm 72 prays for the success of the reigning king by invoking images of the Davidic ideal. Isaiah 11:1–5 prophesies the future coming of a king who will realise this ideal through the power of God's spirit. God will succeed where human beings have been shown to fail. Eschatological proclamations such as this may be grand and rhetorically uplifting, but do they ease present affliction? The question that was often on the lips of psalmists is the same question that faced the prophets—'how long, O Lord?' How long before hope is confirmed by experience? For people of faith the proclamation itself may serve as a kind of confirming experience.

Some prophetic books emphasise the time dimension and speak of the days that 'are surely coming' when God will establish a new covenant of blessing and peace (eg Jer 31:31–34). Others focus more on the transformation of creation that will take place (eg Isa 65:17; 66:22). While a prophet may focus on creation or history for rhetorical and / or theological purposes, the other is always implied. Whatever the future is to unfold, it will take place in the order of creation and according to the order of creation. Whatever shape the renewal of creation is to take, it will take place at some time, as a stage in human history and world history.

7. Conclusion

Given the richness and diversity of the OT, there is much that has escaped notice in this paper, much that has had to be passed over. To provide a satisfactory summary of OT theodicy would therefore be presumptuous. The following statements attempt only to gather together some of the ideas that have been aired in the paper.

The OT proclaims a theodicy that is drawn from the experience of creation and history but it contains texts—also based on experience —that profoundly challenge this theodicy. In other words, the goodness of God cannot be justified from human experience.

The OT persists in proclaiming the goodness of God even though it cannot be empirically verified. This suggests that although faith draws on experience, if it is to survive and flourish it needs to reach beyond experience.

Nevertheless, OT eschatology promises an experience to come that will confirm faith and hope in God and God's purpose. This suggests that the goodness of God is something that human beings should be able to experience in a definitive way.

The OT does not resolve these differences: they are left to the reader to ponder.

God's Presence and Power: Christology, Eschatology and 'Theodicy' in Mark's Crucifixion Narrative

David Neville

In *Night* Elie Wiesel describes the hanging of a young servant boy in a Nazi concentration camp at Buna, near Auschwitz. Witnessed by thousands of prisoners, the hanged boy's life ebbs away slowly because he is so light. Wiesel recalls somebody asking:

> 'Where is God now?'
> And I heard a voice within me answer him:
> 'Where is He? Here He is—He is hanging here on
> this gallows . . .'[1]

For Wiesel, this devastating experience signified the death of God in terms of loss of faith. Brought up in a devout Jewish household, Wiesel's childhood experiences in the death camps of Auschwitz and Buchenwald led him to turn against the God of his ancestors.[2]

An execution not unlike that witnessed by Wiesel is recounted in the canonical gospels. Jesus is depicted as an innocent victim, and the

---

1. Elie Wiesel, *Night*, trans. Stella Rodway (London/New York: Penguin Books, 1981), 77. (The French edition was published in 1958.) In recent discussions of theodicy, this incident in Wiesel's life is referred to almost as often as Ivan Karamazov's protest against innocent suffering in Fyodor Dostoyevsky's *The Brothers Karamazov* (1879–80). Kenneth Surin, *Theology and the Problem of Evil* (Oxford/New York: Basil Blackwell, 1986), discusses how Wiesel's and others' holocaust experience forced such thinkers as Dorothy Sölle and Jürgen Moltmann to reconceive how they might address the problem(s) of theodicy. Their work is instructive, but for me Wiesel's haunting experience proved illuminating for thinking about the process of reflection and reinterpretation that must have occurred within the earliest Christian communities as they adjusted their thinking to re-cognise their crucified messiah. This process is what I refer to as an 'eschatological reinterpretation of faith'.

2. Later books reveal that Wiesel continued to wrestle with issues of faith.

manner of his execution was intended to extend suffering and to maximise shame. The gospels were written by people of faith who had come to the conviction that the tortured, maligned and crucified Jesus was, despite appearances and prior beliefs, the locus of God's presence and redemptive power. In answer to the question, 'Where is God now?' their reply was much the same as Wiesel's: 'Here God is—God is hanging here on this gallows . . .' Yet in the case of the gospel writers, this response signified both a reaffirmation and a redefinition—indeed, an eschatological reinterpretation—of faith. It entailed a *reinterpretation* of faith because God's presence and power were reconceived in light of the service, suffering and death of Jesus, the 'messiah'; it was an *eschatological* reinterpretation because what was inaugurated in Jesus' mission (understood holistically to include his exorcisms, healings, parabolic teaching, voluntary suffering and death) is yet to be consummated and must therefore be perceived by faith, anticipated in hope and lived for in love.

Since Leibniz,[3] the task of theodicy has been to demonstrate that evil and suffering are somehow explicable in a world created by a good and omnipotent god. But this is not a biblical response to the evil and suffering that afflicts people everywhere, albeit unevenly. If it is true that God's presence and power are most fully revealed in the crucified messiah, the appropriate Christian response to suffering and evil is not speculation about how these might be explained but discipleship informed by and conformed to the crucified messiah.

How else might a student of the NT address the interrelation between theodicy and eschatology than in light of the crucifixion of Jesus? A complete treatment would also consider the resurrection of

---

3. Gottfried Wilhelm Leibniz, *Theodicy: Essays on the Goodness of God, the Freedom of Man and the Origin of Evil*, trans. EM Huggard (London: Routledge & Kegan Paul, 1952). The publication of Leibniz's book in 1710 is often credited as being the first use of the term 'theodicy'. My thinking on modern theodicy has been influenced by John Howard Yoder, Terrence Tilley, *The Evils of Theodicy* (Washington, DC: Georgetown University Press, 1991), and William Placher, *The Domestication of Transcendence: How Modern Thinking about God Went Wrong* (Louisville, KY: Westminster John Knox Press, 1996), 201–215. Eschatology is intrinsic to the theodicy of Marilyn McCord Adams, *Horrendous Evils and the Goodness of God* (Ithaca, NY: Cornell University Press; Melbourne: Melbourne University Press, 1999), although this is perhaps clearer in her response to Placher's engagement with her book in *SJT* 55/4 (2002): 461–79.

Jesus, understood as God's vindication of Jesus and therefore God's self-vindication, but here I restrict attention to the story of Jesus' crucifixion in the Gospel according to Mark.[4] My reason for focusing on Mark's account is not because his is generally regarded as the earliest of the canonical gospels but because the suffering of Jesus is, so to speak, honoured more in the Gospel of Mark (and the closely related recital in the Gospel of Matthew) by virtue of being depicted in all its stark terror, without amelioration.[5] Only in the Markan/Matthean account does Jesus succumb to his suffering, for only in this version does Jesus cry out, 'My God, my God, why have you forsaken me?' Apart from an ambiguous response to Pilate's query, 'Are you the king of the Jews?' (Mark 15:2; Matt 27:11), and a second death-cry (more obviously another cry in Matthew's version than in Mark's), Jesus is mute from the time he is brought before Pilate until his death. This accentuates his victimisation. In both Luke's and John's narratives, Jesus 'rises above' his suffering to demonstrate control over what has befallen him.[6] Because Mark refused to soften the stark reality of Jesus' suffering, his crucifixion narrative is more likely to provide insight into the realities of evil and suffering as well as resources for grappling with these overwhelming forces.

Mark's story of Jesus' crucifixion presents a harrowing depiction of physical agony and mental anguish, even though he chose not to accentuate Jesus' suffering. Indeed, his account of Jesus' execution is surprisingly understated.[7] But the wider context, beginning with the

---

4. See Ernest Best, *The Temptation and the Passion: The Markan Soteriology*, 2nd edition (Cambridge: Cambridge University Press, 1990), xxiv. Best argued that in Mark's Gospel 'the cross is nullified by the resurrection, which serves as vindication', and therefore cannot be isolated from the resurrection. He then wrote, 'This does not however answer the problem set by Jesus' shameful death.'

5. The crucifixion narratives in the Gospels of Matthew and Mark are so similar in content, narrative order and vocabulary that much of what is said about Mark's narrative can also be said of Matthew's. For an overview of the similarities and differences in their respective passion narratives, see Raymond E Brown, *The Death of the Messiah* (New York: Doubleday, 1994), 26–30.

6. See Brown, *The Death of the Messiah*, 30–35. Luke's Jesus is comparatively verbose (Lk 23:28–31, 34, 43, 46) and tranquil, while John's Jesus debates with Pilate and on the cross 'takes care of business' (Jn 19:25–30).

7. What may explain this is the shame associated with anyone who experienced crucifixion. See John T Carroll and Joel B Green, *The Death of Jesus in Early*

movement of Jesus and his disciples to the Mount of Olives (Mark 14:26), sketches a picture of an ever-increasing burden of suffering borne by Jesus. At Gethsemane, his agony as he anticipates his 'cup of suffering' is intensified by the inability of his friends to support him and by the cumulative experiences of betrayal, abandonment and isolation. Within a short time-frame, his burden of suffering is increased further by interrogation, false accusations, verbal abuse, torture and public humiliation. From the perspective of narrative development, by the time of his execution Jesus' resources are spent; this may explain the atypical detail in Mark 15:21 that Simon of Cyrene was commandeered to carry Jesus' crossbeam.

1. The purpose of Mark's Gospel

Debate continues over the date (shortly before or after the temple's destruction in 70 CE) and provenance (Rome, Syria or somewhere in Palestine) of Mark's Gospel, but it is generally accepted that Mark wrote for a community experiencing persecution.[8] In other words, the gospel's original audience was well acquainted with suffering.[9] Broadly speaking, then, Mark's chief concern was probably pastoral, even if he considered it necessary to address deficient christological or eschatological ideas. His clarifications were probably intended to correct (or enhance) his readers' understanding of what it means to follow one who was crucified. While Mark affirmed the resurrection, it seems that what his readers most needed to hear and to appreciate was a better (or perhaps renewed) insight into the nature of Jesus' messiahship, which for Mark centred on his service, suffering and humiliating death. Hence the dominance of his interrelated themes of christology and discipleship. To offer insight into the precise nature of Jesus' messiahship coupled with a deeper understanding of the

---

Christianity (Peabody, MA: Hendrickson, 1995), 167–70. In their *Social-Science Commentary on the Synoptic Gospels*, 2nd edition (Minneapolis: Augsburg Fortress, 2003), 214-18, Bruce J Malina and Richard L Rohrbaugh emphasise the 'status degradation' of Jesus, especially at his crucifixion.

8. Someone named Mark probably wrote the Gospel according to Mark, but I assume no more about his identity. For good reasons to think that Mark's Gospel was written for a specific community undergoing persecution, see Joel Marcus, *Mark 1–8*, AB 27 (New York: Doubleday, 2000), 25–39.

9. See Francis J Moloney, *The Gospel of Mark: A Commentary* (Peabody, MA: Hendrickson, 2002), 14. For Moloney, the experience of persecution and suffering on the part of the community for which Mark wrote is a 'hard fact'.

renewed call to follow Jesus along the same path of suffering and perhaps even death was more likely to speak meaningfully into a situation of suffering and confusion than polemics. Had Mark's *primary* purpose been to criticise members of the community for which he wrote, this would have exacerbated tensions within an already harassed community.

In *Mark's Gospel: Worlds in Conflict*, John Painter contends that the Gospel of Mark is itself an 'apologetic work' or 'work of theodicy':

> In a world dominated by evil Mark kindles belief in the goodness and power of God . . . Mark integrated the death of Jesus into the good news of the dawning of the kingdom of God in and through him. Consequently, the proclamation of the gospel and the writing of his Gospel are works of theodicy in the face of prevailing evil . . .[10]

This description of the purpose of Mark's Gospel is based on the perception that Mark took for granted an apocalyptic worldview. Therefore, according to Painter,

> The Markan story will not be understood unless the reader recognises that, in this story, it is understood that, although God created the world, the world lies in the power of (the) evil (one). Human lives lie in the grip of evil and human agencies are powerless to break free.[11]

Understood this way, Mark's Gospel was intended to reassure readers that God's sovereignty was re-established (or at least revealed still to be potent) in the mission of Jesus: 'The story of Jesus recounts the strategy and purpose of God to overcome the powers of evil,

---

10. John Painter, *Mark's Gospel: Worlds in Conflict* (London and New York: Routledge, 1997), 14.
11. Painter, *Mark's Gospel*, 14. For alternative perspectives on the relevance of apocalyptic for understanding Mark's Gospel, see Marcus, *Mark 1–8*, 72–73, and NT Wright, *The New Testament and the People of God* (London: SPCK; Minneapolis: Augsburg Fortress, 1992), 390–96.

liberating those who will receive and enter the kingdom of God.' [12] For Painter, Jesus' probable prediction of the temple's destruction was associated by Mark with the coming of the son of man in judgment. Mark, writing around the time of the temple's literal destruction, anticipated the imminent fulfilment of Jesus' saying in response to the high priest (Mark 14:61–62). His theodicy, his proclamation of 'the good news of God in a world dominated by evil',[13] was that the imminent arrival of the Son of Man would demonstrate God's triumph over evil forces. 'Thus, in Mark, faith in God's deliverance through Jesus as the Christ finds expression in eschatological hope, Jesus the coming Son of Man.'[14]

On this reading, Mark's Gospel might have sustained hope for a time, but only so long as believers accepted that the Son of Man's coming was, indeed, imminent. Once it became clear that the Son of Man's arrival was not as imminent as expected, this necessitated revisionist versions of the Jesus-story to account for the 'delay of the *parousia*'. This perspective has a certain credibility about it, but its proponents all too often presume that God defeats or triumphs over evil by exercising superior power. In other words, the hope Mark allegedly strengthened is that when the Son of Man returns, he will dominate evil forces in much the same way—only definitively—as the forces of evil had dominated him. If this accurately represents the hope Mark aimed to instil, it stands in tension with Mark's depiction of Jesus' suffering and death as the precise means by which God undoes evil in the world.

In any case, Mark faced a twofold dilemma. Not only had the mission of Jesus ended in crucifixion, resulting in what Painter has fittingly described as 'a serious plausibility problem',[15] but those who hoped to participate in the kingdom he inaugurated continued to be at the mercy of hostile and oppressive forces. In short, evil still prevailed. How could Mark reaffirm faith in the crucified messiah, and how could he strengthen hope of belonging to God's kingdom?

---

12. Painter, *Mark's Gospel*, 15. For Painter, one dimension of liberation, as Mark presents it, is a 'transformation of human consciousness' made possible by the mission of Jesus, especially his death by crucifixion.
13. Painter, *Mark's Gospel*, 19.
14. Painter, *Mark's Gospel*, 20. Mark's depiction of the coming of Jesus as the son of man is, for Painter, 'the judgement of God for the overthrow of evil and the establishment of the kingdom of God in power' (18).
15. Painter, *Mark's Gospel*, 9.

It is commonly claimed that Mark sought to instil hope that the crucified one would shortly return as the Son of Man in judgment to overwhelm the forces of evil. This is a plausible interpretation of Mark 8:38, 13:26 and 14:62, but another feature of Mark's narrative, which is not entirely compatible with such an interpretation, suggests that Mark's solution to his twofold dilemma was to reconceive the nature of Jesus' messiahship and, on the basis of this renovation, to reinterpret the meaning of God's sovereignty and power.

In an evocative essay on the paradoxical relationship between power and powerlessness in Mark's Gospel, Dorothy Lee has shown that while Mark depicted Jesus' mission as the irruption of God's reign in Jesus' works of power, the epitome of God's power is revealed in Jesus' crucifixion, which stresses his powerlessness.[16] In the first half of Mark's Gospel, Jesus exercises power in many ways (exorcisms, nature miracles and healings, authoritative teaching, challenging tradition and calling disciples), yet the perspective changes after the decisive turning-point in Mark 8:27–30. Lee speaks of a 'profound and disturbing sense of discontinuity in the way that power operates in Mark's interpretation of the ministry of Jesus':

> For, lying between the power already seen in the ministry of Jesus and the power expected in the future, eschatological coming of the Son of Man (9.1, 13.26, 14.62) lies the paradox of the cross. It is here that the real secret of the kingdom is to be found. God's power, as Mark is about to demonstrate, cannot properly be understood except in terms of its opposite, powerlessness. Through it we are compelled to understand the divine power as something entirely new and unexpected—something that overturns our human assumptions about the way God works in the world.[17]

---

16. Dorothy A Lee-Pollard, 'Powerlessness as Power: A Key Emphasis in the Gospel of Mark', *SJT* 40/2 (1987): 173–88.

17. Lee-Pollard, 'Powerlessness as Power', 177–78. Lee posits a parallel between the power of Jesus displayed in the first half of Mark's narrative, although Mark himself emphasised Jesus' *authority* no less than his power, and the power of the coming son of man. Is it not possible that the power of the coming son of man

Lee's discussion of the journey towards Jerusalem in Mark 8:22 – 10:52 and Jesus' agitation in Gethsemane demonstrates that for Mark powerlessness—not, as before, power—characterises God's reign.[18] Yet there is a further twist. Mark's trial scene (14:53–65) and his crucifixion narrative (15:20b–41) point towards the conclusion that because powerlessness is *God's* way of working in the world, it is therefore the most real or effective form of power.[19] From a human perspective, this is nonsensical (see Mark 8:33), but Lee exposits the paradoxical relationship between power and powerlessness in two ways: first, powerlessness is revealed to be God's power to *renounce* power; and second, it is through Jesus' powerlessness, rather than through his works of power, that God's reign is established.[20]

It may be that the tension between hope in the coming of the Son of Man in judgment and Mark's christological subversion of power as powerlessness is unresolvable. As Joel Marcus points out, there is tension in Mark's eschatology between imminent expectation and a sense of present fulfillment. For example, Mark's placement of the transfiguration story in Mark 9:2–8 immediately after Jesus' prophecy in Mark 9:1 'suggests that the Transfiguration is some sort of foretaste of the dominion of God', and Marcus also considers that Mark's passion narrative partially fulfils Jesus' eschatological prophecies in Mark 13.[21] If tension is integral to Mark's narrative, one should not expect tidy resolutions.

2. Christological innovation

That Jesus was crucified as a messianic pretender at the hands of the Roman prefect, Pontius Pilate, is the most historically reliable datum in the gospels. Crucifixion was widely practised in the ancient world, but

---

more closely parallels the divine power revealed in the cross? Cf Paul's teaching in 1 Corinthians 1–2 on the paradoxical power and wisdom of God summed up in his proclamation of 'Christ crucified'.

18.   Lee-Pollard, 'Powerlessness as Power', 178–83.
19.   Lee-Pollard, 'Powerlessness as Power', 183–84. For Lee, Jesus' powerlessness on the cross reveals God's power because it is self-giving rather than self-serving and humanising rather than authoritarian. One might also say that the potency of divine powerlessness is its capacity to effect human transformation, which coercive or self-aggrandising power cannot achieve.
20.   Lee-Pollard, 'Powerlessness as Power', 184–87.
21.   Marcus, *Mark 1–8*, 71–72. Mk 13:26 is not partially fulfilled, however, but rather reiterated in Mk 14:62.

for the Romans it was principally a 'tool of empire'. Reserved for rebels and runaway slaves, crucifixion served Rome's purpose of demonstrating the futility and inevitable consequence of resisting imperial rule. According to Joel Green,

> In the context of any discussion of the material aspects of crucifixion it is crucial to remember that Rome did not embrace crucifixion as its method of choice for execution on account of the excruciating pain it caused. The act of crucifixion resulted in little blood loss and death came slowly, as the body succumbed to shock. This form of capital punishment was savage and heinous, but for other reasons. Executed publicly, situated at a major crossroads or on a well-trafficked artery, devoid of clothing, left to be eaten by birds and beasts, victims of crucifixion were subject to optimal, unmitigated, vicious ridicule.[22]

In a similar vein, NT Wright has emphasised the symbolic value of crucifixion:

> Crucifixion was a powerful symbol throughout the Roman world. It was not just a means of liquidating undesirables; it did so with the maximum degradation and humiliation. It said, loud and clear: we are in charge here; you are our property; we can do what we like with you. It insisted, coldly and brutally, on the absolute sovereignty of Rome, and of Caesar. It told an implicit story, of the uselessness of rebel recalcitrance and the ruthlessness of imperial power. It said, in particular: this is what happens to rebel leaders. Crucifixion was a symbolic act with a clear and frightening meaning.[23]

---

22. Joel B Green, 'Crucifixion', in Markus Bockmuehl (ed), *The Cambridge Companion to Jesus* (Cambridge: Cambridge University Press, 2001), 91.

23. NT Wright, *Jesus and the Victory of God* (London: SPCK; Minneapolis: Augsburg Fortress, 1996), 543.

Neither the term nor the concept 'messiah' is comprehensible outside a Jewish milieu, yet no single messianic expectation prevailed within the various streams of Judaism in the first century CE.[24] However, one dominant image was of a royal warrior who would liberate Israel from its enemies and establish the rule of God, often in connection with rebuilding or restoring the temple in Jerusalem.[25] Within the gospels, the title that best encapsulates this messianic expectation is 'son of David', a royal title also found in Psalms of Solomon 17 (from the first century BCE).

In broad terms, Mark depicts Jesus as a royal messiah. However, a central feature of Mark's story of Jesus is that this messiah's mission can only be accomplished through suffering and death. Yet suffering and death, especially death by crucifixion, was not part of any messianic expectation. As Donald Juel asserted,

> The Messiah in postbiblical Jewish tradition is a royal figure expected to play the role of king. The variety in portraits arises from the range of functions appropriate to a king. There is no evidence of traditions about the suffering and death of the Messiah prior to the Christian era.[26]

Perhaps Juel overstated his case, since 4 Ezra 7:29 refers to the (non-atoning) death of the messiah.[27] However, Jewish traditions before Jesus seem to have been unfamiliar with the notion that the messiah

---

24.   See, for example, James H Charlesworth (ed), *The Messiah: Developments in Earliest Judaism and Christianity* (Minneapolis: Augsburg Fortress, 1992); John J Collins, *The Scepter and the Star: The Messiahs of the Dead Sea Scrolls and Other Ancient Literature* (New York: Doubleday, 1995); Wright, *The New Testament and the People of God*, 307–320. For some sagacious reflections on the evidence for diverse messianic expectations during the first century, see John Painter, *The Quest for the Messiah: The History, Literature and Theology of the Johannine Community*, 2nd edition (Edinburgh: T&T Clark, 1993), 16–18.

25.   See Wright, *Jesus and the Victory of God*, 485: 'Temple and battle were . . . central symbols of a royal vocation.'

26.   Donald Juel, *Messianic Exegesis: Christological Interpretation of the Old Testament in Early Christianity* (Philadelphia: Fortress Press, 1988), 172.

27.   See James Charlesworth, 'From Messianology to Christology: Problems and Prospects', in Charlesworth (ed), *The Messiah*, 8.

would accomplish his mission through suffering and death.[28] Yet Mark's depiction of Jesus as royal messiah is emphasised precisely (and paradoxically) in his account of Jesus' suffering and death. As Christopher Tuckett recognises,

> There is . . . a powerful strain in Mark's passion narrative emphasising that Jesus is a *royal* figure: it is as the messianic king that he goes to his death, even though the very narrative itself, by virtue of the fact that it is recounting a violent and shameful death, implies an almost complete reversal of previous ideas of what royalty and messiahship involved.[29]

This 'reversal of previous ideas of what royalty and messiahship involved' had profound implications, not only for understanding Jesus' identity and mission but also for understanding the kingdom of God (God's mode of ruling) and one's place in it (discipleship). The death of Jesus at the hands of Israel's oppressor ought to have convinced those who believed him to be the messiah that they had been badly mistaken. Yet, as Juel argued, Mark chose to emphasise the disparity between traditional messianic speculation(s) and the inescapable fact that Jesus was crucified, using '. . . the tension between Jesus the crucified Christ and messianic tradition as an interpretive key for understanding not only Jesus but God and the human situation'.[30]

---

28. See Carroll and Green, *The Death of Jesus in Early Christianity*, 170: '. . . the notion of a suffering Messiah runs counter to everything we know of varieties of messianic expectation in Second Temple Judaism'.

29. Christopher M Tuckett, *Christology and the New Testament: Jesus and His Earliest Followers* (Louisville: Westminster John Knox Press, 2001), 115. Cf Donald Juel, *Messiah and Temple: The Trial of Jesus in the Gospel of Mark* (Missoula, MT: Scholars Press, 1977), and Frank J Matera, *The Kingship of Jesus: Composition and Theology in Mark 15* (Chico, CA: Scholars Press, 1982), each of whom has emphasised the significance of Jesus as a royal figure in Mark's passion narrative.

30. Donald H Juel, *A Master of Surprise: Mark Interpreted* (Minneapolis: Augsburg Fortress, 1994), 103.

3. Intertextuality as reinterpretation in Mark's crucifixion narrative (Mark 15:20b–41)

Given the fact of Jesus' crucifixion, perhaps the most effective means by which the gospel writers reinterpreted their conception of God's way of working in the world was by rereading their scriptures in light of their transformed understanding of the messiah's identity and mission. Whatever experience or insight stands behind the Emmaus road episode in Luke 24:13–35, the process of identifying scriptural texts that could be read as pointing toward a suffering messiah was a crucial stage in the life of the early Jesus-movement.[31] Indeed, without the impetus to demonstrate that the hideous and humiliating execution by crucifixion occurred, in the case of Jesus, 'according to the scriptures' (1 Cor 15:3), the Jesus-movement might not have lasted beyond the end of the first century CE. Only by showing that Jesus fulfilled traditional expectations was the nascent Jesus-movement able to sustain itself and engage in mission.[32]

Mark's crucifixion account, the climactic scene in his passion narrative, follows the interrogation by Pilate (who *before* hearing the chief priests' accusations asks Jesus in Mark 15:2, 'Are you the king of the Jews?'), the release of Barabbas instead of the king of the Jews (Mark 15:9, 12) and the mocking of Jesus by Roman soldiers who salute Jesus as king of the Jews (Mark 15:18). This emphasis is consistent with the inscription detailing the 'charge' on which he was executed, 'The king of the Jews' (Mark 15:26). Mark could not have been clearer that Jesus was crucified as a messianic pretender.

A transitional passage, Mark 15:20b–21, begins with the phrase, 'And they [the soldiers] lead him out so that they might crucify him.' Mark 15:20b is in some sense resumptive of Mark 15:15, which indicates that Pilate 'hands Jesus over' to be crucified. In the intervening passage, Mark took pains to point out that in the governor's strong-hold (*praetorium*) Jesus is mockingly hailed 'king of the Jews' by an entire cohort (normally comprising about 600 men),

---

31.   Juel, *A Master of Surprise*, 103–105, considers Luke's interpretive strategy to differ from Mark's, but it is nonetheless a reinterpretation of biblical tradition.

32.   Green, 'Crucifixion', 99–100, identifies four interrelated Jewish traditions that served as resources for interpreting Jesus' death on a cross: (1) the suffering of the prophets; (2) psalms of the suffering righteous; (3) the idea that Israel's deliverance would come as a result of great suffering; and (4) the 'suffering servant' tradition.

which in some sense anticipates the centurion's confession of Jesus as 'son of God' in Mark 15:39. In Mark 15:21 the soldiers compel a certain Simon of Cyrene to carry Jesus' cross, presumably the crossbeam (*patibulum*), but Mark did not specify their reason for doing so. Since it was customary for anyone condemned to be crucified to carry the cross-beam, it is reasonable to suppose that Jesus was too weak to do so, but at this point Mark was more concerned to expand on Simon's identity by naming his sons.

Mark's crucifixion narrative proper commences at Mark 15:22 and comprises two subsections, the crucifixion of Jesus (15:22–32) and his death (15:33–41).[33] Given the methods and purpose of crucifixion, it is remarkable (to us) how restrained Mark's crucifixion narrative is. No reference is made to Jesus' suffering, and the initial reference to his crucifixion in Mark 15:24 occurs in the most sparing detail (three words, one being Mark's ubiquitous conjunction καί). Since such executions were both public and commonplace, perhaps there was no need to recount the gruesome details. Yet Mark used repetition to ensure that his readers (most of whom were *hearers*) could not escape the ignominy of Jesus' crucifixion.[34]

Mark's first obvious allusion to scripture in his crucifixion story follows his understated notice, 'and they crucify him' (Mark 15:24). Indeed, the emphasis in Mark's initial reference to the crucifixion of Jesus in Mark 15:24 is on the soldiers' action, 'and they divide his clothing, casting lots for them'. This is the first of a number of echoes of Psalm 22 in Mark's crucifixion account; that it is this intertextual echo that Mark emphasised, rather than the mechanics of crucifixion, indicates what Mark wanted to be uppermost in the minds of his audience, namely, that despite Jesus' humiliation and suffering, his crucifixion accords with scripture and so fulfils a divine purpose. The cumulative effect of further allusions is to reinforce this conviction.[35]

---

33. Moloney, *The Gospel of Mark*, 318, makes a good case for dividing Mark 15:20b–32 into two further subsections, 15:20b–25, 26–32.
34. In Mk 15:12–32 there are ten references to 'crucify' or 'cross' (15:13, 14, 15, 20, 21, 24, 25, 27, 30, 32), and in Mk 15:32 there is an additional reference to 'those co-crucified with him'.
35. See RT France, *The Gospel of Mark: A Commentary on the Greek Text* (Grand Rapids: Eerdmans; Carlisle: Paternoster Press, 2002), 640.

After relating Jesus' crucifixion in Mark 15:24 using the historical present,[36] Mark reiterated the point in the following sentence, using the aorist tense, to connect Jesus' crucifixion with the first of three time-notices. This reiteration appears to be retrospective,[37] although Mark's use of καί rather than ὅτε disallows certainty. Perhaps we should read Mark's inelegant syntax as *emphatic*: 'It was nine o'clock, and they *crucified* him!' Although Mark chose not to narrate the sickening and shameful details of Jesus' crucifixion, he repeatedly called attention to this brutal fact.

Mark 15:27 reiterates the point further by noting that 'with him [Jesus] they crucify two bandits, one at [his] right and one at his left'. The phrase, 'one at [his] right and one at his left', is redundant, unless Mark intended to recall the exchange between Jesus and the two sons of Zebedee in Mark 10:35–40.[38] Whereas James and John thought that to be with Jesus (Mark 3:14) entailed positions of honour and prestige, Jesus taught that to be with him and to follow him entailed suffering alongside him. By being placed at the right- and left-hand side of the 'king of the Jews' (Mark 15:26), these two bandits were in a position to suffer in solidarity with Jesus.

Following the reference to two bandits being crucified alongside Jesus, Mark alluded a second time to Psalm 22. The note in Mark 15:29 about passers-by ridiculing Jesus and 'wagging their heads' recalls Psalm 22:7 (21:8 in LXX). Although Mark used the term 'blaspheme' rather than 'mock', which appears in the LXX version of the psalm, the allusion is clear enough.

---

36. On the frequency and purpose of Mark's use of the historical present tense, see Elliott C Maloney, 'The Historical Present in the Gospel of Mark', in Maurya P Horgan and Paul J Kobelski (eds), *To Touch the Text* (New York: Crossroad, 1989), 67–78. Maloney concluded that like other hellenistic writers, Mark used the historical present to make the major events of his narrative more vivid. One might also suggest that in a predominantly oral environment, Mark's use of the historical present made his narrative more immediate to his hearers and perhaps encouraged them to feel as though they were participants in his story.

37. See Adela Yarbro Collins, *The Beginning of the Gospel: Probings of Mark in Context* (Minneapolis: Augsburg Fortress, 1992), 112: 'The aorist tense is used [in Mark 15:25] because the verse is retrospective; it comments on an event already narrated.'

38. The vocabulary of Mark 15:27 more closely matches Mark 10:40, where Jesus recalls James and John's initial demand, but the linguistic construction more closely matches James and John's initial demand in Mark 10:37.

Mark 15:32b returns the reader's (or hearer's) attention to 'those co-crucified with him', again reiterating the ignominious culmination to the story of Jesus and emphasising the shame attached to Jesus' death by noting that even his co-crucified reviled him. 'Jesus is completely alone; he has no allies, not even among those who share his fate . . . The mockery of Jesus is now complete.'[39]

Mark's story of the crucifixion of Jesus progressively underscores his ignominy, shame and isolation. The most reasonable conclusion to draw from what has befallen him is that his mission was not authorised by God. His death by crucifixion at the hands of Israel's oppressor leaves his followers with no alternative but to accept that their hopes had been betrayed or had at least been misplaced. Yet Mark's stark story subverts this reasonable conclusion. While the remainder of his crucifixion narrative continues to emphasise the anguish of the crucified one, and even elevates the sense of Jesus' abandonment, his biblical allusions convey a different dimension.

Mark 15:33 recounts that at midday, the brightest time of day, darkness encompasses the whole land for the second of two three-hour periods. This is almost certainly an allusion to Amos 8:9–10, although other biblical texts may well have been in mind, especially those associated with 'the day of the Lord' (understood to signify judgment).[40] The way in which Mark connected the conclusion of this three-hour period of darkness with Jesus' cry of dereliction suggests that Jesus experiences the darkness as God's judgment. The repetition of timing in Mark 15:34 indicates that Jesus' loud cry, 'My God, my God, why have you abandoned me?', is a response to the darkness.[41] Nothing else thus far in Mark's crucifixion narrative is presented as God's action. The darkness is the first phenomenon suggestive of divine action, and it is to this that Jesus responds for the first time since replying to Pilate's question, 'Are you the king of the Jews?' For Craig Evans, 'The darkness of the land signifies judgment; that Jesus cries out

---

39.   Craig Evans, *Mark 8:27–16:20*, WBC 34b (Nashville: Thomas Nelson, 2001), 506.

40.   See Brown, *The Death of the Messiah*, 1035.

41.   Cf Thomas E Schmidt, 'Cry of Dereliction or Cry of Judgment? Mark 15:34 in Context', *Bulletin for Biblical Research* 4 (1994): 146-47, who accepts a link between the darkness and Jesus' cry from the cross but regards the cry as explicating the darkness to signify judgment.

the way he does suggests that divine judgment has in part fallen on him.'[42] Similarly, Marcus cites Mark 15:33 as an example of 'eschatological exegesis', that is, an allusion to Amos 8:9, which associates the day of judgment ('that day') with the darkness at noon. 'As Jesus dies, then, the eschatological day of God's judgment prophesied in the OT has fallen like a terrible shadow over the earth.'[43]

However, Jesus' cry of abandonment is a direct citation of the opening words of Psalm 22, echoes of which have previously punctuated Mark's crucifixion narrative. Psalm 22 is one of a group of lament psalms or 'psalms of the righteous (innocent) sufferer'. As Marcus has noted, 'The most pervasive source for Old Testament allusions and citations in the Markan passion narrative is a group of psalms in which the speaker laments the persecution that he suffers from his enemies, protests his innocence, and calls upon God to deliver him.'[44] He also points out that the greatest concentration of allusions to an individual lament psalm occurs in Mark's crucifixion narrative, which is replete with allusions to Psalm 22:

> The dividing of Jesus' garments in v. 24 (Ps 22:18), the mockery and head shaking of v. 29 (Ps 22:7), and the cry of dereliction in v. 34 (Ps 22:1) are the most obvious examples. More distant echoes are the demand that Jesus save himself in vv. 30-31 (Ps 22:8) and the motif of derision in v. 32 (Ps 22:6), but in view of the pervasiveness of the influence of the psalm elsewhere in the narrative allusions to it in vv. 30-32 seem likely.[45]

Marcus considers that most of these allusions belonged to a pre-Markan passion narrative but thinks it likely that Mark recognised

---

42. Evans, *Mark 8:27–16:20*, 507.

43. Joel Marcus, 'The Old Testament and the death of Jesus: The Role of Scripture in the Gospel Passion Narratives', in Carroll and Green, *The Death of Jesus in Early Christianity*, 222. Brown, *The Death of the Messiah*, 1460, notes that darkness followed by a loud cry may allude to Psalm 22:3.

44. Joel Marcus, *The Way of the Lord: Christological Exegesis of the Old Testament in the Gospel of Mark* (Louisville: Westminster John Knox Press, 1992; Edinburgh: T&T Clark, 1993), 172. Cf Marcus, 'The Old Testament and the death of Jesus', 207.

45. Marcus, *The Way of the Lord*, 174.

them and expected as much from at least some of his readers. Particularly important for his interpretation of Mark's crucifixion narrative is his view that the way in which biblical allusions are embedded in the text places Mark on a trajectory of postbiblical Jewish exegesis that interpreted psalms of the innocent sufferer eschatologically. This trajectory is at least as early as the Septuagint, in which the heading of most such psalms is translated as εἰς τὸ τέλος ('unto the end'), and is represented in the Qumran literature. Later targumim and midrashim on Psalm 22 indicate that this trajectory extends beyond the first century CE. As a result, Marcus postulates that allusions to Psalm 22 (and other lament psalms) in Mark's Gospel should be interpreted eschatologically.[46]

Placing Mark's allusions to Psalm 22 on an exegetical trajectory that interprets the psalm eschatologically enables one to read the citation of the opening words of Psalm 22 in Mark 15:34 as an allusion to the psalm as a whole, which moves from lament to trust in God's deliverance and beyond trust to praise of God. For Marcus, Mark's placement of the cry of abandonment on Jesus' lips at the moment of his death not only reinforces Jesus' *innocent* suffering but also hints at God's vindication by deliverance from death.[47] As he concludes:

> Although Mark himself is not the source of most of the allusions to the Psalms of the Righteous Sufferer in his account of Jesus' suffering and death, he is aware of their scriptural basis. He is, moreover, the heir of an interpretive tradition that takes these psalms as prophecies of eschatological tribulation and of the establishment of the kingdom of God, which includes the resurrection of the dead. Jesus' suffering, death, and resurrection thus become, in his interpretation, eschatological events prophesied in the scriptures. These scriptures speak of the suffering and vindication of an inclusive figure who incorporates in his own person the experience of the people of God. They are thus an appropriate palette from which to mix the pigments for the Markan

---

46. Marcus, *The Way of the Lord*, 177–79.
47. Marcus, *The Way of the Lord*, 180–82.

> picture of Jesus, for the story of Jesus' martyrdom
> and glorification is also the story of the persecuted
> but divinely empowered Markan community that
> takes up its cross and follows him on the way.[48]

Whatever one thinks of the reasons given by Marcus for thinking that the whole of Psalm 22 was intentionally alluded to in Mark 15:34, the subtlety of this interpretive device suggests that Mark did not intend to minimise the sense of abandonment expressed in Jesus' cry.[49] Moreover, in a careful investigation of Mark's selection of language from Psalm 22, Vernon Robbins has drawn attention to two features of Mark's allusions to Psalm 22 that challenge 'hopeful' interpretations of Jesus' cry in Mark 15:34.[50] First, with regard to the context in which Mark cites the opening words of Psalm 22, Robbins observes: 'The Markan scene occurs when all hope of rescue has disappeared.'[51] And second, with respect to Mark's various allusions to Psalm 22, he points out that the order in which Mark 'borrowed' from Psalm 22 is the reverse of their sequence in the psalm. For Robbins, 'the sequence of Mk 15 inverts the sequence of Ps 22, and with this inversion comes a subversion of its rhetoric. The sufferer in the psalm expresses hope to the end; Jesus on the cross expresses the agony of abandonment by everyone including God.'[52] Since these observations cohere with both the movement and major details of Mark's crucifixion narrative, this 'bleaker' reading of Mark 15:34 is more persuasive than Marcus's 'hopeful' reading.

Mark 15:37 seems to indicate that Jesus cried out a second time at the point of death. Whether this is a second cry in Mark's account, as it clearly is in Matt 27:50, is unclear. Like the two references to Jesus

---

48. Marcus, *The Way of the Lord*, 186. Cf Schmidt, 'Cry of Dereliction or Cry of Judgment?', 145–53, who proposes that Jesus cries out as a representative of the Jewish nation, whose judgment (signified by both the darkness and the rent temple veil) signals the dawning of hope for all nations.

49. France, *The Gospel of Mark*, 652–53, fears this to be the end result of reading Mk 15:34 as Marcus does.

50. Vernon K Robbins, 'The Reversed Contextualization of Psalm 22 in the Markan Crucifixion: A Socio-Rhetorical Analysis', in F Van Segbroeck *et al* (eds), *The Four Gospels 1992: Festschrift Frans Neirynck*, BETL 100 (Leuven: Leuven University Press; Uitgeverij Peeters, 1992), 1161-83.

51. Robbins, 'The Reversed Contextualization of Psalm 22', 1179.

52. Robbins, 'The Reversed Contextualization of Psalm 22', 1179.

being crucified (Mark 15:24, 25), Mark's second reference to a loud cry may simply reiterate that Jesus died in this way—by shouting. For Painter, this is another Markan resumption: 'What Mark has done is to show the response to the loud cry of Jesus before noting that, having given the loud cry, Jesus breathed his last; he died.'[53]

The darkness before Jesus' death, to which he responds with his cry of dereliction, is matched after his death by the violent 'splitting' (ἐσχίσθη) from top to bottom of 'the veil of the sanctuary' in Mark 15:38. 'This gives us two God-given, eschatological signs forming an inclusion on either side of Jesus' death agony.'[54] Both the use of the passive voice and the note that the veil was torn *from top to bottom* imply divine action.[55] Such divine 'ripping' recalls the beginning of Jesus' mission in Mark 1:9–11, where after his immersion in the Jordan by John Jesus perceived the heavens split apart and the Spirit descending upon himself. He also heard a voice from the heavens, 'You are my dear and only son', echoed in the crucifixion narrative by the centurion's confession, 'Truly, this man was God's son' (Mark 15:39). It is widely acknowledged that Mark intentionally framed his account of Jesus' mission by these references to the 'splitting' of the heavens and the 'splitting' of the temple veil. 'In both cases', according to Adela Yarbro Collins, 'the verb σχίζω signifies the opening of that which normally hides the godhead. Both verses imply a theophany. In its original context, [Mark] 15:38 implies that the death of Jesus was God's will and that Jesus was vindicated.'[56]

In light of the two previous references to the sanctuary in Mark 14:58 and 15:29, Brown also interpreted the rending of the veil as a vindication of Jesus. 'Part of the import of the present narrative, which constitutes a third reference to the sanctuary, must be that Jesus is

53. Painter, *Mark's Gospel*, 206.
54. Brown, *The Death of the Messiah*, 1032-33. Brown's remark occurs in the context of his deliberations on the subdivision of Mark 15:33–41, but this observation is not dependent upon structural considerations. He later observed: 'As a negative sign after the death, the rending stands parallel to the darkness before Jesus' death. The day of the Lord with its burden of judgment was being heralded' (1102).
55. Evans, *Mark 8:27–16:20*, 509, accepts Robert Gundry's suggestion that the tearing of the temple veil is the result of Jesus' expiration in Mark 15:37, but this is far from obvious.
56. Collins, *The Beginning of the Gospel*, 117.

vindicated: Rending the veil of the sanctuary has in one way or another destroyed that holy place.'[57] However, as Brown himself noted, both previous references to the sanctuary in Mark 14:57–58 and 15:29 misrepresent Jesus, so one wonders how the rending of the veil vindicates Jesus' alleged statements about destroying the sanctuary. On the other hand, alongside the obvious symbolism of judgment, the recollection of the baptismal story at the beginning of Jesus' mission reminds the reader that *this* crucified one is none other than he of whom the heavenly voice declared, 'You are my dear and only son. With you I am well pleased' (Mark 1:11; cf 9:7). The dissonance between God's acceptance of Jesus at his baptism and God's abandonment experienced by Jesus at his crucifixion corresponds to the ambiguous context within which disciples of Jesus grapple with the paradox of evil in a world created by a good and just God.

With respect to Mark 15:39, this text makes it difficult to know how the *manner* of Jesus' death evoked the centurion's exclamation, 'Truly this man was God's son!' Various explanations have been offered,[58] yet what matters most for Mark is that the only human confession to match that of the divine voice in Mark 1:11 and 9:7 occurs at the cross on the lips of one whose position directly in front of ('opposite') Jesus makes it impossible to avoid the full impact of Jesus' suffering and shame. Jesus is not 'son of God' in isolation from, nor even despite, suffering and shame, but in the midst of and even by means of these cruel realities. That this confession is made by a gentile may signify that he represents non-Jewish Christianity,[59] but the centurion's confession also illustrates the critical decision required of believers in the Roman empire. As Evans observes, 'The centurion acknowledges that this crucified Jesus of Nazareth is the true son of God, not "divine"

---

57. Brown, *The Death of the Messiah*, 1102.

58. For example, Juel, *A Master of Surprise*, 74, n7, regards the centurion's confession as yet another taunt. 'The centurion plays a role assigned all Jesus' enemies: They speak the truth in mockery, thus providing for the reader ironic testimony to the truth.'

59. See Schmidt, 'Cry of Dereliction or Cry of Judgment?', 152: 'Most obviously, the centurion is a gentile, and as such the sequence of vv. 35–39 [in Mark 15] prefigures the acceptance of the gospel by gentiles following its rejection by the Jews.'

Caesar as the imperial cult would have it.'[60] The good news that Mark proclaimed subverted Roman mythology.[61]

Both the splitting of the veil of the sanctuary and the centurion's confession interpret Jesus' crucifixion eschatologically. According to Francis Moloney,

> Immediately following the death of Jesus, two events take place which indicate the beginning of a new era. The eschatological nature of the death of Jesus, symbolized by the darkness over the whole land between the sixth and the ninth hour, becomes clear. As he dies the separation between the inner Sanctuary, once the preserve only of the priestly cast of Israel, is torn from top to bottom (v. 38), and a Gentile, the Roman centurion, confesses: 'Truly this man was the Son of God' (v. 39). The death of Jesus marks the turning point of the ages.[62]

In other words, the crucifixion of Jesus cannot be adequately understood in isolation from God's presence and powerful action.

4. Theodicy and eschatology in light of Mark's crucifixion narrative

The dynamic of Mark's Gospel is the result of tension, especially the tension emerging from differences between traditional expectations of a Jewish messiah and Jesus' crucifixion as 'king of the Jews'.[63] Tension also exists at the heart of Mark's eschatology, arising from the *apparent* discrepancy between the image of the crucified one and the image of

---

60. Evans, *Mark 8:27–16:20*, 512. Commenting on Mark 15:39, Evans writes, 'The centurion now ascribes to Jesus what he had earlier ascribed to Caesar: Caesar is not *divi filius*, "son of God" (alluding to the title of the great emperor Augustus), but Jesus is . . .' (510).

61. See Ched Myers, *Binding the Strong Man: A Political Reading of Mark's Story of Jesus* (Maryknoll, NY: Orbis Books, 1988), 121–24. Cf Evans, *Mark 8:27–16:20*, lxxx-xciii, whose discussion of the purpose of Mark's Gospel focuses on the many ways in which it presents Jesus in opposition to the imperial cult.

62. Moloney, *The Gospel of Mark*, 328.

63. Cf Juel, *A Master of Surprise*, 101–102.

the Son of Man coming in judgment.[64] As a result, there is in Mark's Gospel no straightforward resolution of the traditional problem(s) of theodicy.

Intertextual allusion was perhaps the primary means by which Mark affirmed the fulfilment of God's purposes in and through Jesus' humiliation, suffering and death. Yet this was an *interpretive*, not empirical, affirmation. This is important for understanding the cry of abandonment in Mark 15:34. Mark probably did not intend to suggest that Jesus himself alluded to the whole of Psalm 22, but the multiple allusions to this psalm in his crucifixion narrative indicate that from a post-resurrection standpoint one can affirm that the experience of godforsakenness does not preclude movement towards trust in God and even praise of God.[65]

Mark used intertextual eschatological imagery to indicate that precisely when Jesus experienced abandonment by all, including God, God was nevertheless present and active. If the eschatological imagery of Mark's crucifixion narrative conveys a christological reversal (divine vindication of the crucified one), the implications for disciples of Jesus are threefold: first, to *perceive* God's presence with and for the suffering one; second, to allow for the possibility that within the mystery of God's creativity, innocent suffering has redemptive significance; and third, to accept that since the way of Jesus is none other than God's way of working in the world, it is also a way to be emulated here and now. In response to evil and suffering in the world, Mark's christology and eschatology imply an ethic of discipleship informed by and conformed to the way of Jesus.

In connection with the first and second of these implications, one may affirm with Moltmann, Sölle and others that suffering is not alien to God. A *theological* extension of Mark's crucifixion narrative is that God somehow participates in innocent suffering, sharing the pain and absorbing it into God's own being to be transformed. This, at least, can

---

64.   The discrepancy is apparent because it is based on a particular interpretation of Mk 8:38, 13:26 and 14:62. In light of Mark's christology, this interpretation of Mark's eschatology needs reappraisal. See, for example, the exegesis of these passages in France, *The Gospel of Mark*, 343–46, 497–505, 530–40, 608–13.

65.   For a somewhat different view that nevertheless emphasises the interpretive significance of Mark's allusions to Psalm 22 and other psalms of lamentation in his passion narrative, see John P Meier, *A Marginal Jew: Rethinking the Historical Jesus, Vol 1: The Roots of the Problem and the Person* (New York: Doubleday, 1991), 170–71.

be affirmed in faith, anticipated in hope and lived out in love. As for Mark's ethic of discipleship, it entails a radical reversal of values, not least with respect to our perceptions of power and suffering. Echoing Dorothy Lee, Richard Hays has observed:

> . . . Mark's Gospel redefines the nature of power and the value of suffering. Because Jesus uses power to serve rather than to be served, authentic power is shown forth paradoxically in the cross. Those who exercise power to dominate others, to kill and oppress, are shown not only as villains but also, surprisingly, as pawns of forces beyond their control . . . On the other hand, Jesus' apparently powerless passion becomes the true expression of the power of God.[66]

Such is Mark's 'theodicy'.

---

66.   Richard B Hays, *The Moral Vision of the New Testament: A Contemporary Introduction to New Testament Ethics* (HarperSanFrancisco, 1996), 90. Hays's 'echo' of Lee is unintentional, resulting from a shared perceptiveness of, and receptivity to, central yet counterintuitive Markan themes.

'The Darkness Did Not Overcome It': Theodicy and Eschatology in the Gospel of John

Dorothy Lee

1. Introduction

The Gospel of John, like the NT in general, contains no treatise on theodicy. Eschatology, on the other hand, is prominent in the Fourth Gospel, although it is a narrative treatment of the theme—narrative that includes discourse and dialogue—rather than a systematic discussion. Still less is the relation between theodicy and eschatology explicit. However, the Johannine text implies a good deal about the nature of sin and evil, and it is these theological implications which this essay attempts to draw out, along with the relationship to the Johannine eschatological vision, a vision that is in NT terms unique. What can be said about theodicy in the Fourth Gospel is thus more tentative than what can be said about Johannine eschatology, although even here there is ambiguity.

Broadly speaking, theodicy means the attempt to give a plausible account of the existence of God, or belief in God, in the face of sin, evil and suffering. Eschatology speaks of God's transforming future, a transformation grounded in the person and work of Christ. The difficulty yet necessity of this endeavour is complicated by the problem of how to define evil. In his study of JRR Tolkien, Tom Shippey speaks of two basic theories of evil, both of which are intertwined in Tolkien's own writings and centred on the question of whether or not 'shadows' actually exist.[1] On the one hand is the apocalyptic view (which Shippey calls the 'orthodox' view) in which evil has its source objectively outside the human heart, where it is an actively malevolent force. The extreme form of this is Manicheism, in

---

1. Tom Shippey, *JRR Tolkien: Author of the Century* (London: HarperCollins, 2000), 112–160, especially 128–35.

43

which good and evil are equal forces pitted against one another. On the other hand is the view that evil has no substance and consists of the privation of good (which Shippey calls the 'Boethian' view, although it goes back to Augustine).[2] In this perspective, evil is seen as the absence of goodness within the human heart rather than an objective external reality.

The problem with the latter view is that it fails to deal adequately with the virulent and aggressive forms evil can take. For example, the opposite of love in such a view is probably indifference, but this does not account for hatred, which is an active force signifying much more than indifference. Both views exist in some tension within *The Lord of the Rings*, a tension that in Shippey's view is philosophically unavoidable and even necessary. While the Fourth Gospel has no overt perspective on this question, Tolkien's own tensions could be said to derive from the Bible itself, which leaves the issue largely unresolved.

2. Darkness and light

John has a number of different ways in which he characterises good and evil, but the primary symbolism is that of light and darkness.[3] Darkness is a broad symbol that denotes both sin and evil, as well as the suffering that evil brings; it also includes death. What John means by darkness (σκοτία) is indicated first in the prologue, where it appears twice in John 1:5 without explanation and then unfolds throughout the Gospel. Darkness and light represent what is often referred to as Johannine dualism;[4] they form a major symbolic

---

2.   Shippey attributes this view to Boethius (*c* 480–524/5), probably because his *Consolations* was translated into Anglo-Saxon in the ninth century and thus likely to have been read by Tolkien. Augustine first promulgated this view in reaction against Manicheism.

3.   See Dorothy Lee, *Flesh and Glory: Symbol, Gender and Theology in the Gospel of John* (New York: Crossroad, 2002), 166-96.

4.   On Johannine dualism, see CK Barrett, 'Paradox and Dualism', in his *Essays on John* (London: SPCK, 1982), 98–115, and John Ashton, *Understanding the Fourth Gospel* (Oxford: Clarendon Press, 1991), 205-237. The dualism is not ontological, however. See also Rudolf Bultmann, *Theology of the New Testament*, 2 vols (London: SCM Press, 1955), 2:15-32.

opposition in the narrative. This moral or spiritual dualism closely parallels OT wisdom literature in its contrast between the way of wisdom and the way of folly.

Craig Koester notes that in the Fourth Gospel, darkness can be interpreted in a threefold sense.[5] First, darkness signifies 'the powers that oppose God', which are demonic in origin but manifest themselves in human actions, particularly the rejection and crucifixion of Jesus. Secondly, darkness is symbolic of the 'lethal estrangement from God' resulting in death, both physical and spiritual, an estrangement typified by various figures in the Gospel. John does not make Paul's direct connection between sin and death (Rom 5:12), but there can be no doubt that the Johannine Jesus stands for life over against death. His grief and anger as he approaches the tomb of Lazarus (11:33, 35, 38)—admittedly ambiguous emotions (11:36–37)[6]—reveal that death is the enemy of God; Jesus' victory over the world (16:33b) is the victory also over death. The contrast between the stench of death from which Martha recoils (11:39) and the fragrant odour of life at the banquet to celebrate the raising of Lazarus in Mary's anointing (12:3) makes the same point.[7] Ironically, the richly scented oil also commemorates Jesus' death (12:7), through which life will be victorious and death itself undone.

Thirdly, and rather differently, darkness is also a way of characterising human 'ignorance and unbelief' in the face of revelation, a state that is not in itself culpable. The man born blind, for example, lives in a state of darkness because literally he cannot see and metaphorically he is ignorant of Jesus' identity; yet Jesus refuses to associate his 'darkness' with sin or evil (9:3). Whereas the

5.   Craig R Koester, *Symbolism in the Fourth Gospel: Meaning, Mystery, Community*, 2nd ed (Minneapolis: Augsburg Fortress, 2003), 143-44.
6.   See Rudolf Schnackenburg, *The Gospel according to St John*, 3 vols (London: Burns & Oates, 1968–1982), 2:335-37; Brendan Byrne, *Lazarus: A Contemporary Reading of John 11:1-46* (Collegeville: Michael Glazier, 1991), 57-60; and Dorothy Lee, *The Symbolic Narratives of the Fourth Gospel: The Interplay of Form and Meaning* (Sheffield: JSOT Press, 1994), 208-212.
7.   On this contrast, see Lee, *Symbolic Narratives*, 222, n2; also Gail R O'Day, 'John', in Carol A Newsom and Sharon H Ringe (eds), *The Women's Bible Commentary*, expanded ed (Louisville: Westminster John Knox Press, 1998), 386-88.

religious leaders excommunicate the man after his healing and revile him as a sinner (9:34), embracing Jesus in their accusation for his breach of the sabbath, Jesus vindicates the man of sin and illuminates his life, physically and spiritually. Indeed, the man both sees and 'sees' Jesus for the first time at the end of the story, and responds by acknowledging his identity and worshipping him (9:35–38).[8] By the end, the authorities who have persecuted the man are revealed to be the real sinners, their sin lying not in their ignorance but rather in their arrogant assumption that they possess light (9:39–41). Their darkness is dark indeed.

Two points about the Fourth Gospel's perspective on darkness flow from this, both equally important for John's understanding of evil. First, sin and evil are portrayed as being in violent opposition to light and goodness. They are not merely passive forces, as in the Augustinian/Boethian notion of the absence of good. They possess an objectivity that can be seen and felt. This objectivity expresses itself fundamentally in personal terms. The personality who embodies evil in the Fourth Gospel is 'the ruler of this world' (ὁ ἄρχων τοῦ κόσμου [τούτου], 12:31; 14:30; 16:11), 'the devil' (8:44; 13:2),[9] 'the Satan' (13:27), or the 'evil one' (or 'evil', 17:15). Even Judas Iscariot is described in the context of Jesus' betrayal as 'a devil' (διάβολος, 6:70), and his betrayal of Jesus is identified as demonic and associated with darkness (13:27, 30).[10] Evil is a terrifying force that can infiltrate even the most harmonious and intimate circle.

---

8.   There is a textual problem in Jn 9:38-39a, some textual witnesses omitting them. See Raymond E Brown, *The Gospel According to John*, 2 vols (New York: Doubleday, 1966–1970), 1:375. Arguments for their inclusion, however, are strong; see Bruce M Metzger, *A Textual Commentary on the Greek New Testament* (London/New York: United Bible Societies, 1975), 229, and Schnackenburg, *St John*, 2:254, 499. The Johannine Jesus is the object of worship; thus the verb προσκυνέω is entirely appropriate in this context.

9.   Although etymology is a limited guide to semantic meaning, it is of some significance to note that the Greek word 'symbol' has to do with 'putting' or 'throwing together' (σύν + βάλλω), whereas the word 'devil' has to do with 'dividing', or 'putting/throwing apart' (διά + βάλλω).

10. Note that Jesus himself is accused of sin (5:9-10, 16; 9:14-16, 24-33; 18:23, 30; 19:7) and of being possessed by a demon (8:48-49, 52).

Apart from Judas Iscariot, the evangelist characterises evil in the response of the religious authorities, 'the Jews', who stand over against Jesus though claiming the same God as their Father (8:41). Their rejection of Jesus as the Son of God is the great tragedy and quintessential act of evil in this Gospel.[11] Later in John, the evangelist associates 'the Jews' with the unbelieving κόσμος—that realm which, in various contexts in the Fourth Gospel, exists in opposition to and rebellion against God.[12] The religious authorities, whom John generally refers to as 'the Jews' or the Pharisees (sometimes interchangeably), are in a real sense the human embodiment of the unbelieving κόσμος. Such people, despite their religiosity (and, in the case of Judas Iscariot, their attachment to Jesus), become the epitome of evil, displaying the influence of 'your father, the devil' (8:44). Their rejection of Jesus reveals their true origins and identity, which is the very opposite of what they claim.

Secondly, the Gospel of John makes it clear that, whatever the seeming reality in human life, evil is secondary to goodness. Despite the aggressive activity of evil in the Fourth Gospel, encapsulated in its capacity to crucify the Son of God, the evangelist demonstrates from the beginning that light and darkness are not equally balanced forces. The first stanza of the prologue begins with the pre-existent Logos who stands in radical relationship to being—sharing in pre-existence, existing in face-to-face relation to God (πρὸς τὸν θεόν) and existing as God (1:1–2). As the coeternal source of life, the Logos is the giver of light, the first created entity in Genesis 1:3–5. All created life derives from this divine source. Only then does the prologue introduce darkness, with overtones of the waters of chaos from which the world was formed: 'and the light shines in the darkness, and the darkness did not overcome it' (1:5; cf Gen 1:2).

In the first creation account, God makes the world by overcoming both the deep and the darkness; the latter is overcome on the first day, with darkness turning into night and being banished each day

---

11.   The term 'the Jews' (οἱ Ἰουδαῖοι) is by no means consistently negative in the
      Fourth Gospel (see, eg, 4:22; 11:33–35, 45).

12.   This is not true of all contexts. The word κόσμος can also have a positive
      meaning, where it stands for the creation which, as the work of God's hands, is
      the object of divine love (1:10; 3:16). For a summary of John's symbolic usage
      of κόσμος and also οἱ Ἰουδαῖοι, see Lee, *Flesh and Glory*, 181–88.

by the dawn, while the former is overcome on the second day by the emergence of land and the forming/naming of the seas (Gen 1:3–8). John reflects the language of the first day, yet moves also from the literal to the metaphorical. The double sense of the verb καταλαμβάνω ('to grasp', 1:5) suggests both overpowering and comprehending; the darkness can neither overcome nor understood the light. This statement moves between protology and eschatology,[13] just as the verbs move between present tense (φαίνει) and past tense (κατέλαβεν, aorist), the latter indicating completed action. While the sense of completion refers in the first place to creation, it extends to an eschatological vision that the Gospel itself will fulfil. John's mode of expression is never linear in its logic, particularly in the prologue. The tense of φαίνει suggests that the evangelist is summarising the Gospel narrative; this is an eschatological promise in which the end replays the beginning. As elsewhere, John's purpose is christological. The Logos who entered the world in human form is also the one who created the world. Just as the darkness of creation never conquered the light when the world was made, so too eschatologically the reader can be assured that once more light will triumph over darkness. As Jesus assures his disciples at the end of the farewell discourse: 'Fear not: I have conquered the world' (16:33).

Tolkien's two views of evil are apparent here. Inasmuch as darkness is personified, John portrays it as an active force attempting to gain power over light yet perpetually unable to do so, its efforts directed against God as the source of life (ζωή). At the same time, the symbolic polarities show that John is speaking of the realm of shadows. Darkness does not participate in either the *being* of God (εἶναι) or the *becoming* (γίνεσθαι) that characterises the creation of the world and, later, the incarnation (1:14).[14] It has in one sense no substance of its own, yet it plays an active role in the world,

13. Brown, *John*, 1:26–27, sees John 1:5 as a reference to the Fall, but the present tense of the verb ('shines') indicates an ongoing reality; so Francis J Moloney, *The Gospel of John* (Collegeville, MN: Liturgical Press, 1998), 36–37.

14. For this distinction within the prologue (between εἶναι where it is used of God and γίνεσθαι in relation to creation), see Frank Kermode, 'John', in R Alter and F Kermode (eds), *The Literary Guide to the Bible* (London: Fontana, 1987), 443–48. Kermode quotes John Chrysostom.

possessing its own fierce energy focused on death and destruction.[15] In one short verse, therefore, the shadow actively threatens the creation formed by the Logos. The beginning is seen from the perspective of the end. The darkness has not succeeding in either comprehending the light or preventing its shining forth. In characteristically Johannine style—like waves on the shore with the incoming tide, where each restatement advances the reader's understanding[16]—the prologue moves towards the passion and the eschatological triumph of God over darkness.

At the end of Jesus' public ministry, the evangelist sums up the first half of his Gospel with the symbolism of light and darkness. The imagery is that of discipleship, where the choice is to walk in darkness or in company with the 'light of the world'. The darkness is a threatening power that will finally 'overcome' the misguided pedestrian who imagines it possible to walk without light: 'walk while you have the light, lest the darkness overtake (καταλάβῃ) you' (12:35). Again, the symbolism of light is linked to faith (12:36).[17] The purpose of Jesus' coming is to illuminate the world and overcome its darkness, drawing people into the light of faith: 'I have come as light into the world, in order that everyone who believes in me may not abide in darkness' (12:46). In relationship with Jesus, his followers can become true 'children of the light' (12:36), unable to be overcome by the darkness.

---

15. In Revelation, evil seems to possess a derivative substance that is counterfeit. M Eugene Boring, *Revelation* (Louisville: John Knox Press, 1989), 154–57, speaks of a 'counterfeit "trinity"' of evil corresponding to the heavenly world: the dragon is a parody of God (Revelation 12); the beast from the sea, which is mortally wounded, parodies the crucified Christ (Rev 13:1-10); and the beast from the land (Rev 13:11–18), who is associated with the false prophet (Rev 16:13; 19:20; 20:10), is the parodic counterpart to the Holy Spirit.

16. Moloney, *John*, 34.

17. John finds the source of this symbolism in Isa 6:10 where darkness is linked to blindness, a blindness that is far from innocent but knowing and freely chosen (12:40; cf Mk 4:12 and parallels; Acts 28:16; Rom 11:8).

3. The meaning of sin and evil

With the use of such imagery, John does not offer a concise or abstract definition of sin or evil. He is more concerned with warning and transformation: 'The prophet does not "reflect" on sin; he "prophesies" against.'[18] Throughout the Gospel, the evangelist is more concerned with 'sin' than 'sins'. The singular form occurs thirteen times (ἁμαρτία, 1:29; 8:21, 34 [twice], 46; 9:41 [twice]; 15:22 [twice], 24; 16:8, 9; 19:11), whereas the plural is found only four times (ἁμαρτίαι, 8:24 [twice]; 9:34; 20:23).[19] To two of his own disciples, John the Baptist describes Jesus in the opening narrative as 'the Lamb of God who takes away the sin (τὴν ἁμαρτίαν) of the world' (1:29; cf 1:36). This ascription is powerful enough to make them abandon the Baptist and follow Jesus (1:37–40). The preponderance of the singular throughout the Gospel indicates that, for John, sin is a fundamental underlying problem rather than a series of immoral acts.[20] Indeed, one could argue that John is more concerned with the brokenness and alienation from which actual sins derive than with individual moral failings. Bultmann argued that Jesus' response to the marital ambiguities of the Samaritan woman's life, for example, is directed towards spirituality rather than moral failing; Jesus addresses 'the restlessness of her relationships', which reveals her 'thirst for life' and thus her need of living water (4:16–19).[21] On the other hand, 'sin' characterises the religious authorities who persecute the man born blind and arrogantly assume they possess an insight they self-evidently lack (9:39–41).

---

18. Paul Ricoeur, *The Symbolism of Evil* (Boston: Beacon, 1967), 54.
19. In addition, John uses the cognate verb 'to sin' (ἁμαρτάνω, 4:14; [8:11]; 9:2, 3) and the noun 'sinner' (ἁμαρτωλός, 9:16, 24, 25, 31).
20. Note that at Jn 8:24, which uses the plural (twice, ἁμαρτίαις), this usage is a restatement of the singular (ἁμαρτία) at 8:21. The plural 'sins' is used of the man born blind by the authorities at 9:34, but Jesus speaks a few verses later of their 'sin' abiding (singular, 9:41). The fourth reference to sins is an unusual (Johannine) reference to the authority of the Easter community, bestowed by the risen Jesus for the church's mission, to 'release and retain' sins (20:23).
21. Rudolf Bultmann, *The Gospel of John: A Commentary* (Oxford: Blackwell, 1971), 188. See also CM Conway, *Men and Women in the Fourth Gospel: Gender and Johannine Characterization* (Atlanta: SBL, 1999), 116–19.

John also uses other related language. He speaks of 'evil' in three synonymous terms (πονηρός, 3:19; 7:7; 17:15; φαῦλος, 3:20; 5:29; κακός, 18:23, 30), which describe the opposition of the unbelieving world. In the tabernacles discourse (John 7–8), he speaks of 'false-hood' (ψεῦδος, 8:44) and describes the devil as a 'liar' (ψεύστης, 8:44, 55). Here evil stands over against truth, embodied in Jesus (8:32; 14:6). The devil is the great lie, the deceiver of the world, whose utterances are never to be trusted; nothing he says or does partakes of the truth. In the same discourse, John describes sin as enslaving, particularly for those who lack self-awareness and who imagine that their status before God is free. For John, they are slaves and their state one of wilful yet tragic enslavement to the power of sin (δοῦλος and δουλεύω, 8:33–35). These accusations attack the assumption of 'the Jews' that their physical descent from Abraham guarantees their status as children of God.

With the exception of the woman caught in adultery (not originally part of the Johannine text, 7:53 – 8:11),[22] John is thus not concerned with sin as a series of discrete acts of moral transgression, but rather with the theological and spiritual root of evil within the human heart. The evangelist employs a number of different symbols, including the use of representative figures.[23] As we have seen, the symbol of darkness incorporates images of untruth, self-deceit, wilful ignorance, slavery, death and unbelief. Where human beings reject the light, they enter into league with the forces of darkness. Sin is a fundamental disorientation in relationship to God that can only be removed by a divine miracle (1:12–13; 3:1–8).

Of equal import for exploring the Johannine notion of sin is the theological context which outlines Jesus' saving role; the one who

---

22.   The story is absent from the oldest and best manuscripts (eg, *P*66, *P*75, Sinaiticus and Vaticanus, et al), and also a wide variety of other ancient authorities. See Metzger, *Textual Commentary*, 219–22; also E Hoskyns and FN Davey, *The Fourth Gospel*, 2 vols (London: Faber & Faber, 1947), 2:673–78; Brown, *John*, 1:335–36; CK Barrett, *The Gospel according to St John*, 2nd ed (London: SPCK, 1978), 589–92; and Lee, *Flesh and Glory*, 177–78.

23.   On the use of representative figures in John's Gospel, see RF Collins, 'Representative Figures of the Fourth Gospel', *Downside Review* 94 (1976): 26–46, 118–32.

deals with sin, who 'takes it away', is the one who also defines it.
Throughout the Fourth Gospel, sin is articulated in people's response
to Jesus. Towards the end of Jesus' unsatisfactory conversation with
Nicodemus, Jesus speaks of eschatological judgment already taking
place in confrontation with the light (3:19–21). Sin comes into effect
with the rejection of Jesus, with all that that implies—the rejection of
God, eternal life and identity. For Bultmann, such rejection is linked
directly to the revelation:

> What the world does is sin, because it turns itself
> against Jesus, who has shown himself to be the
> Revealer by his words and his actions. If there were
> no revelation then there would be no sin either, in
> the decisive sense of the term.[24]

For the evangelist, sin is neither moral lassitude nor even a failure of
recognition, an absence of knowledge; rather, it is the active rejection
of light embodied in the Johannine Jesus.

In eschatological terms, what Jesus does in saving the world is to
remove sin at its root by restoring God's image in humanity. Human
beings are given the authority 'to become children of God' (1:12–13),
a status they have forfeited, as manifested in the tragic inability to
recognise their own Creator (1:10–11).[25] Because of the loss of the
divine image, and the light and love which flow from it—because
human beings have forfeited the 'glory' of their status as children of
God[26]—the Light enters the world in flesh to restore the image. As
Gregory of Nazianzus says of the fall and incarnation: 'I received the

---

24. Bultmann, *John*, 551.
25. Whether 'his own' (1:11) is a form of synonymous parallelism (meaning the
      same thing as the κόσμος, 1:10) or whether John is narrowing the focus from
      'the world' to 'the Jews' is unclear. In either case, the rejection of 'the Jews'
      stands for the rejection of the world, 'his own' acting here in a representative
      role.
26. The Greek Fathers tried to distinguish between 'image' and 'likeness' (Gen
      1:26-27), arguing that only the latter was lost in the fall. See JP Smith, *St
      Irenaeus: Proof of the Apostolic Preaching* (Westminster: Newman Press,
      1952), 126, n70. While the distinction cannot be sustained linguistically, the
      attempt to present the fall as partial rather than total is theologically important.

image (εἰκών) and I did not protect it; he received a share in my flesh so that he might even save the image and make deathless the flesh.'[27] Likewise, for Athanasius, humankind, already made in the image of the Logos, can only be restored by the Son: 'therefore the Word of God came through himself, in order that, being the Image of the Father, he might re-create humanity according to the image'.[28]

The notion of the fall as the loss of human glory goes back to Judaism. The Rabbinic commentary on Gen 2:3 speaks of the removal of Adam's glory after the fall: 'The glory stayed the night, but at the end of the Sabbath, [God] took the splendor from him and drove him out of the Garden of Eden' (Gen Rabb IX.5). This same tradition is found in the Gnostic Apocalypse of Adam, where Adam, speaking to his son Seth, recounts the story of the fall: 'Then we became two aeons, and the glory in our hearts deserted us, me and your mother Eve . . . And the glory fled from us' (1:5–6). In the Fourth Gospel, the giving of δόξα to believers (17:22) signifies the restoration of the image, since humankind's original relationship to God has been ruptured and the divine glory, given in creation, lost. As the eternal Son of God, Jesus takes on flesh, entering the realm of matter in full identification with humankind, an identification never made in the OT even though, for John, everything in the OT points to it. Because the Son bears flesh in his humanity, human beings can now become sons and daughters of God.

This means that the filiation of believers is dependent on Jesus' identity as the eternal Son who has taken on flesh. The risen Christ makes this point in the Easter garden in his commission to Mary Magdalene. He identifies himself with the believing community, yet also carefully distinguishes himself from them: 'I am ascending to my Father and your Father, my God and your God' (20:17). The careful nuance of this verse is vitally important—not 'our Father and our God' but *my* and *your*. Significantly, only a few verses later in the climactic faith confession of this Gospel, Thomas acclaims the risen Jesus 'my Lord and my God' (20:28). The evangelist stresses that

27. *In Sanctum Pascha*, in J-P Migne (ed), *Patrologia Cursus Completus, Series Graeca* (Paris: Garnier, 1844–1891), 36.XLV.633-36.

28. *De Incarnatione: An Edition of the Greek Text*, edited by FL Cross (London: SPCK, 1957), XIII.7.

Jesus stands not only on the human but also on the divine side. The Fourth Gospel here returns to its beginnings in the revelation of Jesus' divine identity (1:1–2, 18).

In this way, the Gospel according to John defines sin in relation to its saviour. As Barrett observes, both sin and its remedy are christological: 'Since sin is concentrated into the rejection of Christ it is clear that sin can be removed only by Christ'.[29] Final judgment, for John, is realisable in the meeting with Jesus. As the Light of the world (8:12; 9:5), the Revealer both illuminates and exposes, vindicating and condemning. Eschatological judgment lies in the past for believers who have already crossed over from death to life (μεταβέβηκεν, 5:24); no future judgment awaits them. Yet not only has final judgment already taken place; so also the meaning of sin has become decisively apparent. To stand before the Johannine Jesus is to come face to face with both sin and salvation simultaneously. The one assists in defining the other. Judgment is the ensuing response to this definitive encounter. Sin, in this sense, is discerned and defined eschatologically.

John's understanding of sin and evil is thus christological and eschatological; both take shape in relation to Jesus. How the characters of the Gospel respond to Jesus as the revelation of God is the only determinant in naming sin: 'the Revealer uncovers the essence of sin'.[30] To belong to the realm of sin and evil, to side with the darkness, is exemplified in the refusal to believe in Jesus as the Light of the world, the Wisdom of God, the only Son of the Father who shares the life of God. In the Johannine worldview, it means to reject life itself and, in doing so, to reject both self-knowledge and the knowledge of God. The 'sin of the world' taken away by the Lamb of God is the sin of unbelief. Sin exposes itself in the choice of death over life, darkness over light, deceit over truth, slavery over freedom, self-delusion over self-knowledge, 'the ruler of this world' over the Κύριος. It means choosing the good opinion of other people over

---

29.   Barrett, *St John*, 80.
30.   R Metzner, *Das Verständnis der Sünde im Johannesevangelium* (Tübingen: Mohr Siebeck, 2000), 113.

God's esteem.[31] In the Fourth Gospel, sin is the unbelieving rejection of life as it is disclosed in Jesus Christ, a rejection epitomised by darkness:

> From a Johannine perspective, walking in darkness means persisting in unbelief, since antipathy toward God and Jesus is the sin at the root of all other sins. Conversely, walking in the light means living by faith in Jesus.[32]

Even religion itself (including forms of faith in Jesus) is no proof against sin and evil. On the contrary, for this evangelist there are no more culpable sinners than those religious leaders who lack self-knowledge and are filled with self-delusion; who harm those entrusted to their care; who abuse others to gain power; who rob and deceive the innocent; who place the demands of goodness and justice beneath their own self-preservation; who close themselves against the very light they claim to radiate. The darkness here is wilful, self-conscious and self-chosen, the most destructive form of all, implying an alliance with the forces of darkness. Such unbelief and rebellion against the God of Jesus Christ is the true manifestation of sin and evil in the Fourth Gospel.

4. An eschatology of presence

John's peculiar eschatology, with its shift from a strictly apocalyptic time-frame, understands that everything representing ultimacy in Christian faith belongs firmly in the present. Schnackenburg has described this as 'the magnificent one-sidedness of Johannine escha-

---

31. In the Fourth Gospel, embracing death and darkness means also a turning away from divine glory (δόξα), manifest in the incarnate flesh of Jesus. Such a disorientation results in turning to others for good opinion and esteem (δόξα, 5:41–44)—the word in this context reverting to its original, classical meaning of 'opinion' instead of 'glory'—rather than to God as the author and giver of life. See Metzner, *Das Verständnis der Sünde*, 231, 246–47.

32. Koester, *Symbolism in the Fourth Gospel*, 160.

tology'.[33] No longer is salvation of the future; now it has definitively engaged and transfigured the present.[34] The glory of God is unveiled in the incarnation, a glory that Paul and the synoptic gospels associate with the future (eg, Rom 8:17–22; Mark 8:38 and pars; 13:26 and pars). John understands the incarnation as '"the Son of Man coming in the clouds" with great power and glory' (Mark 13:26; cf Dan 7:13). In the Fourth Gospel, this eschatological glory, present already in the flesh, unfolds throughout the ministry of Jesus, reaching its climax on the cross; everything about Jesus reveals the life-giving, loving, self-giving nature of the Father. In this sense, Jesus can speak of himself as 'the resurrection and the life' in the greatest of the 'I am' sayings, revealing to Martha a reality that can be grasped in the here-and-now, even in the face of death (11:25–26).

In the Fourth Gospel, it is the incarnation that is salvific, and John views the incarnation through the lens of the resurrection. The result of Jesus' enfleshment is his death on the cross; yet because he is Lord of life from eternity before time, the creator and source of life, the eternal Son, he possesses the uniquely divine power to 'lay down my life in order that I may take it up again' (10:17). The incarnation implies Jesus' death if his mortality is genuine; in turn, the giving up of life implies, for him (and him alone!), the resurrection. The 'logic' is suggested by the unusual construction of the sentence in John 10:18b. Jesus does not just speak of his authority to lay down his life *and also* to take it up again; he speaks instead of laying it down *for the purpose of* (or *with the result of*)[35] raising it, as if the raising were entirely dependent on the laying down. The incarnation implies death and the death implies resurrection because of the unique identity of the one who is the source and giver of life.[36] Jesus' death

---

33.   Schnackenburg, *St John*, 2:426–37, especially 437. Schnackenburg sees this one-sidedness as corrected somewhat by the evangelist's disciples.

34.   John's use of νῦν, 'now', is often significant in this respect (4:23; 5:25; 12:31; 13:31 [twice]; 16:32).

35.   See below.

36.   There is little in John about the disciples misunderstanding the necessity of Jesus' passion, especially compared to the three passion predictions in Mk 8:31; 9:31–32; 10:32-34, although at the arrest Simon Peter cuts off the ear of the high priest's servant (Jn 18:10–11) and later denies his relationship to Jesus (18:15–18, 25–27). Perhaps the death and resurrection of the Johannine Jesus is

results in the release of life, as illustrated in the main events of the passion: the inscription (19:19–22); the seamless robe (19:23–24); the founding of a new community around the mother of Jesus and the beloved disciple (19:25–27); the giving of the Spirit (19:30); and the flow of blood and water (19:31–37). Incongruously, these become vibrant and fecund symbols of life.

Moreover, because of Jesus' identity, the same authority is given to believers as children of God. The raising of Lazarus, who is one of the 'friends' of Jesus (and thus one of God's children), points to the raising of all believers who follow the path opened for them through death and resurrection.[37] Believers find eternal life in the present, a life that will carry through in and beyond death. At John 6:54, Jesus confirms that 'one who eats my flesh and drinks my blood has [present tense] life in me, and I will raise him/her up on the last day'. These are not really two separate stages—eternal life given now followed by a future resurrection of the dead. Rather, one flows from the other; the one implies the other. Believers will be raised because of the life they already possess.

There is an arresting parallel in the Greek myth of Demeter and Persephone. After being seized by Hades, god of the Underworld, to be his queen, Persephone mistakenly eats seeds of the pomegranate, condemning herself to the realm of the dead. Although she can return half-yearly to her mother Demeter, the corn goddess (thus ensuring the seasons of the year), she must return to Hades at the end of each summer. In John, by contrast, the believer eats the fruit of life which Jesus, in the eucharist, both *gives* and *is* (6:51–58), thus consuming the 'seeds' of eternal life (cf 12:24). These seeds—that is, in the imagery of John 6, the bread that has come down from heaven—bestow a life that even the darkness of death cannot overpower. The believer lives now in an eternal summer that the onset of winter cannot destroy.

---

more self-evident to those who know his true origins and destiny, ie, identity (cf Jn 16:29–32).

37. The point is emphasised in the distinctive parallels between the raising of Lazarus, which is, strictly speaking, still on a literal or material level, and that of Jesus. See Lee, *Flesh and Glory*, 219.

The peculiar shape of Johannine eschatology means that what is forged by the incarnation (with all that it implies about death and resurrection) is an eternal present that is no longer susceptible to the constraints of time. The eternal Logos enters the transient and ephemeral world of time, passing through it as we do, yet also transforming it. The incarnation—the revelation of divine glory in human flesh—is an event that comes 'from above', entering the realm that John describes as 'from below'. In Jewish apocalyptic thinking, the resurrection is a future event, signalling the end of history and the winding up of the world in its present form. Here John stitches together Jewish thinking, which is eschatological, and vestiges of Greek (Platonic) philosophical thought, with its ontological distinction between a domain above that is the source of being and the world below which shadows it. Jewish apocalyptic categories predominate, but Greek influences are also present. Yet the differences are important. The earthly is not denigrated in John's understanding; indeed, the earthly serves its true function by pointing symbolically to the heavenly (cf 3:12–13, 31). Moreover, unlike Greek philosophical conceptions, the divine enters the material world and becomes part of it, dissolving any possibility of ontological dualism.

Even the Jewish apocalyptic influence is qualified in John's symbolic worldview. For the believing community, the human mortality Jesus takes upon himself is not simply an event in the past. The resurrection creates an eternal sense of presence and releases life, especially in the giving of the Spirit-Paraclete who is 'the personal presence of Jesus with the Christian while Jesus is with the Father'.[38] Not only does the farewell discourse make plain the vital relationship between Jesus and the Spirit in the context of Jesus' departure; the resurrection narrative works in a similar way. Between the two encounters with the risen Christ—those of Mary Magdalene (20:1–18) and Thomas (20:24–29)—is the formal giving of the Spirit on the evening of Easter Sunday. One week later, on the Sunday following (when the community gathers to celebrate the resurrection), Jesus pronounces a beatitude on those who, unlike Thomas (and the other disciples), come to faith without seeing the

---

38.   Brown, *John*, 2:1139.

risen Christ in the flesh (20:29). This blessing is directed more at
future believers for their assurance—that is, the readers of the Gospel
—than reproachful of Thomas. John's point is that, though separated
from Jesus by time and space, and though dependent on the witness
of the apostolic community, future believers are in no way inferior to
the earliest community; they, too, stand in direct relationship to Jesus
through the Spirit and the life of the church.[39]

Furthermore, not only is the risen Christ present, but his wounds
are still on display. This is a peculiar feature of the Johannine and
Lukan resurrection narratives—that the Risen One bears the marks of
his suffering and death (Jn 20:24–29; Lk 24:39–40). Theologians point
to the function of the wounds in confirming the continuity between
the Jesus of history and the Christ of faith. But more is intended by
the exposure of Jesus' wounds to Thomas. In terms of Johannine
symbolism, the wounds are themselves the source of life (19:34). The
piercing of Jesus' side, whatever it may mean on a literal level,
reveals the death of Jesus to be life-giving and death-defying
(19:35–37). The wounded side, from which blood and water flow, is
now paradoxically the source of life—both blood and water being
sacramental symbols of the Spirit in the Fourth Gospel. There are also
overtones of birth in this scene; in an eschatological sense, the death
of Jesus represents the birth of the new community, the beginning of
the end.[40] Jesus stands before Thomas, and thus before the readers of
the Gospel, with his side still open, his wounds exposed, blood and
water flowing out to the community and thus to the world. The
Fourth Gospel captures the Crucified One in a moment of time that is
eternal.

This means that the signs of sin and evil are transformed eschatologically to become symbols of life. Jesus' death is the attempt of
the darkness to snuff out the light, an unholy alliance between the
Roman Pilate, along with the secular 'justice' for which he stands,
and the religious authority of 'the Jews', whose piety and desire for

---

39. See Dorothy Lee, 'Partnership in Easter faith: The Role of Mary Magdalene
     and Thomas in John 20', *JSNT* 58 (1995): 37–49.
40. On maternal imagery in the Fourth Gospel, see J Massyngbaerde Ford,
     *Redeemer—Friend and Mother: Salvation in Antiquity and in the Gospel of
     John* (Minneapolis: Augsburg Fortress, 1997), 168–201; Lee, *Flesh and Glory*,
     135–65.

ritual cleanliness drives their conduct during the trial and crucifixion.[41] In purely human terms, their attempt succeeds; the darkness does overthrow the light. Yet in terms of Johannine irony (prominent throughout the passion narrative), the symbols of death and darkness—the overcoming of the light by the darkness—are transformed into their opposite through the identity of the one who suffers and dies. The cross becomes a symbol of glory, unity, community, life and light. In the crucified and risen Jesus the Light of the world shines with unsurpassed splendour. The intimacy Jesus shares with his disciples, his role as the bridge between heaven and earth, his divine identity, the authentic nature of his fleshly existence, his giving of life to those who believe—all these are confirmed and even heightened in the cross and the Easter garden.[42] That which speaks of death becomes symbolic of life. While the unenlightened reader might assume from the prologue that Jesus can never be killed by the darkness, John shows that the darkness itself is revelatory; even in death, the light of life shines forth. The signs that in human terms denote the victory of sin, evil, death and darkness are transfigured into radiant symbols of eternal life. In the end, even death (despite itself) reveals the glory of God, for through its signs the Son of God gives birth to life and brings salvation to the world.

Nevertheless, John does not abandon traditional eschatological language of a future self-manifestation of God. Sometimes it is difficult, particularly in the farewell discourse, to know whether the language is ecclesiological (the giving of the Spirit to the believing community through Jesus' death and resurrection), thus locating

---

41. The trial before Pilate, in seven scenes, makes this point (18:28–19:16a), with Pilate shuttling between the inside of the praetorium, where Jesus is, and the outside, where 'the Jews' insist on remaining because of their reluctance to incur impurity (see also 19:31). Arguably the characterisation of Pilate, despite his attempts to release Jesus, is every bit as negative as that of 'the Jews'; so David Rensberger, *Overcoming the World: Politics and Community in the Gospel of John* (London: SPCK, 1988), 87–106. Against this view, see Brown, *John*, 2:794–95, 860, who, reflecting a scholarly consensus, sees John as whitewashing the character of Pilate.

42. This is powerfully conveyed in the garden imagery, which with its paradisal overtones is the place of Jesus' arrest, burial and resurrection (κῆπος, 18:1; 19:41).

itself in the present, or whether it retains something of its future, apocalyptic force. The Gospel is undoubtedly aware of a still-future dimension. The world and its prince, though already conquered, persist, projecting their hatred and hostility onto the believing community, just as they have with Jesus (15:18 – 16:4a). Believers continue to die, and 'human death is brutally real',[43] yet it does not have eschatological victory either now or in the future (11:4). With the prospect of a divine future still to be fulfilled, the community lives under protection in the here-and-now, with a sense of consecration that preserves its ecclesial identity and draws it into the life of the triune God (17:20–23). The church's eschatological deliverance from sin, evil and suffering is already spelt out, already given in the incarnate presence of Jesus, awaiting only the fullness of revelation.

5. A Johannine theodicy?

In three passages the fourth evangelist refers explicitly to the connection between sin and suffering, offering what seems to be a Johannine theodicy. In the story of the man born blind, the disciples assume that the man's disability is the direct result of sin, either the man's parents or his own (foetal!) sin (9:2).[44] At first glance, this view ties in with the parallel story of the disabled man in John 5, where Jesus appears to make a link between the man's disability and sin (5:14). Yet in the case of the man born blind, Jesus categorically rejects his disciples' theodicy (9:3–4). And in John 5, the healed man never comes to faith in Jesus; indeed, he cooperates with the authorities in their persecution of Jesus (5:15–16). The accusation of sin, in his case, more likely relates to his unbelief.[45]

However, Jesus' reply to his disciples in John 9 creates further theological problems. The literal translation of his reply is: 'Neither

---

43. Sandra M Schneiders, *Written that You May Believe: Encountering Jesus in the Fourth Gospel* (New York: Crossroad, 1999), 154, and on the theme of death in the Fourth Gospel, see 149–61. Cf Sandra M Schneiders, 'Death in the Community of Eternal Life', *Interpretation* 41/1 (1987): 44–56.

44. For the notion of parental sin transmitted to children, see Ex 20:5 and Deut 5:9 (also Lk 13:2-5). On this issue, see Bultmann, *John*, 330–331, n8.

45. Metzner, *Das Verständnis der Sünde*, 52–53, 61.

this man sinned nor his parents, but in order that the words of God
may be manifest in him [it?]' (9:3). The main clause of 9:3b must be
supplied by the reader, presumably, 'he was born blind in order that
the works of God might be manifest in him'.[46] This seems to imply
that God deliberately blinded the man in order to reveal his glory.
Similarly, in the case of Lazarus' illness, Jesus replies to the sisters:
'This sickness is not towards [πρός] death but for the glory of God in
order that the Son of God may be glorified through it' (11:4). This is
hardly a more satisfactory theodicy than the disciples' view at 9:2,
contradicting the notion that God's sending of the Son is motivated
fundamentally by love of the world (3:16).

It is likely, however, that the use of ἵνα at John 9:3 expresses not
purpose but result, as at 9:2, 'Rabbi, who sinned, this man or his
parents, in order that [ie with the result that] he was born blind?'[47]
In Semitic thought the distinction between purpose and result is
often blurred.[48] The same can be argued for 11:4. The preposition
πρός expresses either purpose ('not for the purpose of death but on
behalf of the glory of God, in order that the Son of God may be
glorified through it') or result ('this illness will not result in death but
the glory of God, with the result that the Son of God is glorified
through it'). The text itself, in both cases, is ambiguous. It is true,
more generally, that the Fourth Gospel articulates belief in divine
sovereignty that, while permitting evil and suffering, remains
ultimately in control of the world and its destiny. This is very
different, however, from arguing that God deliberately causes
suffering in order to gain glory.

46. GR Beasley-Murray, *John* (Waco: Word Books, 1987), 151, proposes that we
translate it as an imperative: 'Let the works of God be manifest in him', but this
is unlikely and ignores the parallel with 11:4 (so Moloney, *John*, 297). Talbert
suggests that one possibility is to punctuate 11:3-4 differently: 'But in order
that the works of God might be manifest in him, it is necessary for us to work
the works of the one who sent me . . .' See CH Talbert, *Reading John: A
Literary and Theological Commentary on the Fourth Gospel and the Johannine
Epistles* (London: SPCK, 1992), 158-59.
47. Barrett, *St John*, 335; Ben Witherington III, *John's Wisdom: A Commentary on
the Fourth Gospel* (Cambridge: Lutterworth Press, 1995), 182-83.
48. See CFD Moule, *An Idiom Book of New Testament Greek*, 2nd ed (Cambridge:
Cambridge University Press, 1965), 142-43.

The only resolution to these exegetical problems is to recognise that John addresses illness and disability eschatologically. Despite touching on issues of theodicy, John is more concerned with eschatology—with God's purpose for the world revealed in the incarnation. In the narratives of John 9 and John 11, the evangelist is speaking eschatologically. These evils are caused neither by God nor by individual sin, but their end—the giving of sight, the raising of the dead—reveals their transformation. Theodicy cannot explain why such evils occur, but eschatology reveals that God's ultimate purpose will be fulfilled; and that purpose is loving and life-giving. The works of God and the glory of God are the end results of human life, indeed, of all creation; through the Johannine 'signs', Jesus reveals God's eschatological purpose to bring salvation and life. God's life-giving Word, in this Gospel, has the final word. The problem of theodicy is not resolved from a theoretical viewpoint, but it is 'resolved' in the lives of those who are reborn to become God's children. Jesus' response to the man born blind thus 'shifts the problem of providence and suffering',[49] and sets it within an eschatological framework: 'The man's blindness will be made to serve God's larger purpose.'[50] Similarly, the sickness of Lazarus 'provides an occasion upon which . . . God may bestow glory upon his Son'.[51] In other words, these three passages—particularly John 9 and 11—provide not so much a theodicy as an eschatology. Evil and suffering are interpreted from the perspective of their final defeat in Christ. John's Gospel offers no overt theodicy but it has vital things to say about the nature of sin and evil; the only 'resolution' to be had emerges from the evangelist's unique eschatology.

6. Conclusion

Two concluding points emerge from this survey of the Fourth Gospel's eschatological vision in relation to sin and evil. First, in apocalyptic terms, evil and sin stand over against everything the

---

49. RA Culpepper, *The Gospel and Letters of John* (Nashville: Abingdon Press, 1998), 175.
50. Witherington, *John's Wisdom*, 183. See also Barnabas Lindars, *The Gospel of John* (Grand Rapids, MI: Eerdmans, 1981), 342.
51. Barrett, *St John*, 390.

Johannine God represents;[52] in this Gospel the battle between good and evil has already been waged and won. Evil represents a tragic distortion in the world that God has created. In the prologue this tragedy is indicated by the failure of the world and of 'his own' to recognise or receive its creator. Death, too, is part of that which is hostile to God. The darkness of Lazarus' tomb, the decay of his body after being four days dead and the bindings around his body all signify the stranglehold that death has over human life. As the 'resurrection and the life', Jesus has divine authority to unsay death and to wind back its bands, summoning those imprisoned in darkness into the light of day (5:25-29; 11:38-44).[53]

Secondly, darkness viewed in an eschatological perspective cannot overcome light—indeed is already overcome in the defeat of 'the ruler of this world'. The power of evil lacks ultimacy and in the end is banished by the light that shines in the darkness. God incarnate enters the world and takes up the darkness, including the darkness of death, defeating it from within. God is not the cause of evil but rather has taken responsibility for the world by taking on flesh. Thus in the Fourth Gospel, God's 'explanation' for evil is God's answer in the incarnation. By living our life and dying our death, Jesus the incarnate Logos transfigures life and death, forging a new humanity, a new filiation, a radical renewal of creation that derives from his identity. In this Gospel, it is enough for God to cross the divide between heaven and earth—divine and human, spirit and matter—for the breach to be repaired, the chasm bridged, the wound healed. The advent of God, the flesh of God, the death of God—these are what destroy the realm of shadows and overcome the darkness.

Near the beginning of his quest in *The Lord of the Rings*, Frodo the ring-bearer is caught in a 'barrow', an ancient tomb, trapped in the dark on cold stone in the place of the malevolent dead. To his horror, he sees the shadow of the barrow-Wight slowly approaching, its arm

---

52.   On the characterisation of God in the Fourth Gospel, see MM Thompson, *The God of the Gospel of John* (Grand Rapids, MI: Eerdmans, 2001).

53.   John's 'sabbath christology' in John 5 and 9 outlines his understanding of the unique authority Jesus possesses in this Gospel, an authority he shares with the Father and is witnessed in his work of giving life and judging. On this theme, see Lee, *Flesh and* Glory, 116-17.

outstretched to seize him. In terror, Frodo calls out to Tom Bombadil, the master of wood and dale, to save him. Tom appears almost at once in his blue jacket and feathered hat, bringing with him the warm light of day that floods the chill darkness of the barrow. He enters the tomb and releases Frodo at once, singing merrily:

> Get out, you old Wight! Vanish in the sunlight!
> Shrivel like the cold mist, like the winds go wailing,
> Out into the barren lands far beyond the mountains!
> Come never here again! Leave your barrow empty!
> Lost and forgotten be, darker than the darkness,
> Where gates stand forever shut, till the world is mended.[54]

In the Gospel of John, the light has already shone, warming and illuminating the chill of death, and the shadows have fled. The barrow-Wights may stretch out deathly hands, but they cannot harm the children of light, protected by the divine name (Jn 17:11-12). With the coming of Christ, the darkness is swallowed up, leaving only joy and life, salvation and light, even in the deepest pit of death. For John, it is not we who explain evil but God who defines and destroys it in the one act of sending the Son to mortality and death.

---

54.   JRR Tolkien, *The Lord of the Rings, Part 1: The Fellowship of the Ring* (London: George Allen & Unwin, 1966), Book 1, 153-54.

Making Excuses for God: Theodicy and Eschatology in the Patristic Era

Kim Power

The first draft of this paper was written as the 'Coalition of the Willing' bombed Iraq into submission in the paradoxical hope of enforcing democracy with aggression, while media covered it as if it were a video game. We live in apocalyptic times as war and rumours of wars abound. Questions of theodicy and eschatology confront us inescapably. Modern science offers no easy alternatives to religious reflection on this question. If there is to be hope for a future, we will find it in our hearts and souls, not in our academies or our laboratories. As a global community we are challenged to justice and the alleviation of suffering; consequently the topic of this conference is not simply timely, but prophetic.

Theodicy and eschatology are both related dynamically to our objective and subjective images of God. They are structural threads constructing our webs of religious meaning. An alteration of one, forces alteration of another. Traditional doctrines inherited from the second to the sixth centuries, known as 'the patristic age' have done yeoman service for almost two millennia. More recently, the interest of secular historians in this period which established the foundations of Western culture has led historians to speak less of patristics and more about 'late antiquity'; that is, studying these centuries from perspectives that integrate religious systems with culture, and bridging the boundaries of classics, theology and history. Now new scientific and theological paradigms threaten to destroy, disrupt or subvert traditions, yet the questions themselves do not retreat.

However, because we speak of an era, we should not slip into assuming one common theology. We can become so accustomed to theology's use of Tradition, with a capital 'T', that we easily forget that at any given time there is a spectrum of theological positions. In late antiquity, doctrine was still fluid, and local churches had a great deal of autonomy. Christian apologists were beginning to write for a pagan audience and in dialogue with Judaism.[1] Not only did neoplatonism emerge, but Christian authors accepted scientific premises, unless they directly conflicted with Scripture. The Gnostic movement was also in dynamic dialogue with early Christianity.[2] Many aspects of Gnostic thought were compatible with Christian belief, and second century theologians can be extremely difficult to categorise.[3] The foundations of Christian doctrines of theodicy and eschatology were forged from the debates and tensions within Christian communities engaged with their own zeitgeist. The interpretations that emerged the victors in those patristic battles became enshrined in dogmas so perduring that it could seem as if they were always the sole tradition: a perception that overlooks their reinterpretation in every subsequent age.

The emergence of Christianity from intertestamental Judaisms created a unique problem for Christianity. The dominant Judaic theodicy believed suffering signalled a rupture of the Covenant, individual or collective, that demanded suffering at once punitive and purgative. But the Christian Scriptures confronted Judaic theodicy with the gospel of Jesus Christ, who reconciled God and humanity through a gratuitous act of loving atonement (John 1:14; 3:16–7), and who taught that God's perfection lay in the divine capacity for merciful forgiveness (Matt 5:43-48). This made a punitive theodicy more difficult to maintain—yet the Incarnation did not end suffering! Nor does it answer the question: Why did the Judeo-Christian God create a world in which suffering is endemic? The suffering of the innocent holds God accountable. God's nature is implicit in this discourse, because theodicy poses problems about divine compassion, justice and omnipotence. Moreover, as we are made in the image of God, beliefs about God shape our anthropology. God's responses to evil and suffering must be ours. Christian theodicy is integrally related to eschatology, the study of the 'last things' and the beginning of God's reign, the moment of justice, reward and punishment. Since the

1.   'Justin Martyr', Apologia 1 & II; Dialogue with Trypho the Jew.
2.   Examples are Origen, Commentary on the Song of Songs 9. Athanasius, On the Incarnation, 54.11; Ambrose, Hex 3.6.26; Gregory of Nyssa, On the Creation of Man 30.1.
3.   Mark Edwards, 'Origen No Gnostic: Or, on the Corporeality of Man', *JTS* 43. 1 (1922), 23–37.

beginning of the twentieth century, eschatology has become a far more pervasive theological theme.[4] It returns us to biblical and patristic texts for insights, where we discover that God's eschatological promises can be seen as fully realised in earthly life, fully deferred until the end of the world or partially realised now to be fully realised in eternal life.

I will examine two Christian writers, Irenaeus of Lyons and Augustine of Hippo, in the context of their responses to Gnosticism. Irenaeus was the first to confront Gnosticism systematically, whilst Augustine's doctrine of original sin unquestionably set the parameters for all further theodicies in the West. However, firstly, I will spend some time exploring Gnosticism since:

Gnostic thought pervaded late antiquity.

The engagement with Gnosticism led to the articulation of our traditional theodicies and eschatologies.

Gnosticism is still less well understood than orthodox Christianity.

1. Gnosticism and Christianity[5]

1.1 Methodological concerns

Polemic texts are the usual contexts for either justifications for, or denuncations of, Gnosticism. Apologists and critics are identical in their need to define themselves in relation to other groups. Similarities are minimised, differences are emphasised. Sometimes, cultic practice is chosen simply to reinforce the politics of difference. Another problem is that Gnostic texts are often extremely obscure. The further they were from mainstream thought, the deeper they hid their meanings in symbolic language which only initiates understood, as the Gospel of Philip illustrates:

> Light and darkness, life and death, right and left, are
> brothers of one another. They are inseparable. Because
> of this, neither are the good good, not the evil evil, nor
> is life life, nor death death. For the reason that each

---

4.   Michael Scanlon, 'Eschatology', *Augustine through the Ages: An Encyclopedia*, general editor Allan D Fitzgerald (Grand Rapids: Eerdman, 1999), 316.

5.   The origin of Gnosticism is the subject of academic debate and will not be treated here.

one will dissolve into its earliest origin. But those who
are exalted above the world are indissoluble, eternal.[6]

To outsiders, the meaning is virtually impenetrable. However, this
alone does not distinguish Christian from Gnostic discourse. Cryptic
sayings of Jesus constitute the Gospel of Thomas, many of which we
only 'understand' because we have read seventy per cent of them in
explanatory gospel narratives. Others are as opaque as Philip's gospel,
as Jesus' explanation of how the childlike enter the kingdom illustrates:

> When you make the two one, and when you make the
> inside like the outside and the outside like the inside,
> and the above like the below, and when you make the
> male and female be one and the same, so that the male
> not be male nor the female female; and when you
> fashion eyes in place of an eye and a hand in place of a
> hand, and a foot in place of a foot, and a likeness in
> place of a likeness; then will you enter.[7]

In late antiquity, Gnosticism was one factor which mediated
Christianity's reception. Gnosticism was as much a worldview or a
theodicy as a specific religion, because it was a systematic approach to
evil easily adaptable by other religious systems.[8] So widespread was it
that gnosticising tendencies appear in all ancient religious traditions.

The Gnostics themselves were never a homogeneous group.[9]
Indeed, an emphasis on individual authority was one of their critics'
objections. The danger was that theological diversity would proliferate

---

6.   The Gospel of Philip, II.53.15–24. All Gnostic texts are translated in *The Nag
     Hammadi Library* [NHL]. Revised edition, general editor James M Robinson,
     (San Francisco: Harper, 1990).

7.   The Gospel of Thomas, Saying 22.

8.   For an excellent accessible discussion of Gnosticism and its principal schools, see
     Denis Minns, *Irenaeus* (Washington, DC: Georgetown University Press, 1994),
     1–35.

9.   Helmut Koester's 'Introduction to the Gospel of Thomas,' states they were
     actually the first to call themselves monks, or solitaries. *NHL*: 126. On the
     principal Gnostic sects, see Giovanni Casadio, 'Gnostic Womanhood: Preliminary
     Notes for a Typology of the Feminine in Second Century Gnosticism', edited by
     EA Livingstone, *Studia patristica* (Leuven,1989), 307.

to the extent that Christianity would splinter into smaller and smaller sects. Conversely, though Gnostics argued vehemently for the authenticity of individual revelation, the purported authors of Gnostic writings are Jesus himself, James the Just, the Lord's brother, the apostles Peter, John, Thomas, Philip, Paul and Mary Magdalene. It would be naïve to think that this in no way relates to issues of authority.

Robin Lane Fox looks further than the argument for a conflict over institutionalised versus charismatic authority to a deeper, perhaps less conscious motive. He argues that, despite being under interdict, Christianity was still growing and winning converts from paganism because its strong faith in humanity's redemption through God's love cut through the doubts of pagan schools and the worries of an era that led one scholar to characterise the second century as the 'Age of Anxiety'.[10] Simultaneously, Christian apologists like Justin Martyr stressed Christianity's continuity with older wisdom traditions. Groups that later Christians labelled Gnostic usually held to a radical form of life they believed was more authentically Christian: typically ascetic, ostensibly non-hierarchical, they perceived their rebirth in Christ as a fundamental separation from past traditions, Judaism included.

Nonetheless, Gnostics usually agreed on two basic issues. A core belief was that Gnosticism conferred special access to divine revelation, usually through teachings said to have been handed down secretly from Christ to the disciples. Gnostic categories were less saint versus sinner than enlightened versus the unenlightened. Hence Gnosticism was the ground on which Christianity wrestled with the question, 'Is knowledge or faith the way to salvation?' As our own age is self-consciously aware, claims to élite knowledge are also claims to power and result in hierarchical social relations. In fact, it is difficult to resist the judgment that some Gnostic texts are not simply arrogant, but are downright offensive.

Gnosticism's second crucial tenet, which eventually caused its ultimate split from Christianity, was its reconciliation of God's infinite justice and goodness with the existence of evil by positing two

---

10.   Robin Lane Fox, *Pagans and Christians* (New York: Harper Collins, 1986), 330–4; ER Dodds, *Pagan and Christian in an Age of Anxiety* (Cambridge: Cambridge University Press, 1965).

existential and eternally opposed spiritual principles, one of which created the spirit and belongs to the light, and one which is responsible for evil through created matter. Effectively, this split Genesis' Creator from Jesus' *Abba*. Because Christian bishops acknowledged continuity between the Creator and the Father, Gnostics considered them deluded and could therefore reject the authority of the elected leader of their community. Elaine Pagels would add a third fault line between Gnosticism and Christianity. Orthodox Christians believed that Jesus was Lord and Son of God in a unique way, forever distinct from the rest of humanity, whereas the Gospel of Thomas recognises that Jesus and Thomas share the same source.[11]

Pagels tried to demarcate orthodoxy and heresy in each of these categories, yet found that there was too much diversity among Christian authors. For example, the Gospel of John's high christology and structural oppositions between light and darkness, good and evil made it a Gnostic favourite. Despite its authentic Christian provenance, John barely made it into the canonical Christian Bible. Moreover, the Gospel of Thomas, which grounded much of Pagels's argument, is no longer considered Gnostic, due to its seventy per cent overlap with the synoptic gospels.

The moderate Valentinian School's elaborate cosmology traced creation back to a single source, while exonerating Jesus' Father of any responsibility for evil. Paradoxically, given the claim that Gnosticism privileges divine immanence, Valentinian Gnosticism distanced the true God from humanity by a series of minor deities or emanations, also called aeons or hypostases. They are usually paired figures, male and female. Together with their source, they constitute Fullness of Spirit (the Pleroma). The Old Testament's Creator God was a lower emanation, a demi-urge whose name and role have parallels with matter's creator in Platonism.[12] Yet, how could an emanation descending from the infinitely good high God become monstrously evil enough to create matter to ensnare spirit? In the Valentinian

11. Pagels's, *The Gnostic Gospels* 1979 (later reprinted in Vintage Reissue editions, 1989) is often cited as the definitive text. However, she acknowledged that delays in publishing meant that further scholarly discussion had already overtaken some of her material. But as her text is still in print, it is worthwhile examining her arguments.

12. Casadio, 'Gnostic Womanhood', 312.

version, Sophia is the daughter of a primal couple.[13] She yearns to know her Father, interpreting yearning as love. It is only through 'The Limit', the power of order, that she conquers passion and accepts her rightful place in the universe.[14] Other narratives depict Sophia trying to emulate higher masculine deity's power to create in and from itself. Any resulting conception had to be malicious and insane.[15] In some versions, her son's behaviour distresses her so much that she abandons him altogether and flees to the higher heavens. Consequently, he thinks he is the only God, thus becoming ever more arrogant and outrageous. To the Gnostics, he is a false God, trying to pass himself off as the true All Father, Jesus' *Abba*. The Wisdom imagery is why some scholars perceive Gnosticism as woman-friendly, notwithstanding that Wisdom in the Old Testament is a glorious feminine figure, and Judaism is condemned by certain of these same writers as being patriarchal. This requires nuancing. In the Greco-Roman world, where women metaphorically played matter to man's spirit, the Sophia myth is hardly elevating for women. Like Eve, Sophia tries to act on her own authority, introducing death into creation, through her son. Indeed, Valentinus sometimes named her Eve.[16]

1.2 Eve
The Gnostic portrait of Eve is important, and less ambiguous than Sophia's. Eve's disobedience took on new meaning. Eve became a positive model because she defied the arrogant minor emanation that was the demi-urge and ate the fruit that would bring her wisdom —true esoteric knowledge that she then passed on to Adam. The Apocalypse of Adam therefore construed the loss of Paradise as a petty tyrant's unjust vengeance which destroyed humanity's primal unity, leaving it to fall from its celestial status into ignorance and servitude to the demi-urge, stumbling in the dark, searching for its lost glory.[17]

---

13. Irenaeus, Against Heresies [*AH*], 1.2.2.
14. Pagels, *Gnostic Gospels*, 160.
15. Casadio, 'Gnostic Womanhood', 320.
16. Pagels, *Gnostic Gospels*, 160.
17. Apocalypse of Adam 5.64.5–30. George MacRae, 'Introduction' to the Apocalypse argues AA may be an intermediate stage between Judaism and Gnosticism because it does not really draw on Christian motifs. *NHL*: 277.

Gnosticism cannot be simply categorised as either sexist or proto-feminist. Some communities reviled anything symbolically feminine.[18] Others revered feminine emanations, permitting women strong leadership roles within the community. According to Tertullian, the Carpocratian teacher, Marcella, claimed that they preserved secret teachings handed down from the women disciples Mary, Salome, and Martha, and the Coptic *Pistis Sophia*. Such groups believed that Christ had 'made Mary male'. Hence, Mary Magdalene could be the source of definitive doctrine about Christ: hardly an affirmation of woman *qua* woman.[19] In the main, though, female emanations echo Greco-Roman gender stereotypes, being passive, weak and inferior.[20]

In sum, as Minns has observed, Gnostics understand evil as the result of a dysfunction in the divine economy, yet not attributable to the Father himself.[21] In this schema, Christian belief in the incarnation becomes problematic, as does Jesus' passion and resurrection, because each imputes that divinity was itself enmeshed in matter. The radical Gnostic asserted that Jesus was not human but an angel of light who created the illusion he was human. He therefore did not really die. Only the symbolic body did. In one text, an appalling and manipulative Jesus not only eludes death, but laughs while Simon of Cyrene dies in his place:

> It was another, their father, who drank the gall and the vinegar; it was not I. They struck me with the reed; it was another, Simon, who bore the cross on his shoulder. It was another upon whom they placed the crown of thorns. But I was rejoicing in the height over all the wealth of the archons and the offspring of their

---

18. Dialogue of the Saviour 13–14; 91–93. Clement of Alexandria condemned Gospel of the Egyptians' similar argument in *Strom.* 3.9. Methodius, The Banquet 4. 2 and Augustine, The Literary Meaning of Genesis, 12.7.10; 12.3.3 represented respected Christian women as 'honorary men'.

19. The Gospel of Thomas, Saying 114; cf The Gospel of Mary 9; The Gospel of Philip, 59.1–10, and the Coptic Pistis Sophia, 1.17–19; 33–34.

20. Casadio, 'Gnostic Womanhood', 307. Howard M Jackson suggests Gnostic scholars may have redacted Plato himself. See *NHL*: 318.

21. Minns, *Irenaeus*, 18.

error, of their empty glory, and I was laughing at their ignorance.[22]

For others, Jesus really died, but his resurrection was only symbolic. There were practically as many variations on this theme as there are texts. The letter of James and what we know of Valentinus uphold the suffering of Jesus in the flesh. One's belief about Jesus' passion had very real consequences. When persecution was rife, one's theology could literally mean life or death. Admitting one was a Christian was a sure way to either the salt mines or the arena. There was widespread debate in Christian communities—should they offer themselves for prosecution? Were they unfaithful disciples if they ran away? Was not dying for their faith imitating the actions of Jesus? As time distilled experience, opinion fell upon a middle option. One did not seek martyrdom. That was fanatical. One could legitimately attempt to avoid detection. However, once denounced, one followed Jesus to the cross. The dominant Gnostic response, however, was that what happens in the body is irrelevant, since matter is evil and the body is only the prison of the spirit. Although some self-defined Gnostics did accept martyrdom, Pagels agrees with ancient orthodox theologians who asserted that, in the main, the Gnostics did not put their hands up to be counted. Some texts make it clear that their authors saw only ignorant fanaticism and stupidity where others saw heroic faith.

Instead, the Gnostics' task was to undertake the spiritual journey, enlightened by Christ, to return to the Fullness of Spirit whence all came. This spiritual journey required distancing oneself from matter as much as possible, a stance that sabotaged the sacramental aspects of ecclesial life.[23] The parallel with the Platonic fall of the corrupt soul into a body is so clear that Tertullian denounced Gnosticism with his well-known aphorism, 'What has Athens to do with Jerusalem?'[24]

Gnostic perception of matter as evil could lead to totally opposing practices. Some Gnostic sects advocated rigid asceticism and total

---

22. Second Treatise of the Great Seth, 56.5–19.
23. Irenaeus, AH, 1.21.1; 5.1.3.
24. Tertullian, Prescriptions against the Heretics, 7. Tertullian himself would later join the Montanist movement, another group that eventually split from the mainstream.

sexual abstinence so that spirit would not be further attenuated or diminished by being inserted into ever more matter. Others permitted full-blown hedonism, because indulging the body could not affect the spirit. In both cases, the religious rationale was the same—the body is irrelevant to the spiritual life.

As early as Paul we may have evidence of such gnosticising tendencies. When Paul wrote to Corinth about the sex industry, he did not say, 'Obey the commandments!' He threw their own slogan—'All things are lawful for me'—back at them, with the addition, 'but not all things are beneficial'. 'All things are lawful for me', but 'I will not be dominated by anything'. The body, he decreed, was made for the Lord, and the Lord for the body. Christians were, in fact, the body of Christ. He agreed with the Gnostics that whoever was joined to Christ was one spirit with him. Precisely because of this, the body is a gift of God and is the temple of the Holy Spirit (1Cor 6, *passim*). Paul insisted on this point. Mainstream Christianity affirmed the incarnation and, in doing so, affirmed the body. This is where full-blown Gnosticism is fundamentally self-contradicting. Gnostics past and present accuse Christians of worshipping a distant God, yet they deny the incarnation of the Word, which, traditionally understood, is precisely about God choosing to live amongst humanity as one of us (Phil 4:6–9).

2. Irenaeus's response: recapitulation and the question of authority

Born in Asia, Irenaeus (b 130, d 202 CE), who was learned in Greek philosophy as well as Christian theology, was elected bishop of Lyons, circa 177, shortly after a bloodbath of persecutions there.[25] Some scholars argue that Irenaeus did no more than contribute to the choice of an authoritarian structure in Christianity.[26] Others, myself included, accept that he is significant because of the rich theology he developed in the process of trying to identify and stabilise true

---

25. Stuart G Hall, *Doctrine and Practice in the Early Church* (London: SPCK, 1991), 58. Eusebius's History of the church preserves The Acts of the Martyrs of Lyons.

26. G Vallée, 'Theological and Non-theological Motives in Irenaeus' Refutation of the Gnostics' in *Jewish and Christian Self-Definition: The Shaping of Christianity in the Second and Third Centuries*, edited by EP Sanders (London: SCM Press, 1980). Sociology would suggest that Christianity would not have survived if it had not become institutionalised, and with institutionalisation comes hierarchy and bureaucracy.

Christianity, and to distinguish it from heresy.[27] More recently, John Hick, Simon Tugwell and Matthew Fox argue that Irenaeus is a more optimistic alternative to Augustinian traditions.[28]

Theologically, Irenaeus's key concern was Gnosticism's subversion of the Christian economy and the implications of that for Christianity's self-understanding.[29] He depicted Gnosticism as an anarchic and chaotic patchwork of doctrines.[30] To invalidate the Gnostic claim to an élite, secret revelation, he argued that the apostles had handed down the 'Rule of Truth' to their successors.[31] The core of his argument is found in *Against the Heresies*, 3.3.1:

> It is within the power of all, therefore, in every Church, who may wish to see the truth, to contemplate clearly the tradition of the apostles manifested throughout the whole world; and we are in a position to reckon up those who were by the apostles instituted bishops in the Churches, and [to demonstrate] the succession of these men to our own times; those who neither taught nor knew of anything like what these [heretics] rave about. For if the apostles had known hidden mysteries, which they were in the habit of imparting to 'the perfect' apart and privily from the rest, they would have delivered them especially to those to whom they were also committing the Churches themselves. For they were desirous that these men should be very perfect and blameless in all things, whom also they were leaving behind as their successors, delivering up their own place of government to these men; which men, if they discharged their functions honestly,

27. Hall, *Doctrine*, 59.
28. John Hick, *Death and Eternal Life* (London: Collins, 1976); Simon Tugwell, 'Irenaeus and the Gnostic Challenge', *Clergy Review* (1981); Matthew Fox, *Original Blessings* (Putnam Pbk, 2000).
29. So also Robert A Markus, 'The Problem of Self-definition: From Sect to Great Church', in *Jewish and Christian Self-definition*, 5.
30. Irenaeus, AH, 2.14.2.
31. Irenaeus, AH, 3.1.2; 3.2.2; 3.3.1–4; 3.4.2. The Rule of Truth was not a creedal formulation as such but a set of beliefs. Hall, *Doctrine*, 61–2.

would be a great boon [to the Church], but if they
should fall away, the direst calamity.

Thus, 'true gnosis' is the apostolic Rule of Truth.[32] In explaining
the Rule's content, Irenaeus drew on the Pauline opposition of Adam
and Christ to develop the doctrine of recapitulation, an integrated
theology of creation and redemption that necessarily embraced a
theodicy.[33] A sense of divine love and compassion suffused his
'economy' of salvation.[34] Irenaeus's starting point was that the Creator
and the Father were one. This pre-eminent God created *ex nihilo*
through the Word, and what God creates is good.[35] God endowed
humanity with freedom of choice from the beginning. Therefore, any
fall from grace and concomitant suffering was the result of human
decisions. In the fullness of time, the Word itself became flesh to
redeem humanity, to restore this lost liberty and, most importantly, to
give humans the full gift of righteousness, their adoption as children of
God.[36] For Irenaeus, the incarnation was always a part of God's plan
because, in view of God's nature as saviour, it was 'necessary that
what might be saved should also be called into existence, in order that
the Being who saves does not exist in vain'.[37]

Irenaeus highlights the role of Mary in order to emphasise that the
Word is truly flesh and sanctifies flesh. Through Mary's flesh, Jesus is a
son of Adam standing in solidarity with all human beings, whilst

---

32.   Irenaeus, AH, 1.10.2; 3.1.1–3; 4.33.7–8. However, he established the primacy of
      Rome in appeals to tradition. On this aspect of his thought, see Minns, *Irenaeus*,
      116–122, and Hall, *Doctrine*, 59–61. For the problems inherent in studying
      Irenaeus see Minns, *Irenaeus*, viii–x. The weight of scholarly opinion holds that
      the doctrine of Recapitulation is a unifying theme in Irenaeus's theology. Dai Sil
      Kim, 'Irenaeus of Lyons and Teilhard de Chardin: A Comparative Study of
      "Recapitulation" and "Omega"', *Journal of Ecumenical Studies* 13/1 (Winter
      1976); JND, Kelly, *Early Christian Doctrines* [*ECD*] (San Francisco:
      HarperSanFrancisco, 1978), 174.

33.   Irenaeus, AH, 3.21.10; 5.1.3; 2.22.4; 3.18.7; *A New Eusebius*, [*ANE*] edited by J
      Stevenson (London: SPCK, 1980), #101.

34.   On the significance of 'economy' see Minns, *Irenaeus*, 56. Irenaeus on God's
      tender love, AH, 3.18.5–6; 3.20.1; 5. Preface; 5.14.3; 5.17.1; 5.21.3.

35.   Irenaeus, AH, 2.2.5–5; 2.25.1; 2.31.1–4; 3.25.3; 4.9.1.

36.   Irenaeus, AH, 2.33.4; 3.5.3; 3.9.3; 3.10.2; 3.16.7.

37.   Irenaeus, AH, 3.22.3.

summing up all creation in himself.[38] By re-enacting the experience of all men, Jesus undid Adam's sin.[39] Ecclesially, the incarnation unites humanity to God, and grounds the sacraments, while the spirit unites God to humanity. Thus, an infinitely loving divinity takes responsibility for rebuilding communion from both ends of the matter-spirit spectrum. The incarnation is the heart of the ontological aspect of salvation, for Jesus became 'what we are that he might bring us to be even what he is himself'.[40] Accordingly, Irenaeus demonstrates the integrity of creation and redemption.

Irenaeus's originality appears especially in his interpretation of Genesis 3, where time and timing were clearly important. God did not create humans perfect from the very beginning, but took a developmental approach in which humans grew spiritually as well as physically, intellectually and psychologically. As creatures, a huge rift separated humanity from God. Though God endowed Adam and Eve with an 'ancient human liberty' of reason and free will (the image and likeness of God) and the gifts of the Spirit, they never possessed 'original righteousness'. Because God created Adam and Eve to grow fully into the divine likeness, they were still 'morally, spiritually and intellectually' children in paradise.[41] Immaturity mitigated responsibility. Their motive was not pride or sexuality run rampant, but the childish desire for too much too soon.[42] Adam and Eve were vulnerable to the loss of the divine image precisely because neither they nor God's plan had reached completion. In fact, one might say that impatience was their sin. They did not wish to experience the process of maturation, thus, in Minns' opinion, childishly rejecting the 'divine economy itself'. The outcome was momentous.[43] In this paradigm, humanity's story is the history of salvation because it is the

---

38. Irenaeus, AH, 2.32.5; 3.10.2; 4.33.1; 4.33.4; 5.1.1–2; 5.8.3.

39. Irenaeus, AH, 3.16.6; *Demonstration of the Apostolic Preaching*, 32–34, in *ANE*, #101.

40. Irenaeus, AH, 3.10.2; 3.18.7; 3.21.2; 4.37.3; 5 Pref; 5.1.1, 3; 5.6.1; 5.7.1; 5.23.2; 5.36.2.

41. Irenaeus, AH, 5.16.2. Kelly, *ECD*, 171.

42. Irenaeus, AH, 3.23.3, 5; 4.38,4. It is quite common for the church fathers to link original sin and sexuality. For an overview see J Quasten, *Patrology*, vol 3 (Spectrum, 1960), 97.

43. Minns, *Irenaeus*, 61–2, citing Irenaeus, AH, 5.16.2 and *Demonstration of the Apostolic Preaching*, 12.

history of humanity's development and spiritual growth. Moreover, in his refutation of God's responsibility for evil, Irenaeus emphasised God's patience and mercy, which were so boundless that God used humanity's very apostasy to instruct it.[44] Even death has a merciful aspect.[45] Adam and Eve's sin may be the original sin, but it is more symbolic of the errant ways of a slowly developing humanity than the archetypal sin that stripped humanity of its primal righteousness.[46]

Gnostic privileging of Paul as the source of Christian truth impelled Irenaeus to Paul for a solution, turning their own guns against them. His development of Paul's metaphor of the second Adam was theologically masterful. In tandem with Paul's Adam/Christ parallel, Irenaeus drew parallels between Eve and Mary, effective at the time but with less felicitous results historically.[47] Minns underlines that 'Eve has the same universal significance' as Adam, and even though Mary's humility undoes Eve's disobedience,[48] she does not symbolise feminine inferiority.[49] However, scholars have not engaged with the extent to which Eve's status is a product of the Gnostic controversy, or whether it is indicative of positive perceptions of Eve across many Christian schools of thought. Given the high number of women in early Christian communities, and their egalitarian status in many, denigrating the feminine would not have won Gnostic women to the cause of 'orthodoxy'. Similarly, his notion of Mary as 'the new Eve' elevates Mary to spectacular heights in early mainstream Christian thought. She is Christ's partner in salvation, but her humanity grounds her as a model for all Christians, especially women, for she is Eve's patroness, or *avocata*.[50] As the new Adam and Eve, Christ and Mary reiterate the choices of the primal couple, and this time they get it right.

However, even after the incarnation, Christians had to submit to the economy of salvation, which is inherently developmental.[51] Irenaeus was scathing of those who wished to become gods before they

44. Irenaeus, AH, 1.5.2; 4.28.1; 4.37.1–2, 7.
45. Irenaeus, AH, 3.23.1–7, especially 6; cf 5.23.1.
46. See Minns, *Irenaeus*, 59.
47. Irenaeus, AH, 3.22.4; 5.17.3; 5.19.1; 5.20.1; *ANE*, #101.
48. Irenaeus, AH, 3.22.4.
49. Minns, *Irenaeus*, 58.
50. Irenaeus, AH, 5.19.1.
51. Irenaeus, AH, 2.28.1.

have become human. First, they must partake of God's glory within their human bounds. Metaphorically, humans must await the Potter's hands to finish their work in their due time.[52] The alternative was obnoxious arrogance:

> if any one do yield himself up to them like a little sheep, and follows out their practice, and their 'redemption', such a one is puffed up to such an extent, that he thinks he is neither in heaven nor on earth, but that he has passed within the Pleroma; and having already embraced his angel, he walks with a strutting gait and a supercilious countenance, possessing all the pompous air of a cock.[53]

On the other hand, Irenaeus promised that those who submitted patiently to God's creative work would not only bear God's imprint, but would be so exquisitely adorned that Godself desires them for their beauty.[54] One of the most important aspects of Irenaeus's thought is that those in whom the Spirit dwells are characterised not by an otherworldly distance from matter but by a healed union of body, soul and spirit. The Spirit empowers the redeemed to recognise God as Father, and tends them 'towards perfection, and preparing us for incorruption, being little by little accustomed to receive and bear God'.[55] Moreover, Irenaeus idiosyncratically interpreted Paul to insist that, even in eternal life, 'God should for ever teach and man should for ever learn the things taught him by God'.[56]

Eschatology is integral to the doctrine of recapitulation. Irenaeus believed that a six thousand year period of creation and development culminating with the incarnation[57] must be recapitulated before the eschaton. Through the Antichrist, all the evils and apostasy of the past will be poured out on apostate nations and Rome will be desolated,

---

52.   Irenaeus, AH, 4.39.2.
53.   Irenaeus, AH, 2.28.2; 3.15.2.
54.   Irenaeus, AH, 4.39. 2–3.
55.   Irenaeus, AH, 5.8.1–2.
56.   Irenaeus, AH, 2.28.3. Specifically, he draws on I Corinthians 13:13, that faith, hope and love shall perdure.
57.   Irenaeus, AH, 5.28.2–3.

thereby reiterating all the evils poured upon Egypt for the liberation of the Jews.[58] The fiery purging that ends the world purifies living believers in the refiner's fire.[59] Irenaeus often draws on the prophet Isaiah's description of the Jewish exiles' return from Babylon to describe the new creation's birth pangs.[60] As conqueror, priest and sanctifying bridegroom, Christ opens the new temple in the new Jerusalem to the faithful Christian.[61] Irenaeus is something of a millenarian. A new, resurrected human community will exist in the true Promised Land, the New Jerusalem, where individual virtue determines the social order.[62] There, the eschatological beatific vision, which Irenaeus was the first to articulate, would vivify and immortalise members.[63] The resurrected Christians will have inherited Judaism's birthright. They are metaphorically the children of Jacob, the Jews the children of Esau.[64] Irenaeus insists this incorruptible life of liberty is embodied.[65] God redeemed humans precisely as creatures, never as incorporeal spirits.[66] Those who claim the name of Christian but reject their creatureliness are apostates. They will be judged and cast into hellish darkness, which is eternal exile from the Good. Scripture calls this exile God's wrath or divine judgment, but it is *not* God's punishment, because the apostates' prior choices led them into exile. Having lived so long in darkness, their first sight of the light of the beatific vision perpetually blinds them to it.[67] In terms of his soteriology, they have not become accustomed to receiving and bearing God, and it is as if the divine glory annihilates them. Spiritually they are still children, rejecting the divine pedagogy that would have fitted them for eternity. In essence, they are even now re-enacting the sin of Adam and Eve, but at this time with no excuse, for the Word has not only been spoken in creation, but has been made flesh.

---

58.   Irenaeus, AH, 4.30.4; 5.26.1; 5. 29.2.

59.   Irenaeus, AH, 5.28.4.

60.   Irenaeus, AH, 5.35.1.

61.   Irenaeus, AH, 4.20.11–12; 4.21.3; 4.28.6.

62.   Irenaeus, AH, 5.31.1–34.1.

63.   Hick, *Death and Eternal Life*, 205, Irenaeus, AH, 4.20.6; 5.36.1–2.

64.   Irenaeus, AH, 4.21.3; 4.28.3.

65.   Irenaeus, AH, 4.22.1.

66.   Irenaeus, AH, 5.8.2.

67.   Irenaeus, AH, 4.28.5; 5.27.1–2;

Irenaeus presented a rich anthropology in which human 'becoming' occurs in an ambiguous world that, nevertheless, is never out of God's providence. Irenean theology no more legitimated world order than the Gnostics, but where for them it is a mad world, for Irenaeus it is an incomplete one, whose tragedy was its impatient unwillingness to become what it was created.[68] This theology is ultimately an affirmation of the goodness of material creation, in which a redeemed humanity is united to God through sacramental signs both physical and sacred,[69] as it journeys to its ultimate destiny, 'to [behold] its own Delight'.[70] The one question Irenaeus never answers is why God made Adam and Eve so vulnerably childish when the consequences of their mistakes were so dire.

When Irenaeus's theology was received as the orthodox formulation, it automatically validated the argument that the bishop should be the authoritative leader. We can see how this helped the process of institutionalisation, since the analogy 'one god, one bishop' endowed the leader with power to discern good and bad spirits, if his theological lineage was legitimate. Extending the analogy of Christ the bridegroom and his ecclesial bride to the bishop as proxy bridegroom would reinforce it further.[71] There is no doubt that this meant individual Christians ceding teaching authority to their leader but, in the second century, this may not have seemed too high a price. After all, Christians usually still met on private premises. Communities were not so large that they did not know each other. Functions were not centralised. Teachers and bishops were not necessarily the same. Above all, Christians still elected their bishops.[72] Later Christianity would grow increasingly suspicious of the prophetic charism and the unmediated spiritual power the prophet tapped. Nevertheless, personal revelation, especially when characterised as prophecy, was,

---

68.   Irenaeus, AH, 4.38.4.
69.   Irenaeus, AH, 1.9.4; 1.21.1; 3.17.1–3; 4.17.5; 4.33.2; 4.37.1–5; 5.1.3.
70.   Irenaeus, AH, 5.7.2; see also 4.20.5; 4.37.7.
71.   See my article, 'Eucharist as Holy Marriage: The Impact on Doctrine, Church Order and Social Relations', in *Eucharist: Experience and Testimony*, edited by Tom Knowles (Melbourne: David Lovell Publishing, 2001), 217–230.
72.   Mary Douglas' work on institutional allegiance is pertinent. *Risk and blame: Essays in Cultural Theory* (London and New York: Routledge, 1992), 56.

and still is, an aspect of mainstream Christianity.[73] It is also true that later forms of Gnosticism moved further and further away from mainstream Christianity, so that self-knowledge became identified as knowledge of God, a charge laid against our own contemporaries' investment in 'spirituality'. Irenaeus became the spokesperson for those provoked

> to state their own faith in history and tradition and to set out the texts of their Gospels more firmly and explicitly. Heretical ideas and groups survived, catering for those who wished to be perverse, but by c. 180 Christianity had been strengthened by great conservative statements.[74]

3. Mani and Manichaeism

The battle may have been over, but the war was not definitively won. Gnosticism reappeared rejuvenated in third-century Persia in the teachings of Mani,[75] whose dualism opposed mind/spirit/good to body/evil/chaos, possibly under the influence of Syrian Gnosticism. The Good was the divine essence; Evil was uncreated. In Mani's system, creation and redemption were the Good's efforts to control the essentially chaotic nature of evil incarnate in matter. Gold in mud, particles of light/spirit in darkness/matter were Manichaen analogies. As for earlier Gnostics, the Creator was demonic. Hence Mani interpreted Genesis 1 as the first step in human redemption: rebellion against the Creator's tyranny. He sexualised primal sin, which became Eve's sexual temptation of Adam, for each human conception further attenuated the divine essence by diffusing it through more and more matter. Soteriologically, Christ was the Divine principle and his crucifixion signified the universal suffering of spirit enmeshed in

---

73.   Medieval women writers like Hildegard of Bingen, Catherine of Sienna and Margery Kempe legitimated their teachings by claiming the prophet's role. *A History of Women Philosophers,* edited by Mary Ellen Waithe, vol 2 (Boston: Dordrecht, 1989, reprinted 1991).

74.   RL Fox, *Pagans and Christians,* 332.

75.   For Mani's life, I am dependent on Pheme Perkins, 'Mani, Manichaeism', in *Encyclopedia of Early Christianity,* edited by Everett Ferguson *et al* (New York: Garland Publishing, 1990), 562–3.

matter. Redemption consisted of returning to the light by rigid asceticism, abstention from sexual relationships, or at least from conception. The sect was organised hierarchically. Auditors or hearers were disciples of the celibate and pacifist élite 'elect' of both sexes.[76] They performed certain services for them so that the élite could distance themselves ever further from matter or the destruction of the life imprisoned in it. Therefore, so the élite did not have to cut trees and plants or grind 'living' grain, auditors did this for them. The elect did have to eat, of course, but exonerated themselves before meals by intoning their innocence of the acts of reaping and grinding. Practically, this theology led to some bizarre beliefs: the belching of the elect released 'spirit' from matter. For faithful service, the elect forgave auditors their sins and they held out the hope of their rebirth as elect souls in the next life. Only the elect returned via the stars to the Light's realm at death.

Parallels with earlier Gnosticism are clear, but Mani did not locate the source of evil within a constellation of divine power run awry. Rather Evil is independent and seemingly unconquerable, except for the rigidly ascetic few who can meet the demands of perfection. Eschatologically, the belief in the uncreated nature of evil/matter logically meant that the universe was doomed to an eternal cycle of apocalytic fire followed by a new creation, though this is only implicit in extant texts. Manichaeism became a particular problem in the fourth century, best known to us because the renowned Augustine of Hippo was a Manichee before he was a Christian. He tells us that this system allowed him to avoid dealing with Hebrew scriptural texts which he saw as barbaric by employing inappropriate language about God. Ultimately, dissatisfied with the intellectual shallowness of Manichaen texts and preachers, he found his solution in an allegorical interpretation of Scripture which he learnt from Ambrose of Milan.

4. Augustine of Hippo

Augustine's doctrine of original sin became the orthodox Christian solution to evil. For Augustine, order *(ordo)* was the overarching category that defined the nature of the created world, and which established the criterion for evaluating it in terms of eternal/temporal

---

76.   However, women could not hold office.

dualism. Its concomitant values are justice, hierarchy, dominance, form and rationality in the pursuit of public harmony. Difference can never connote equality, but must be either superior or inferior.[77] *Ordo* as a structural concept fosters a spirituality of control, where sinfulness taints any response not wholly rational.[78] Evil was equivalent to disorder, which implies corruption. For this, he blamed original sin, a doctrine developed in debates over theodicy with Manichees and Pelagians. Where the former blamed uncreated evil, both Augustine and the Pelagians understood evil to be a 'no thing', a negation of the Good, but they differed over the power of the will to choose the good freely. Three potent factors shaped Augustine's thought: First, Paul's anguished cry in Romans—why is he at war with himself?—which resonated so powerfully with Augustine's experience. Secondly, why does not baptism free our wills totally as the Pelagians claimed? Thirdly, if God is both just and powerful, then why do innocent babies suffer as if tormented by demons? The answer he formulated was original sin, though he would move from an allegorical reading to a more literal one as his thought developed.[79]

In his paradigm, Eve falls because of pride, and Adam chivalrously sins so that she will not enter exile alone.[80] The blame for evil and suffering falls on the primal couple, especially Eve, but Augustine never satisfactorily explains how she can be seduced into evil by an angel, who did not share the human capacity for free will, for how could angels have chosen evil when they were perpetually exposed to the vision of the Good?

For Augustine, original sin had several consequences. First, it distanced humanity from God when it corrupted the human spirit, which entailed loss of immortality, so that human nature reverted to a

77. Augustine, On Order 1.8.26; City of God [CD], 22.24; Eighty Questions [Questions] 1.53.
78. Eugene TeSelle concluded that Augustine was a man with a need for control both of himself and others, 'Augustine as Client', 94.
79. Augustine, Against Julian [AJ] 1.2.4; 4.16.83; On Marriage and Concupiscence [On Marriage and Con.]. 2.12.25; Against Two Letters of the Pelagians [Against 2 lett] 1.16.32.
80. Augustine consistently said that pride motivated Eve. Literal Meaning Gen. 11.30.39. He also referred to pride in feminine terms. On Virginity. 30. When chastising women, he attributes independence to pride. Ep. 262.

wild state.[81] The first act of disorderly wills forever imprinted on the body the intimate signs of the revolt that led to death.[82] By this, Augustine meant that men could not control their erections. Their bodies rose up against their will, the way they had rebelled against God, forever reminding them of their disobedience and consequent mortality.[83] Because medical texts assumed women's bodies responded in a similar, but hidden fashion, he thought women experienced the same constant reminder.

Secondly, because of this physiological punishment, sexual metaphors and images permeate his writing on original sin, although Eve's sin was pride. Because the disorder of sexual desire is the fundamental consequence of original sin, it is the most dangerous form of concupiscence. Throughout his treatises, we find the belief that desire contaminated all male/female relationships and that real companionship between genders was almost an impossibility. At best, marriage could be 'a certain friendly and true union of the one ruling, and the other obeying'.[84]

Thirdly, sexual intercourse could transmit this disordered spirituality, because biology attributed conception to the father's spirit. If original sin corrupted the spiritual essence carried into the woman's body during intercourse,[85] then Adam's sin literally passed from father to child, even though the rhetoric blames Eve.

> Evilly did Eve give birth, thereby leaving to women the inheritance of childbirth, and the result that everyone formed in the pleasure of concupiscence and conceived in it in the womb and fashioned in it in blood, in it wrapped as in swaddling clothes, first

---

81. Augustine, AJ. 1.7.32. Cf. 2.9.32; 2.5.11. This argument is present right throughout AJ; On Marriage and Con. 1.19.21. The Literal Meaning of Genesis [Literal Meaning Gen] 10.26.35; Against 2 Lett 1.6.11.

82. Augustine, Against 2 Lett. 1.16.32.

83. Augustine, CD 14.17. Cf. On Marriage and Con. 1.15.17; 1.21.24, 2.12.25; AJ. 4.12.58–59; Against 2 Lett. 1.16.33.

84. Augustine, On the Good of Marriage [Good of Marr.]. 1.

85. Kim Power, 'Philosophy, Medicine and Gender in the Ascetic Texts of Ambrose of Milan', in *Ancient History in a Modern University*, vol 2, edited by TW Hillard, RA Kearsley, CEV Nixon, and AM Nobbs (Grand Rapids: Eerdmans, 1997), 821–32.

> undergoes the contagion of sin before he drinks the
> gift of the life-giving air . . . to weep at birth for the
> guilt he contracted before his birth.[86]

Because children were born corrupted, they did not suffer unjustly,
but as part of the punishment for human choices. This theology led to
an imperative for infant baptism because, until they were baptised,
Satan still held them in thrall. Hell was their destiny, without recourse
to divine mercy.[87] This God is just in the extreme, for there is no
mitigation of punishment due to the infants' objective innocence.

It also created an imperative for the virgin birth. If Christ had had a
human father, original sin would have tainted his humanity.[88]
Conceived of pure spirit in uncorrupted virginal flesh, Christ is able to
free those in bondage to sin:

> The first birth holds man in that bondage from which
> nothing but the second birth delivers him. The devil
> holds him, Christ liberates him; Eve's deceiver holds
> him, Mary's son frees him: He holds him who
> approached man through woman; he frees him who
> was born of woman that never approached man. He
> holds him who injected into the woman the cause of
> lust; he liberates him, who without any lust was
> conceived in the woman.[89]

---

86.   Augustine, AJ. 2.6.15. The permeation of the child by sin is strong in this passage.
87.   Augustine, AJ. 1.7.32. Cf. 2.9.32; 2.5.11. This argument is present right
      throughout AJ. On Marriage and Con. 1.19.21. Literal Meaning Gen. 10.26.35;
      Against 2 lett. 1.6.11.
88.   See Sermon 151.5; Trinity, 13.12.16; 13.16.21; Ep. 217.5. 16; On Christian
      Doctrine, 1.14.13; AJ5.15.
89.   Augustine, On Christian Grace, 2.45. cf 2.43; AJ. 6.22.68. Whereas all children are
      born in sin, Mary, because of her virginal birth-giving, did not need to be purified
      after the birth like other women. Questions, 3.40. How children born of baptised
      parents can inherit and pass on the contagion of sin is beyond the scope of this
      paper, but relevant passages are found in AJ. 2.2.4; 6.7.17, 20; 2.10.33. Julian did
      not believe that men and women sin by intercourse because they live according to
      their created nature. See AJ. 2.2.4; On Marriage and Con. 1.19.21; Against 2 Lett.
      11.7.

Baptism is the efficacious sign of this liberating and immaculate grace.[90] It signifies the only authentic, life-giving birth, where children become members of the body of Christ. Fathered by God, mothered by the church, human beings move from death to life and from sadness to the anticipation of blessedness.[91] In this paradigm, all maternal virtues are attributed to the church, which is the true mother. Augustine compares human mothers, who can only give birth to wretchedness and death, to 'stepmother' nature, whom philosophers saw bringing children into a life of suffering.[92]

Although the irresistible grace of Augustine's God is at work in the human heart, God dispenses justice at the expense of mercy. His God is not Origen's tender spouse, Irenaeus's gentle moulder of souls, or Ambrose's chastising but erotic bridegroom. God's grace comes in harsh, punitive discipline. The soul must leave God's maternal mercies to encounter the Father's authority.[93] In De Doctrina Christiana, he argued, 'Every severity and every apparent cruelty, either in word or deed, that is ascribed in holy Scripture to God or his saints, avails to the pulling down of the dominion of lust'.[94] From such a perspective, Augustine could, and did, validate the beating of women, children and slaves to inculcate virtue.[95] He instructed an abbess that fear and love are the wise leader's tools.[96] Moreover, the maintenance of authority is so important that, if superiors are mistakenly being too harsh, they

---

90. Augustine, Trinity, 13.16.21; AJ. 5.15.56; 6.16.50.
91. Augustine, Sermons 216.8; 151.8.
92. It also is an example of the way philosophy permeated Augustine's thinking. AJ. 6.21.67. Cf 1.3.10, where he speaks of the sinfulness of all human conception and children being born in the inequities of their parents.
93. Augustine, Con. 13.22. Cf. 10.4.
94. Augustine, On Christian Doctrine. 3.11.17.
95. Augustine, *Con.* 9.9; Ep. 246.3; the exception is a man beating his mother, which is punishable with excommunication. Ep. 35.1. Beatings should always be for the right reason, Eps. 35.4; 246.2. See John A Sanford, *The Man Who Wrestled With God: Light from the Old Testament on the Psychology of Individuation* (New York: Paulist Press, 1981), 30, on wives and mothers as extensions of the male self. Augustine's own perception of the role of women in his life fits neatly into this category.
96. Augustine, Ep. 211.14–15; On Continence. 9.23. Cf G Lawless, Monastic Rule, 117.

should not ask forgiveness, lest their humility impair their authority.[97] Such teachers are channels of God's grace, for anything or anyone who makes people good has its source in God. In this world, suffering is never unjust. It is either purgatorial or punitive.[98]

The grace of God empowers human beings by teaching them what they have to do and how to do it lovingly. All goodwill has its source in divine grace.[99] Both virtue and sin are incremental, conditioned by habitual behaviours. Virtue engenders a mystical ascent, sin a descent until the sinner is lost in the illusions of corporeality, blind to truth and wisdom and entirely incapable of extricating herself. Her only hope is her Maker's grace offering repentance and forgiveness.[100] The *Confessions* depicts such a graced redemption for both Augustine and Monica, which culminates in their shared vision of the Good at Ostia. In Augustine's account, they ascend from sacred speech, through exquisite sensual delight, to contemplation of the Light, ultimately transcending even their own souls to sip at the fountain of life, 'eternal Wisdom, life-giving and the source of all being . . . the joy of the Lord'.[101] Mortals cannot sustain such ecstasy more than momentarily, but we catch a glimpse of the eternal and ultimate intoxication of the soul in his vision of his dead friend, Nebridius, whose thirst is slaked, his joy unending. Here we catch a glimpse of a gentler God. Nebridius will never forget his friend, for he is united to a Lord ever mindful of his servants.[102]

Througout Augustine's thought, sexuality is enmeshed in sin and comes perilously close to evil itself, though under pressure from Julian of Eclanum in his later years, Augustine came to accept that sexuality and gender existed in Paradise. He could even permit the possibility of desire perfectly responsive to the will; although he would have wished desire to have been entirely absent.[103] Human beings embraced in

---

97. Nevertheless, they must ask God's pardon. Ep. 211.14.
98. Augustine, CD. 21.13.
99. Augustine, Ep. 188.2. 7–8.
100. Augustine, Trinity, 12.10.15–11.16.
101. Augustine, Con. 9.10.23–6. I am not concerned here with the debate as to whether the Ostia experience was true Christian mysticism or the attainment of the heights of philosophic experience.
102. Augustine, Con. 9.3.
103. Augustine, Against 2 Lett. 1.5.10; 1.17.34–35. AJ. 5.9.8.

peace of soul and integrity of body, and Eve remained *uirgo intacta,* receiving Adam's seed in the same way that a virgin menstruates.[104] Augustine argued this strongly against Julian, who asserted that sexual desire was from God, because without desire there would be no intercourse.[105] For Augustine, any pleasure should lie in the desire for children, not sexual yearning.[106] Desire 'is not a good which comes out of the essence of marriage, but an evil which is the accident of original sin'.[107] Scholars still debate to what extent this anthropology retains elements of Manichaeism, but Augustine is not a dualist and is far more positive about sexuality in his later life than Ambrose or Jerome ever were.

Perhaps it is not surprising then that, to overcome such corrupted concupiscence, grace had to be stern and virtually irresistible as an aspect of God's omnipotence. What creature could resist it? Yet, clearly some did. Augustine finally concluded that, if grace could not be resisted, then sometimes God withheld grace. Therefore he justified his argument that redemption was predestined with Romans 8:28–30. As Mathijs Lamberigts explains:

> Predestination was not based upon God's foreknow-
> ledge of human deeds, but was to be situated in God's
> eternal decree and was therefore unfailing. This also
> meant that human beings had no right to claim God's
> grace. Predestination, moreover, was for some, and not
> all. The grace of perseverance in faith was no longer
> set aside for all the baptized, but only the faithful
> people chosen by God from the *massa damnata . . .*
> God's *Electi.*[108]

---

104. Augustine, CD. 14.26; On Christian Grace, 2.41.36.

105. Augustine, Against 2 Lett. 1.15.30.

106. Augustine, Good of Marr. 3. Augustine distinguishes between desire and pleasure. Where desire for children motivated sexual intercourse, then a certain 'grave pleasure' is permissible. He may have been influenced by Aristotle's significant belief that conception would not occur without the experience of some pleasure. A. Rousselle, *Porneia: On Desire and the Body in Antiquity*, translated by Felicia Pheasant (Oxford: Basil Blackwell, 1993), 40.

107. Augustine, *On marriage and con.* 1.17.19.

108. Lamberigts, 'Predestination', in *Augustine through the Ages*, 678.

It has always seemed to me that Augustine, in his desire to protect God's justice, has ended by subverting it. All the good choices a human makes are graced and, in this sense, predestined. Sin is always a product of free will which God has chosen not to grace. God gets all of the credit and none of the responsibility. Mainstream orthodoxy did not endorse predestination, mindful that it was polemically driven against what Augustine considered the Pelagians' overly trusting attitude to, and reliance on, free will. They, in their turn, were combatting the fatalism of Manichaeism.[109] Thus tradition, at least until the Reformation, retained a creative tension between free will and divine grace which it allied with Augustine's tension between the hope of the blessed life and eternal suffering in hell. This tension offers us a way into his eschatology.

There can be no doubt that Augustine's eschatology was influenced by the fall of Rome, which led him to write the *City of God*—a city that stands in stark contrast to the secular city, sometimes called the devil's city:

> Accordingly, two cities have been formed by two loves: the earthly by the love of self, even to the contempt of God; the heavenly by the love of God, even to the contempt of self. The former, in a word, glories in itself, the latter in the Lord. [110]

Millenarianism appears in Augustine's thought also.[111] However, it is a far cry from Irenaeus's beatific vision. Instead, Augustine's millennium is the period between Christ's resurrection and his second coming, when the battle for the city of God is fought in every human heart. Socially, politically and personally, God's city is besieged throughout history. Thus, Augustine's eschatology creates an ethical imperative for the Christian in the world. That it still stands is due only

---

109. Lamberigts, 'Predestination', in *Augustine through the Ages*, 678.
110. Augustine, CD, 14.28.
111. Karla Pollman, 'Moulding the Present: Apocalyptic as Hermeneutics in *City of God*, 21–22, in *History, Apocalypse, and the Secular Imagination: New Essays on Augustine's City of God* edited by Mark Vesey, Karla Pollmann, and Allan D. Fitzgerald, OSA (Bowling Green, OH: Philosophy Documentation Center, 1999), 165–82.

to grace, for God has bound Satan and he cannot bring full power to bear against the church.[112]

However, at the second coming, God will release Satan so that God can manifest divine power absolutely. Satan will marshal God's enemies against the church until evil is definitively defeated and every demonic power, with all the human *massa damnata*, are flung into everlasting fire.[113] Augustine resists any argument that such fire is purgatorial, though he does consider it possible that even the blessed may need fiery purification after death. Alternatively, the church's purification may simply be the purging of the wicked from her membership.[114] A further paradox is that the very glory of heaven may lead to theological *schadenfreude* as Christians contemplate the damned in hell. Thomas Smith argues that Augustine's vision of hell can be stripped of its 'abominable fancy' and recovered as an 'erotic counterweight' of 'architectural beauty' which preserves order in the universe and appropriate punishment for those who offend God. It is not persuasive.[115] Smith falls into the same trap as Augustine. The focus on God's greatness and beauty, which renders any offence against God as infinite, ignores the humility of the incarnation and Jesus' forgiveness from the cross.

Karla Pollman has argued that Augustine's apocalyptic thinking has two aspects. These equate to what I earlier called partially realised and future eschatology. The first, she believes, is pragmatic, operative in both the soul and the church. This is the realised eschatology of the City of God that exists in the church and the soul. The second is totally transcendent and beyond history. This is the Christian hope for the future.[116] Yet, as Scanlon has observed, they function dynamically because focus on Christ's redemption creates anticipation of a future when intimations of joy give way to reality. The pardon of sin and the grace to persevere in discipleship are the 'now' of 'not yet', conferred through the Holy Spirit's grace.[117] The rebirth from sinful death to life

---

112. Augustine, *CD*. 20.8.
113. Augustine, CD. 20.5, 8; 21.3.
114. Augustine, CD. 20.5; 21.13.
115. Thomas A, Smith, 'The Pleasure of Hell in Augustine's *City of God*', in *History, Apocalypse, and the Secular Imagination, op cit*, 203–4.
116. Pollman, 'Moulding the Present', 169.
117. Scanlon, 'Eschatology', 316.

in Christ is the first resurrection that anticipates the second.[118] So it should not surprise us that Augustine would see 'the future as the Christian's favourite tense'.[119]

5. Conclusions: Can patristics contribute?

From such disparate theodicies and eschatologies, the *sensus fidelium*, that is the teaching assented to by all the faithful, wove what we modern Christians call Tradition. Conditioned perhaps by a *zeitgeist* that understood suffering as determinative of existence, it adopted more pessimistic than optimistic alternatives. This is understandable given the omnipresent threat of death from disease, childbirth and war, the ubiquity of slavery and the poverty of the majority and, in Augustine's era, the fall of Rome, the disintegration of the Empire and the barbarian invasion that would restructure Europe and North Africa. Nevertheless, we can discern threads of hope. The emergent orthodox tradition selected common themes. Against diverse heretics, including the Gnostics and Manichees, Christians insisted that the church was a community of sinners, not a fortress inhabited by a spiritual aristocracy, thereby validating inclusivity against elitism. They retained the unity of creation and redemption and affirmed that the created world is good; the body is good and ordinary human life demands respect. God's goodness, creation's goodness and human responsibility for evil are constants. However, particulars may change radically. Although Augustine adopted Irenaeus's doctrine of recapitulation and even further elevated Mary's role, he did not retain the delight in creation and the compassion for humanity that so characterises Irenaeus. A platonic dualism, if not Manichaeism, infiltrates the gospel and makes the world suspect, though Augustine is poignantly aware of the world's beauty. However, owing to his primal parents' perversion of the human will, its very beauty was a snare that seduced him from seeking Beauty itself. Augustine accepted the science of his day which could accommodate the biological transmission of spiritual flaws. Paradoxically, just as contemporary Christians reject the doctrine of original sin, theologically and practically—infants are rarely presented for baptism today within days

---

118. Augustine, CD. 20.6.
119. Scanlon, 'Eschatology', 316.

of birth—evolutionary psychologists are bringing it back in the tension between our hard wiring for survival and for altruism.

Patristic theodicies and eschatologies reveal that we are all constrained by our historical concerns and horizons as we struggle to identify the source of evil within ourselves, to discern our moral responsibilities and to articulate our ultimate hopes. These men all shared a passionate commitment to the search for a language, in Augustine's words, for those 'precious cups of meaning', with which to do so. The tension in their eschatologies between the present and the future is evidence that they were well aware that there was no access to unmediated and transparent truth in this life. Yet, their yearning for it is often tangible, and they knew it mattered to persevere on the journey. However they imaged their God, for all of them the love that constitutes Godself impelled God to become one with them to save them, and their experience of grace was its proof.

Theodicy and Eschatology

Christiaan Mostert

1. Introduction

To speak about theodicy is to venture on to dangerous and holy ground. It is dangerous for several reasons. First, one may give the impression of thinking that there is an explanation for what is truly inexplicable. There is no explanation for how evil and suffering fit into a world held to be created by God and created fundamentally good.[1] Here theologians discover what is true of all their work—but nowhere more so than in this area of theological thought—that their best ideas and most articulate sentences are mere stammering and that, if they are not careful, they can easily over-reach themselves. This explains why some practitioners unwisely say too much in the way of theodicy and others, wisely but unsatisfactorily, say too little. As Kenneth Surin puts it, 'evil, in its root and essence, is a mystery'.[2] This has to be evident in any discussion of evil and the suffering which is its result. Second, there is the danger of offering an account of suffering which trivialises it by giving it a tidy place in a theological system. The equally dangerous result of this is abstraction. Any attempt to make intelligible by neat logical moves what is not intelligible—and what should never be stripped of its 'outrageous' quality—is not far off offensive, however philosophically smart it might be.[3] There are perhaps two

---

1. 'Evil' and 'suffering' are typically mentioned in the same breath but they are not the same, though they are closely connected. Though untold suffering is the result of evil, the policies and actions of morally evil people, there is also suffering that is not the result of evil but of natural disaster, and thus morally neutral. There is also a category of suffering that is just. All of it, however, reflects the brokenness (the 'sinful' character) of human experience in the world.
2. K Surin, *Theology and the Problem of Evil* (Oxford: Basil Blackwell, 1986), 162. Of all the books written on theodicy this slim volume is one of the most valuable.
3. This criticism is levelled in particular against some exponents of the 'free will defence', notably Alvin Plantinga, *God, Freedom, and Evil* (Grand Rapids: Eerdmans, 1977) and Stephen T Davis, 'Free Will and Evil', in *Encountering Evil: Live Options in Theodicy,* edited by ST Davis (Atlanta: John Knox Press,

ways to avoid this second danger. The stories of suffering must be in our ears whenever we attempt to speak theologically of evil and suffering,[4] and our speech must be such as to engage us more tenaciously in the struggle against evil, whatever its form, and in action to alleviate suffering. No other kind of speaking about theodicy will do. A third danger in speaking about theodicy, accentuated by the introduction of eschatological considerations, is that of thinking that the end justifies the means. The purpose of this essay is to examine what place there might be for eschatological thinking in the discussion of evil and suffering, but we have to be very wary of any tendency to think that if the (eschatological) end is sufficiently positive the fact that there is suffering in the world—indeed the sum total of actual suffering in the world—is an acceptable condition.[5] This would be a trivialisation of evil, an implicit statement that evil is not really evil when seen in the light of the good, the glory that is in store for us (Rom 8:18–21).

To embark on any kind of theodicy is also to stand on holy ground. It has this character, first, in the same sense in which all speaking of God does. Theology in the best sense is speech *to* God, even though its form may be speech *about* God. What is said about God is always said in the presence of God, whether acknowledged or not. Simply for this reason—and all the more when our thought brings the reality of God into relation with the reality of suffering—we cannot but be aware of the enormous ontic and epistemic distance between God and our-

---

1981), 69–83. Davis distinguishes between the 'logical problem of evil' and the 'emotive problem of evil', and claims to solve the former. What is problematic about his discussion is that he is satisfied with his attempt to answer philosophical difficulties with the problem of evil, undeterred by the criticism that it is implausible.

4.   Surin cites Elie Wiesel: 'Let us tell tales. Let us tell tales—all the rest can wait, all the rest can wait. Let us tell tales—that is our primary obligation . . . Tales that bring men close to the abyss and beyond—and others that lift him up to heaven and beyond.' 'Art and Culture after the Holocaust', in Surin, *Theology and the Problem of Evil*, 150.

5.   This is the danger, in particular, of theodicies of the type of John Hick's 'Irenaean' or 'soul-making' theodicy, in which evil will 'prove to have been interim evil out of which good will in the end have been brought'. J Hick, *Evil and the God of Love*, edited by Fontana (London: Collins, 1968), 399f. See also J Hick, 'An Irenaean Theodicy', in *Encountering Evil*, edited by ST Davis 39–52. It should be added that Hick's theodicy is more nuanced than this and that it contains many important elements.

selves. We have, as it were, to take off our shoes (Exod 3:5). But it is holy ground for an additional reason: theodicy is speech about the dead who have suffered and the living who suffer. We do not speak with a loud voice in the presence of the dead, and less so in the presence of those who have been the victims of persecution, tyranny and genocide. The test of credibility is set very high; we dare not speak other than concretely about suffering and its relation to the purpose of God. Dare we give any 'answers' that we could not give in the presence of those who have been the victims of systematic, cold-blooded killing? This is why Auschwitz casts such a long shadow over the discussion of God and evil, God and suffering, even though theodicy has a long history before the death-camps (and, we might add, the killing-fields). Remembering the horrors perpetrated even on innocent children, would it be enough simply to deflect Irving Greenberg's startling judgment that 'no statement, theological or otherwise, should be made that would not be credible in the presence of the burning children'?[6] While ever Christians speak about a loving, merciful, benevolent, all-powerful God, the dead will claim a hearing, rightly and necessarily so. The ground on which we venture theological ideas about the relation between God's love and power, on the one hand, and human evil, natural disaster and suffering on an incalculable scale, on the other, is holy indeed.

2. The problem of evil philosophically approached

However, nothing in what has been said so far means that there is not a problem to be addressed with as much intellectual subtlety as possible and necessary; and indeed there is no shortage of attempts to meet the need. But how is the need to be understood? What exactly is to be addressed? At its simplest, there is felt to be a problem—perhaps a logical problem—about holding together the belief that God exists (and is all-powerful and perfectly good) with the reality that evil exists. Boethius, who wrote early in the sixth century, is reported to have said, 'if God is righteous, why evil?', at least hinting at the tension. David Hume, in the eighteenth century, stated the problem with characteristic clarity and simplicity: 'Is [God] willing to prevent evil, but not able?

6.   I Greenberg, 'Cloud of Smoke, Pillar of Fire: Judaism, Christianity, and Modernity after the Holocaust', quoted by Surin, *Theology and the Problem of Evil*, 147.

then he is impotent. Is he able, but not willing? then he is malevolent.
Is he both able and willing? whence then is evil?'[7] Since evil obviously
exists, doubt is thrown either on God's omnipotence or God's
goodness or both.

In recent times JL Mackie has been among the more vigorous
protagonists of this atheistic (or atheological) position.[8] Mackie asserts
that there is a very telling criticism of the belief that God exists, by way
of 'the traditional problem of evil'. 'Here it can be shown', he states,
'not that religious beliefs lack rational support, but that they are
positively irrational, that the several parts of the essential theological
doctrine are inconsistent with one another . . .' In fact, a theologian
must believe 'not merely what cannot be proved, but what can be
disproved from other beliefs that he also holds'.[9] Mackie argues that
the truth of any two of the following statements logically entails the
falsity of the third: (1) God is omnipotent; (2) God is wholly good; (3)
yet evil exists. To succeed in this argument, he realises that he needs
additional premises ('quasi-logical rules'). Thus, (4) 'omnipotent' has to
mean that there is nothing that an omnipotent being cannot do, and (5)
'good' has to mean that a good thing opposes evil and eliminates it as
far as it can. It follows that (6) 'a good omnipotent thing eliminates evil
completely', in which case 'the propositions that a good omnipotent
things exists, and that evil exists, are incompatible'.[10] Of course,
theism can survive—at least until other arguments are brought to bear
against it—if any of propositions 1–3 are modified, eg by using the
term 'omnipotent' in a modified sense, but such 'solutions', despite
being common, are, in Mackie's view, soft or 'half-hearted'.

Mackie examines a number of attempts to solve the problem of
reconciling traditional theism, strictly understood, with the existence of
evil, before concluding them all to be fallacious. Thus he reiterates his
conviction that 'there is no valid solution of the problem which does
not modify at least one of the constituent propositions in a way which
would seriously affect the essential core of the theistic position'.[11] Two

7.   D Hume, *Dialogues Concerning Natural Religion,* Part X, in *Hume on Religion,*
      edited by R Wollheim (London: Collins, 1963), 172.

8.   See his essay, 'Evil and Omnipotence', published in various collections, including
      The Problem of Evil: Selected Readings, edited Michael L Peterson (University of
      Notre Dame Press, 1992), 89–101.

9.   J Mackie, 'Evil and Omnipotence', 89.

10.   J Mackie, 'Evil and Omnipotence', 90.

11.   J Mackie, 'Evil and Omnipotence', 101.

kinds of response can be made to this conclusion. The first is to attempt to refute the charge, by arguing that an omnipotent God—in the strongest sense of the term—will not necessarily eliminate evil completely. Plantinga, when confronted by the proposition that an omniscient and omnipotent God would eliminate every evil state of affairs, argues that it is not necessarily true, on the grounds that there are some kinds of values that cannot exist without at least some kind of evil.[12] It is not at all uncommon for people to turn a situation of evil —and certainly a situation of suffering—into a situation of good. All kinds of adversity are overcome by people and all kinds of suffering and injustice are overcome and turned to good. It is unlikely that the good done by Nelson Mandela would have been done if he had not experienced the evil of apartheid in general and the injustice of imprisonment in particular. This 'good' does not diminish the evil he suffered and does not turn it into a form of good; the evil he suffered was evil! But neither does such a 'good' cease to be a good just because it involved suffering and evil. It is a question of balance; some goods do not out-weigh the evils which they presuppose, but others do. Therefore, it is not necessarily the case that an omnipotent deity—who must be presumed, as wholly good, also to want to maximise good, as opposed to merely opposing evil—would be able to eliminate every evil state of affairs. This argument, though offered by Plantinga, is a core element in theodicies very different from his, viz theodicies of the 'soul-making' type.[13]

The second kind of response to Mackie's conclusion is to acknowledge that there are theodicies in which one of the core propositions is modified, typically Mackie's point (4) above, about the divine attribute of omnipotence. There are two main ways in which Mackie's insistence that there is nothing that an omnipotent being cannot do is challenged. There is, first, a radical response: the attribute of omnipotence can simply be denied. This is the solution offered by theodicies of a

---

12. A Plantinga, *God, Freedom, and Evil*, 22f.
13. In these theodicies God creates a world which is conducive to the making of souls, ie the development of that quality of life that is truly human and reflective of the image of God. Such a process necessarily involves pain and suffering and the evil from which these often result. The best-known example of such a theodicy is John Hick's *Evil and the God of Love*. 'We have to ask ourselves', Hick asks,'whether a world from which suffering was excluded would serve what we are supposing to be the divine purpose of soul-making', (358).

'process' type. David Griffin says, 'My solution dissolves the problem of evil by denying the doctrine of omnipotence fundamental to it'.[14] His way of denying the essentially unlimited power of God is to deny the doctrine of creation *ex nihilo* and to propose instead that there has always been 'a plurality of actualities having some power of their own'; this ipso facto limits the power of God. This is, moreover, a true limitation of God's power, being neither a self-limitation—which could in principle be reversed—nor a limitation to what is logically possible—which might well be regarded as not a real limitation on God's power at all. This kind of proposal may be thought to solve the problem of evil for belief in God, but it leaves one with a rather diminished theism. Can such a God do very much? In a response to Griffin's theodicy, John Roth says—with understandable hyperbole —'A God of such weakness, no matter how much he suffers, is rather pathetic. God though he may be, Griffin's God is too small. He inspires little awe, little sense of holiness. History shows that this God's persuasive power is too scant to make a difference that is decisive enough . . .'[15] There is also, secondly, a more subtle response: the attribute of omnipotence can be qualified. Even Mackie himself doubts that the idea of divine omnipotence can remain unqualified, at least 'for any being that continues through time'.[16] Plantinga argues that God's omnipotence has to be qualified at least to some extent. It is not a denial of divine omnipotence to restrict God's power to the capacity to bring about logically possible states of affairs. In other words, there are at least logical limits to what God has power to do; God cannot create square circles or married bachelors.[17] One might not place any non-logical limits on God's power, and thus be entitled to claim to be upholding God's omnipotence. The implication is that logical limits on God's power are not significant or real limits; non-logical possibilities are not part of any real world. Plantinga concludes, 'What the theist typically means when he says that God is omnipotent is not that there

14.   David R Griffin, 'Creation out of Chaos and the Problem of Evil', in *Encountering Evil*, edited by ST Davis 105.

15.   John K Roth, 'Critique [of Griffin's Theodicy]', in *Encountering Evil*, edited by ST Davis, 121.

16.   J Mackie, 'Evil and Omnipotence', 101.

17.   A Plantinga, *God, Freedom, and Evil*, 17. Plantinga points out that there have been theists who deny that God is limited to what is logically possible, but the whole 'problem of evil' would, of course, not be regarded as problematic by them.

are no limits to God's power, but at most that there are no nonlogical limits to what He can do'.[18] On this basis he is willing to agree with Mackie that there are no limits to what an omnipotent being can do. However, as noted above, Plantinga does not accept that God, understood as omnipotent and as wholly good, will eliminate every evil state of affairs. His disagreement with Mackie remains, for it is impossible, in his view, to show that any five of his following set of six propositions logically entails the denial of the sixth.

(1) God is omnipotent;
(2) God is wholly good;
(3) God is omniscient;
(4) Evil exists;
(5) An omnipotent and omniscient good being eliminates every evil that it can properly eliminate;
6) There are no non-logical limits to what an omnipotent being can do.[19]

Where have these considerations taken us? The essay began with observations about the hazardous nature of any discussion about evil, suffering and theodicy, and made the suggestion that keeping close to the stories of suffering—rather than becoming buried in treatises about it—might serve as a kind of 'reality check' in any discussion of the problem. Then, at the risk of appearing to ignore the warnings, soundings were taken of the major points in the discussion of the problem among philosophers and philosophical theologians. Is there much value in the results of this discussion? It has to be acknowledged that, whatever the benefits of this philosophical/theological discussion, the essential mystery of evil and suffering in a world created by God is not resolved. Any slight illumination of the problem still leaves us far from an explanation. Also, it has given us no excuse to turn away from the task of resisting and removing evil and alleviating suffering. The answers to our questions in this difficult area still leave

18. A Plantinga, *God, Freedom, and Evil*, 18.
19. A Plantinga, *God, Freedom, and Evil*, 21. These six statements are Plantinga's modifications of Mackie's six points, reported above, which led him to conclude that 'the propositions that a good omnipotent things exists, and that evil exists, are incompatible'. (See note 10 above.)

us mostly dissatisfied and we hardly rush to share them with those whose actual experience of suffering is arduous in the extreme. But there is arguably at least some benefit in being assured by people with nuanced arguments that, whatever remains unexplained and unresolved, belief in God—understood broadly in a Christian way—is not rendered logically untenable by the existence of evil and suffering.

Yet surely something more should be said, both about the narrower discussion immediately above and the broader question about possible ways forward in theodicy. First, the discussion of theodicy quite properly takes place at different levels and in very different ways. The stories of suffering endured and faith held make their quite indispensable contribution. However, the more abstract discussion of issues can also contribute something. The point is well made by Marilyn McCord Adams, who says near the end of her book on the subject, 'I have meant to chart a via media that rejects the dichotomising of philosophical reflection on horrors, on the one hand, and praxis that copes with them, on the other. If they are not the same, I nevertheless envision a marriage between them'.[20] Adams has some complaints about the philosophical discussion which she observes and in which she is an active participant. In particular, she considers that the discussion has been conducted at too high a level of abstraction. This has several aspects. It is not sufficiently anchored in particular religious traditions and therefore speaks about God too abstractly; it does not get beyond 'restricted standard theism',[21] and lacks the particularity of the Jewish, Christian, Islamic or other understandings of God. The other major point of abstraction is the tendency to subsume actual evils, especially the most horrendous, under the generic category of 'evil'. This is too far away from the concrete, no matter what light such theoretical discussion throws on particular difficulties. The way forward is by both particularising and widening the terms of the discussion. Instead of working on the basis of a standard general theism, we will get further by using the resources of the particular religious tradition in which we stand. Once we do so, however, Adams—writing from her own Christian faith—is confident

20. Marilyn McCord Adams, *Horrendous Evils and the Goodness of God* (New York: Cornell University Press & Melbourne: Melbourne University Press, 1999), 186. This book is also among the best of its kind.
21. Marilyn McCord Adams, *Horrendous Evils and the Goodness of God*, 3. She borrows the phrase from William L Rowe, 'Evil and the Theistic Hypothesis', *International Journal for Philosophy of Religion* 16 (1984): 95–100.

that 'the wider resources of Christian theology can be deployed to formulate a family of solutions to the so-called logical problem of evil'.[22] This is an approach we now consider.

3. The shape of a Christian theodicy

In seeking a way through the problematic reality of evil and suffering, the tradition in which one stands makes a decisive difference to the shape of any answer that may be found. It is one thing to stand in a tradition of faith in the biblical God and from within this tradition to struggle with the problem of evil and suffering. It is another thing entirely to stand outside any tradition of faith in God and to consider whether the existence (and especially the magnitude) of evil and suffering constitutes a reason for rejecting belief in any substantial kind of God.[23] The reality of evil and suffering has always been a problem inviting serious thought for Christian thinkers, even if the idea of putting God 'on trial' for creating evil would have been far from their minds.[24] However, in the wake of the Enlightenment the question took on a radically different form, God being more or less banished from the universe. Belief in God had already become problematic, and the existence of evil and suffering in the world was yet further grounds for stepping outside the tradition of belief in God, or at least for questioning the notion of a wise Providence. In short, as Surin puts it, 'the "problem of evil" metamorphosed into the problem of the coherence and intelligibility of Christian belief per se'.[25] Ironically, it did not follow that evil and suffering ceased to be problematic, for in a

---

22. Marilyn McCord Adams, *Horrendous Evils and the Goodness of God*, 4.
23. Here 'substantial' is used in its contemporary sense of 'real' or 'actual'. It is conceivable that, given the reality of evil and suffering, a person might be inclined to believe in a deity who is less responsible for, less affected by, and less engaged in the transformation of a sinful and suffering world, eg a deistic God.
24. W Pannenberg observes, 'On the soil of belief in God the Creator a problem of theodicy—a demand for God's justification of the world he has created—cannot seriously arise'. The clay does not accuse the potter (Isa 45:9); *Systematic Theology,* Volume 2 (Grand Rapids: Eerdmans, 1994), 163. Pannenberg acknowledges that this does not prevent the question from being asked.
25. K Surin, *Theology and the Problem of Evil*, 9.

mechanistic world perfectly regulated by mathematical rules the
burden of the problem of evil shifted from God to humanity itself.[26]

To state the obvious, the Christian faith has always been much
more than a theodicy. It offers a theological account of the being and
activity of God and of everything that exists in the world, seen in its
relation to God. This must include the existence of evil and suffering in
the world, but these are only a part of a much larger story. The word
'story' is the right word, for Christian discourse about God, the world
and the self has, at least on one side, the form of narrative.[27] The
grammar of this story is trinitarian; it cannot be told adequately any
other way. The subject of the narrative is the triune God; the plot is the
creation, reconciliation and transformation of the world, understood as
a work of the divine love. The story has a beginning and—nota
bene—an ending, though the end is a matter of anticipation and hope
rather than something already arrived at. The ending is a necessary
part of the story, notwithstanding its open-endedness; it is not a
dispensable part. It affects proleptically every part of the story; no part
can be considered apart from it. Likewise, every problem that is
addressed theologically—the metaphysical counterpart to the narrative—must be considered in the light of the anticipated ending. This
presents significant challenges to theological work, not least when it
comes to addressing the problem of evil and suffering, but it cannot be
bypassed. Regardless of how unexpected or incongruent the end of a
story is, it is decisive for the story's meaning.

Although, as suggested at the end of the previous section, there
may be value in a philosophical theodicy, a Christian theodicy will be
different because of its embeddedness in a narrative. Surin expresses
astonishment at the failure of modern 'theodicists' to take this into
account when considering Augustinian and Irenaean options in
theodicy, as if Augustine and Irenaeus were participants in a post-Enlightenment discussion.[28] In the process, the narrative from which
much later the Irenaean theodicy was extracted is forgotten. But this
narrative and the theology it carries contain resources which are far
from marginal in the Christian attempts to make theological sense of

26.   K Surin, *Theology and the Problem of Evil*, 43.
27.   Nicholas Lash observes, 'The forms of Christian discourse are set between the
      poles of metaphor and analogy, of narrative and metaphysics.' 'Ideology,
      Metaphor, and Analogy', edited by S Hauerwas & LG Jones, *Why Narrative?:
      Readings in Narrative Theology* (Grand Rapids: Eerdmans, 1989), 117.
28.   K Surin, *Theology and the Problem of Evil*, 12–15.

evil and suffering. Both Irenaeus and Augustine in their different ways have a theology of history—the incarnation at its centre—by means of which they understand the events and realities of human life in the framework of the divine purpose. In doing this they provide a model for addressing the problem of evil and suffering in a way that differs greatly from a judgment about the logical coherence of a set of propositions. Surin advocates a 'narrative resolution'[29] of crises of meaning which are precipitated by powerful experiences of evil and suffering, one's own or those of others. The Christian narrative does not solve the problem of evil and suffering in a neat, logical way, but it offers a framework for understanding the problem and resources for working with it. It can perhaps best be thought of as working in two ways: as a narrative of the 'economy' of salvation and as an invitation to people to understand themselves as addressed and engaged in particular ways.

Christian faith is nourished by the story of salvation, which theology understands in terms of a divine 'economy' (*oikonomia*) of salvation, the activity of the triune God in creating and redeeming a contingent world, including the human being as a special covenant-partner who is destined to be the image of God. In thinking of the problem of evil and suffering, some particular elements in this narrative can be highlighted.

(1) God the Father, the first Person of the Trinity, has brought into being a finite universe through the Son and the Spirit.[30] Creation is the work of the triune God. All things, visible and invisible, have been created through the agency of God and remain in being only through God's sustaining power. Christian theology has been unwilling to attribute the existence of evil to God, except in the most oblique way; instead it prefers to attribute it to creaturely beings, angelic or human. However, the concern to absolve God from responsibility is, at best, only partially successful, for even where the blame is laid with angels or humankind, the Creator brought into being—arguably for good

---

29.   K Surin, *Theology and the Problem of Evil*, 27. (Italics added.)
30.   Although the naming of God as 'Father' creates difficulties, it is extremely
      difficult, and requires very awkward prose, to avoid referring to the first Person of
      the Trinity as 'Father'.

reasons—this particular world with this particular possibility.[31] In any
case, we cannot speak with the certainty and clarity we would like
about the origins of evil. Pannenberg reflects the mystery of evil's
origins. 'God did not will wickedness and evil as such. He could not
take pleasure in them. They are not an object of his will. Nevertheless,
they are in fact accompanying phenomena. As such they are conditions
of the realising of his purpose for the creature . . .'[32]

(2) The human being, who suffers as a result of the imperfection
and brokenness of the world but who also actively contributes to evil
and suffering, knows itself to be made for communion with God, but is
aware of the estrangement from God in which it lives. This is the
condition in which we live, the unavoidability of which is denoted by
the problematic but necessary concept of 'original sin'. The reasons for
this may lie in the way in which human beings seek to exercise the
independence for which they were created, viz in self-assertion over
against God and creation, including other people. Yet God does not
turn against humankind or leave it to its own devices, but reaches out
to it in reconciling love and with the promise of redemption and
renewal. Evil and suffering, and the estrangement which they both
generate and express, are not to have the last word.

(3) In the incarnation of the Logos-Son, God enters fully into the
human condition. The God who is 'with us', the Immanuel-God, could
not identify more closely with human existence in this world. In the
particularity of Jesus of Nazareth the universal love of God is
expressed once for all. God enters into human experience, its tragedies
as well as its joys, its weakness as well as its strengths. Jesus knows
first-hand the evil that human beings can do to each other. He suffers
as others suffer; perhaps more profoundly. He confronts the sufferings
of many with the healing and liberation that will characterise the reign
of God when it comes, and in his person it comes into the very present
of those who encountered him. On the cross he knows estrangement
even from God, his Abba, not to mention the hostility and abandonment of the world. On the cross God does not only identify with all

31. W Pannenberg writes, 'Concern to absolve the Creator has been a mistake in
      Christian theodicy. The attempt cannot succeed, nor does it accord with the NT
      testimony, for in and with the crucifixion of his Son God accepted and bore
      responsibility for the world that he had created.' *Systematic Theology*, volume 2,
      166.
32. W Pannenberg, *Systematic Theology*, volume 2, 167.

who suffer rejection and pain, but above all accepts and bears responsibility for the world which God has created.[33]

(4) In the resurrection of Jesus from death God defeats the power of death and the power of evil. Not only is it a vindication of the authority of Jesus' claim to speak and act in the name of God, but it is a proleptic coming of God's eschatological reign into the time and space of the world. As Jesus is raised from death, so it will be for the dead who die 'in Christ'. The new creation that is associated with the end of the age, in which there will be no more tears and suffering and in which even death will be no more (Rev 21:4), is manifest in the risen Christ. Here above all we see the 'Yes' to all God's promises (2 Cor 1:20), the victory that seals the defeat of evil. In the resurrection of Jesus we see the nature of the future that, although still outstanding, is in Christ and through Christ the future of humankind. For in Adam all die, but in Christ all will be made alive (1 Cor 15:22). So much hinges on the resurrection of Jesus that the apostle Paul says that, if we are mistaken about this, our faith is in vain and we will have been misrepresenting God (1 Cor 15:14f).

(5) If we are to narrate this story of redemption trinitarianly we must also speak of the Holy Spirit, the third Person of the Trinity. This is the Spirit who, according to Paul, raised Jesus from the dead and who will also give life to our mortal bodies (Rom 8:11). The Spirit is the life-giving energy in all creation (Ps 104:30), but in the light of the resurrection this has to be understood from the perspective of the eschatological future.[34] The one who is the source of all life is also the source of the new life, the life that is 'wholly penetrated by the Spirit and remains related to him',[35] the life in which the power of evil is already broken (though, empirically speaking, not yet fully) and in

---

33. Note Bonhoeffer's statement that 'God allowed himself to be pushed out of the world on to the cross'. For the idea of God's acceptance of responsibility for a world in which there is evil and suffering see W Pannenberg, *Systematic Theology*, volume 2, 166. 'Responsibility for the coming of evil into creation unavoidably falls on the God who foresees and permits it, even though creaturely action is the immediate cause. God did not shirk the responsibility but shouldered it by sending and giving up his Son to the cross. In this way, as Creator, he stands by his responsibility for the work that he has made. Evil is thus real and costly enough for God himself as well as for creatures.' (169)

34. See W Pannenberg, *Systematic Theology*, volume 2, 98.

35. W Pannenberg, *Systematic Theology*, volume 3, 622.

which the reality of suffering, though still pervasive, is also being transformed through the compassionate presence of Christ and the hope generated by his resurrection.

From this story of creation and redemption several things follow for our self-understanding and our vocation as human beings.

(1) Through this narrative human beings are set free from both pessimistic and optimistic views of human nature and society. We are not people on whose shoulders the weight of the world's evil and suffering can be placed; nor does it have to be. We are not creatures who are incapable of any good, Calvinistic conviction notwithstanding. Neither are we creatures who are only victims of other people's limitations and evils. We are perpetrators of evil—in word and deed, as well as by neglect—not only its victims; we are agents of suffering, not only its recipients. We are 'fallen' beings, not angels. We are implicated in society's injustice and evil 'up to our necks', even if we are not personally responsible for injustice done and suffering inflicted in times before our own.[36] The Christian narrative calls us to the salutary practice of confession, in which we might be confronted with the ambiguous reality of our lives.[37] Above all, we must see the truth of what we are, and not be satisfied with self-deception. But in the light of the cross, we are also people embraced by the forgiveness of God, and are therefore set free from the failures of the past to embark on a new course of life and to do new things in the power of the Spirit.

(2) The Christian narrative also calls us to conversion, for we are not created to be captive to the power of evil, let alone its agents. Rather, we are called to live in fellowship (*koinonia*) with the triune God, whose divine life is open to us. Part of the symbolic power of the ascension of Christ to the right hand of the Father is its encouragement to us to think that our humanity has been taken by Christ into the very centre of the life of the Trinity. There lies our true orientation, even while we struggle on in this life under the sign of the cross. It follows that our vocation is to live in conformity with the image of God which

---

36. This alone is reason enough for a clear and unqualified apology from the Prime Minister to Aboriginal people for past injustices. His unwillingness to do so ignores our 'solidarity in sin' even when we in our generation are not directly responsible. We remain the beneficiaries, to a greater or lesser extent, of these injustices.

37. Donald MacKinnon speaks of 'the dark ambivalence of human action'; 'Subjective and Objective Conceptions of Atonement', quoted in K Surin, *Theology and the Problem of Evil*, 155.

Jesus Christ has actualised and which, in him, is our eschatological future. We are also called, in the koinonia of the church, the community of faith, hope and love, to be renewed in our minds, to discern what is good, and to live lives that are holy and acceptable to God.[38]

(3) The narrative of divine reconciliation with the world enlists us in the service of reconciliation. We are called into partnership with God in the divine work of setting things to rights in the world. This work is the diaconal responsibility of the church, in which, thankfully, it is joined by people of goodwill from every religious or political commitment. It is, at the most basic level, a diakonia to those who suffer, whether physically, emotionally or spiritually, and whether through neglect and marginalisation or through abuse and exploitation. This is the ministry of caring for the sick and the poor, the unloved and those who fall by the wayside in an increasingly hectic and pressured world. There is also the patient and persistent task of exposing, fighting and resisting evil in whatever forms and on whatever scale it exerts its power. This, too, is part of the Christian vocation, collectively and individually.

(4) The 'economy of salvation' is not given to us in word only but also in action, notably in the church's liturgical action, particularly in the sacraments. If in our baptism we become part of this great story, so that the small narratives of our lives are meshed with the great narrative of divine redemption, in the eucharist and other 'sacramental' acts of the church we are called back repeatedly to this story and given strength for the task. As one Australian church's confessional statement puts it, 'In [the] sacrament of [Christ's] broken body and outpoured blood the risen Lord feeds his baptised people on their way to the final inheritance of the Kingdom'.[39] Sacred places and times, sacred things, sacred words, all in the service of sacred people,[40] inspire and challenge, encourage and re-engage us in the fight against evil and the alleviation of suffering.

---

38. This is a very rough paraphrase of Romans 12:1–2. See further on the pursuit of holiness, K Surin, *Theology and the Problem of Evil*, 23.

39. The Uniting Church in Australia, *The Basis of Union*, 1992 edition (Melbourne: Uniting Church Press), §8.

40. I owe these phrases to Gordon Lathrop, *Holy Things: A Liturgical Theology* (Minneapolis: Fortress Press, 1993), esp. ch. 4.

In all these ways the narrative of salvation, the great story of God's action to heal and liberate, addresses the problem of evil and suffering. They are an integral part of a theodicy, not a philosophical theodicy concerned primarily with logic but a narrative and dramatic theodicy, which tells of the 'mighty deeds of God' in respect of evil and suffering, all that God has done, is doing and will yet do to 'deliver us from evil'. It is a practical theodicy rather than a purely theoretical one. It would be strange, however, if its 'practical' character should disqualify it from being considered a theodicy, for the statement of how God engages with evil and suffering and how they are to be finally overcome is as integral a part of theodicy as the question of their origin and their possibility in a world created by God. The Christian narrative, both in general and in its function as a theodicy, includes the recognition that although we live from the future we do not yet live in the future. We do, however, have anticipations of this eschatological future; already Christians claim to experience something of the new for which they hope. The impact of this hoped-for new, the eschatological future, on theodicy must now be considered more explicitly.

4. Eschatology and theodicy

In the course of this essay it has not been possible to suppress the theme of eschatology at various points in the argument. The very idea of a 'narrative' of God's work in the universe implies, as was noted, a plot, with a beginning and an ending. This ending is not just the final line in the story but a conclusion, a telos toward which the story has been moving and in the light of which every element in the story takes on its meaning. Certainly, not all endings are clear; many are ambiguous. Perhaps the best endings are surprising, even subversive. However, as Paul Fiddes argues, an ending is acceptable or satisfying if a reader can 'make order', even where the author denies it or leaves it in doubt. This making of order requires an end 'that opens possibility'; 'like the ends in Christian apocalyptic it will have an openness about it, but it is the opening of hope'.[41] The Christian narrative—'grand' in its scope, since it claims to incorporate (by perfecting or subverting) the narratives of all people—opens possibilities where otherwise none are thought to exist. It is an entirely

---

41.   Paul S Fiddes, *The Promised End: Eschatology in Theology and Literature* (Oxford: Blackwell, 2000), 50.

fair question to ask whether these possibilities are grounded in or consonant with some aspect of present reality, or whether they are so discontinuous with it that many will judge them to be illusory; to this question we must return. For now the point being made is that the Christian attempt to say something about the mystery of evil and suffering in a world created and (to be) redeemed by God necessarily includes an eschatological aspect. But is any kind of reference at all to eschatology permissible in relation to theodicy and, if not, is there a criterion by which to distinguish legitimate from dubious reference?

Any view of life in this world which suggests that it is of little or no significance in the light of eternal life (or 'life after death') is to be rejected on the grounds that it fails to see the divine intentionality in created life and must therefore be based on an inadequate doctrine of creation. This is true *a fortiori* of those views of suffering which gloss over it in order to emphasise the wonders of the heavenly life. The promise of 'pie in the sky when you die' has no resonance any more when offered as a compensation for deprivation and suffering in this life. Any spiritual advice to endure one's sufferings patiently in the expectation of heavenly rewards is, to say the least, both theologically and morally dubious. When the apostle Paul considers that 'the sufferings of this present time are not worth comparing with the glory about to be revealed to us' (Rom 8:18), he is not giving a licence to anyone to say that the sufferings to which he refers are insignificant. He does, of course, 'set them within a wider framework that looks beyond the present to the full realisation of God's design for human beings and their world',[42] but there is no trivialisation of suffering in the passage from which these lines come.

There is probably a strong sense that the glory that is in store for us cannot compensate people—certainly not those who have suffered terribly or really had no life at all—for the evil which has been done to them or for the suffering that has afflicted their lives. Dostoyevski's Ivan Karamazov speaks for many when he asks whether one would accept the torture of even one child as the condition of a peaceful and restful human destiny for all people; he himself would not! Divine providence is too costly. For Ivan the sufferings of humankind cannot

---

42. Brendan Byrne, *Romans*, Sacra Pagina Series, volume 6 (Collegeville: The Liturgical Press, 1996), 257.

be redeemed, not in this life and not in any subsequent life.[43] Theodicies of a 'soul-making' type are often criticised for requiring suffering for the sake of a greater good. In Hick's view, the idea that people gradually become children of God, through their experiences and choices, requires a world something like ours, 'not a pain-free and stress-free paradise'. It has to be a world with the possibility of 'hardship, disaster, failure, defeat and misery'.[44] Hick's theodicy also requires an eschatological fulfilment, for clearly the divine purpose is not realised for many people by the time their earthly life comes to an end. However, he is careful to say that this eschatological fulfilment is not a reward or a compensation for the experiences of suffering during a person's life on earth; he rejects any 'book-keeping' view. What he does propose is that people's sufferings, which vary greatly in intensity and duration, 'will in the end lead to the enjoyment of a common good which will be unending and therefore unlimited, and which will be seen by its participants as justifying all that has been endured on the way to it'.[45]

The conclusion is inescapable that eschatology cannot be kept out of Christian theodicy, despite the fact that it is sometimes invoked too glibly. Christiaan Beker understands Paul as believing that the pain of suffering, like all other riddles of life, will 'only be resolved in God's coming eschatological glory when through the tears of suffering we may nevertheless confess in hindsight that "all things work together for good to those who love God"'.[46] It will often be impossible to repeat this Pauline assurance in the presence of suffering! However, without suggesting that here we have an explanation of suffering, let alone a justification, this is the hope by which Christians live. Beker distinguishes between the Christian disposition of hope and the content of hope in which it is anchored. The content of hope is 'the forthcoming apocalyptic triumph of God'.[47] The triumph of God is the fullness of God, when God will be 'all in all' (1 Cor 15:28), and the glory of God. The Christian hope is that the glory of God will include a transformed and glorified creation, in which God can fully glory. Such

43. See further K Surin's discussion of this; *Theology and the Problem of Evil*, 98.
44. J Hick, 'An Irenaean Theodicy', ST Davis (ed), *Encountering Evil*, 48.
45. J Hick, *Evil and the God of Love*, 377.
46. J Christiaan Beker, *Suffering and Hope: The Biblical Vision and the Human Predicament* (Philadelphia: Fortress, 1987), 76.
47. J. Christiaan Beker, *Suffering and Hope*, 76f.

glory will have to mean a very great reversal for those who have suffered much or whose lives have been severely cut short. Jürgen Moltmann concludes some personal thoughts on this subject with these lines:

> . . . I would think that eternal life gives the broken and the impaired and those whose lives have been destroyed space and time and strength to live the life which they were intended for, and for which they were born. I think this, not for selfish reasons, for the sake of my personal completion, and not morally, for the sake of some kind of purification; I think it for the sake of the justice which I believe is God's concern and his first option.[48]

If the issue is indeed the justice of God, eschatology must be allowed to play a significant part in the articulation of a theodicy, which is precisely the attempt to show that God is just despite the magnitude of evil and the intensity and extent of suffering in the world.

If it is a question of the justice of God the question must be asked, who is the judge? Whose responsibility is it to make the judgment about God's justice? Understandably, the clay not being in a position to criticise the potter, Christians are not strongly inclined to put God 'on trial'. Who are we to make a declaration that God is, or is not, just—the one whom the Psalmist praises for being 'just in all his ways' (Ps 145:17)? Shall not the judge of all the earth do what is just? (Gen 18:25).[49] Theodicy, as suggested at the beginning of this essay, is

---

48. J Moltmann, *The Coming of God: Christian Eschatology* (London: SCM, 1996), 118.

49. It should not be assumed, however, that theodicy is necessarily negative or critical. To the extent that it is, it will be found by many Christians to be impious, even blasphemous. It is true that Job is put in his place by the reply of God (Job 38–41), but God's greater judgment is against the 'friends' of Job, who had not spoken rightly about God, 'as my servant Job has'. (Job 42:7ff.) The psalms of lament, essentially prayers, cry out *to* God and sometimes *against* God, and might be taken as providing space, also in later times, for the expression of deep anguish and the voicing of questions that have their origin in profound experiences of suffering.

dangerous, and we embark on it only because the stakes are high. Account must be taken of both the goodness of the divine purpose and the magnitude of human suffering. Any judgments made about God and the implications of the eschatological consummation for which we hope are utterly provisional, since we see, for now, 'in a glass, darkly' (1 Cor 13:12a).[50] The confirmation of our stammering judgments is itself eschatological. For it is the Spirit who, in the eschatological transformation of all things and the eschatological glorifying of the Son (and the Father in the Son), will deliver the final verdict on the Father, whose project, through the Son and the Spirit, creation is.[51] The question that is now open will then be definitively answered. The debatability of God, both God's existence and God's justice, will then give way to unimaginable clarity—when we shall know as fully as we are now fully known (1 Cor 13:12b)—and the whole project of creation will appear as a work of the world-encompassing love of God.

This demonstration can only be eschatological; so it is itself a matter of hope. On two counts, then, Christian theodicy cannot be attempted without eschatology: not only in its reliance on an eschatological verification of its hope but also in the substance of this hope. The world's evil and suffering cannot make theological sense in any other framework; neither can it be incontrovertibly demonstrated other than eschatologically. This double conviction has been stated strongly and subtly by Wolfhart Pannenberg on the penultimate page of his *Systematic Theology*.

> Only in the light of the eschatological consummation
> is the verdict justified that in the first creation story
> the Creator pronounced at the end of the sixth day
> when he had created the first human pair: 'And God
> saw everything that he had made, and behold, it was
> very good' (Gen 1:31). Only in the light of the
> eschatological consummation may this be said of our
> world as it is in all its confusion and pain. But those
> who may say it in spite of the suffering of the world
> honour and praise God as their Creator. The verdict

---

50. The King James Version of this text cannot be surpassed by any modern translation.

51. W Pannenberg entitles the last section of his final chapter of theology 'The Justification of God by the Spirit'; *Systematic Theology*, volume 3, 630–646.

'very good' does not apply simply to the world of creation in its state at any given time. It is true, rather, of the whole course of history in which God is present with his creatures in incursions of love that will finally lead it through the hazards and sufferings of finitude to participation in his glory.[52]

If it is obvious that the Christian narrative about a cosmos created, broken ('fallen') and to be perfected requires for its coherence an eschatological promise and hope, it is far from clear that such a hope coheres with the possible scenarios of the world's future being drawn in other quarters, notably cosmology. Christian eschatology envisages transformation and renewal; cosmology speculates about stars running out of fuel and an eventual 'galactic graveyard'.[53] The cosmological speculations are, of course, far from uniform. Paul Davies also speculates about the possibility of 'genuine immortality', not just for the descendents of *Homo sapiens* but for universes as well![54] Nevertheless, the reality of death, cosmic death, is pervasive in the pictures painted of the ultimate future of the universe, prompting the irrepressible question of the purpose and worthwhileness of it all.[55] A new phase of the dialogue between scientists and theologians focuses on these questions. It is not an area for simplistic ideas, neither in science nor in theology; only a commitment to articulating 'a *thick, many-layered* account of reality' is likely to advance the conversation.[56]

---

52. W Pannenberg, *Systematic Theology*, volume 3, 645.

53. The phrase is Edward Harrison's, *Cosmology* (Cambridge: Cambridge University Press, 1981), 360. It is quoted by Paul Davies, *God and the New Physics* (London: Penguin Books, 1983), 201.

54. Paul Davies, *The Last Three Minutes: Conjectures about the Ultimate Fate of the Universe* (London: Weidenfeld & Nicolson, 1994), 138.

55. John Polkinghorne and Michael Welker ask, 'What are the true purposes of the Creator of such a world of change and decay? What ends are being brought about within it by the divine purpose?' *The End of the World and the Ends of God: Science and Theology on Eschatology* (Harrisburg: Trinity Press International, 2000), 10.

56. *The End of the World and the Ends of God*, edited by John Polkinghorne and Michael Welker, 11. The essays in this collection testify to such a commitment.

In particular, a major challenge this sets for theologians is to consider how their understanding of eternal life, the new creation, the future that God has in view for the cosmos, can be brought into relation with the core of cosmological understandings of the future of the universe. Clearly, a theological understanding of these things requires fresh articulation in the light of these new challenges. On the other hand, the ground of Christian hope for the future—both of the cosmos as a whole and individual persons—remains the resurrection of Jesus from the dead.[57] Accounts of the universe that leave the last word with its death and its ultimate futility cannot remain unchallenged from the side of theology. Neither, on the other hand, can constructive theology be done without serious engagement with those best equipped to speak about the origins and the likely future of the universe, physically speaking. Each side has a critical task in relation to the other.[58] However, the critical task is not exhaustive; there is also a constructive aspect in each side's task. If the fundamental category of Christian reference to the resurrection of Jesus is *transformation,* the same might be true analogously of the new creation that is promised, the resurrection of the dead. In any case, as John Polkinghorne suggests, the new creation is better thought of as a 'divine redemptive transformation of the old creation' than a second creation *ex nihilo;* it is 'a resurrected world created *ex vetere'.*[59] The relation between the old creation and the new will then be one of both continuity and discontinuity, with cosmology and theology making their distinctive contributions to the former and the latter respectively.

---

57. Michael Welker expresses amazement at 'how resistant the belief in resurrection, or at least the tolerance of the church's insistence on that belief, has been despite the severe doubts and attacks on it since the Enlightenment'. He concludes that 'the knowledge of Jesus' resurrection is just as little an illusion as the discovery of justice or of mathematics'. 'Resurrection and Eternal Life', in *The End of the World and the Ends of God,* edited by John Polkinghorne and Michael Welker 279, n.1, 283.

58. Walter P Carvin describes the relation between religion and science as 'subtle and intriguing'. In addition, he issues an instructive warning: 'Religion must learn to live with whatever cosmology, whatever theory a science provides; but on no account must it ever marry any of them.' 'Creation and Scientific Explanation', *Scottish Journal of theology,* volume 36, no 3, 1983, 306.

59. John Polkinghorne, 'Eschatology: Some Questions and Some Insights from Science', in *The End of the World and the Ends of God,* edited by John Polkinghorne and Michael Welker, 30.

If theology speaks of the transformation of all things, cosmology will at least insist that the matter-energy of the world to come would have to differ greatly in its properties from the matter-energy of the present world.[60] It does not appear to be an unthinkable idea.

Christian eschatology is challenged not only by discoveries in cosmology during the twentieth century; it is also challenged by the idea of closure as such. It must therefore think afresh about what Christian faith means by the promise and hope of a consummation, an end, a closure to the course of history as we know it. Paul Fiddes begins his *The Promised End* with the observation that 'many modern novelists seem to find it difficult to bring their books to an end'.[61] This parallels the difficulty of the idea of an end to history, especially when 'end' is understood as *telos* or conclusion rather than simply as ending. The idea of a final resolution of all discord, a final harmony and reconciliation of all things, is suspect in a time when history is generally no longer understood as a divine project. It may offer consolation and have an element of moral appeal, but it is dismissed as wishful thinking.[62] In addition, deconstructionists are sceptical of all meta-narratives, the Christian story among them, for seeking to impose a single structure of meaning on historical events. Meaning—if there is any—remains open and dispersed;[63] closure is not permitted. In responding to this apparently pervasive mood, theology must work with a multiplicity of images and metaphors. The notion of 'closure' is as misleading as it is pertinent. Christian faith certainly speaks of an end to this age, a completion or fulfilment, meaning by this an end to spatio-temporal existence. But it does not mean the cessation of creaturely existence. If the idea of closure is to be used it cannot mean the closing of a door or the lowering of a curtain with nothing on the other side of it. Pannenberg makes the point that *'God and not nothing is the end of time'*.[64] Eternal life is not nothingness; it is the fullness of life, nothing less than participation in the eternal life of God. This should not be understood as suspended animation or a sleep-like state in

---

60. John Polkinghorne, 'Eschatology: Some Questions and Some Insights from Science', 39.

61. Paul S Fiddes, *The Promised End*, 1.

62. Paul Fiddes speaks of 'consoling deceptions'. *The Promised End*, 13.

63. Paul S Fiddes, *The Promised End*, 32.

64. W Pannenberg, *Systematic Theology*, volume 3, 594 (Pannenberg's italics).

which nothing really happens. The eschatological future for which
Christians hope is one in which God reigns in and over all things, not
over nothing! From the side of the creation, we must at least speak in
terms of the knowledge of the glory of God and the *enjoyment* of
God.[65] Eschatological life is a feast, not a famine; the symbol of the
heavenly banquet expresses its festive quality.

To conclude, I have argued for an approach to theodicy which does
not put all its eggs in any one of the logical-philosophical, the practical-
vocational or the narrative baskets but combines elements of each. Of
the available approaches, the narrative resources of the Christian faith
have been found to be most productive. Surin's theodicy, oriented to a
narrative resolution of crises of meaning rather than the demonstration
of the logical consistency of a set of carefully qualified propositions,
appears to take us furthest. Everything depends on the persuasive
power of the Christian 'grand narrative', not only its capacity to
provide a framework for thinking about evil, suffering and their
redemption, but also its power to draw us beyond paralysis or despair
and recruit us in the service of resisting evil and alleviating suffering.
The central place of a hoped-for eschatological closure—a notion that
needs particular care—was argued strongly; without this ending the
whole narrative collapses. Two particular problems were noted: the
need to bring this narrative about the cosmos and human existence
into connection with cosmological thinking about the likely future of
the universe and the need to enter into dialogue with the pervasive
mood of suspicion about universal narratives and final endings. These
two 'conversations' are ongoing. In the meantime, impelled by the
message of Christ crucified and risen, Christian theology has no option
but to articulate as clearly and cogently as possible the hope that
nothing in creation can separate us from the love of God and nothing
can finally diminish or obscure the glory of God.

---

65.   I have long been fascinated by the idea, expressed in the Westminster Catechism
      of 1647, that the chief purpose of humankind was 'to glorify God and to enjoy
      [God] for ever'.

Natural Theodicy in an Evolutionary Context: The Need for an Eschatology of New Creation

Robert John Russell

In a universe of blind physical forces and genetic replication, some people are going to get hurt, other people are going to get lucky, and you won't find any rhyme or reason in it, nor any justice. The universe we observe has precisely the properties we should expect if there is, at bottom, no design, no purpose, no evil and no good, nothing but blind, pitiless indifference.[1]

There is every reason for a Christian of today to embrace both the theological teachings of Genesis and the theory of evolution. But holding together the Christian view of God and the insights of evolutionary science does demand a rethinking of our theology of the trinitarian God at work in creation.[2]

1. Introduction

Life is filled with beauty, joy, creativity, hope and peace. From an azure sky above a Tahitian atoll, whose choral reefs team with abundant multicoloured fish and plants, to the craggy Rocky Mountains and the soaring Swiss alps, from the taste of delectable food to the ecstasy of sexual intercourse, from the glorious photos of stars being born in deep space to the astonishment at the birth of one's child, life is, as the Priestly account proclaims, 'very good' (Gen 1:1 – 2:3). But

---

1.   Richard Dawkins, *River Out of Eden: A Darwinian View of Life* (New York: Basic Books, 1995), 133.

2.   Denis Edwards, *The God of Evolution: A Trinitarian Theology* (New York: Paulist Press, 1999), 13.

life is also torn by the pain of hunger, cold and bodily wounds, threatened by hurricanes, drought and earthquakes, vulnerable to bacterial and genetic diseases, a fierce combat zone in the Caribbean tropics and the African savannah. Most living creatures are caught up in endless cycles of predation that compose the food chain, and most animals are fated to an agonising death.

The Bible is striking, compared to the views of its neighbouring cultures of Greece and Babylon, in bringing both sides of life under the rubric of radical monotheism; God as the creator of the world, though working even through the tragedies of life, is the source of all that is, and, ultimately, all that is is good. Suffering, disease and death are the universal consequences of an inestimably tragic and singular event, the Fall. Yet they will be removed in the coming reign of God when all living creatures are restored to their original, right and harmonious relations (Isa 11:1–9) and, even more so, when they are transformed into creatures of everlasting life in the new creation (Rev 21:1 – 22:5).

This historical/theological explanation of the two sides of life as created good and only *consequentially* evil is severely challenged by neo-Darwinian evolution, from which perspective natural selection, and with it death and extinction, is integral to what drives evolution and thus becomes *constitutive* of life. This paper focuses on the 'underside' of the picture of life on earth where 'natural evil' (suffering, disease, death and extinction) raises the challenge of 'natural' or 'evolutionary' theodicy: How can we believe in the goodness and power of the God who creates life through the very processes of evolution that constitutively involve natural evil? This challenge is one believers must address as we struggle with our faith in God, as we watch friends turn away from faith because of natural evil and as we attempt to respond to the atheistic challenge to faith based on natural evil.[3]

---

3. Other accounts of what drives evolution, such as punctuated equilibrium, panadaptionism, neo-Lamarckian effects, self-organisation, cooperation and symbiogenesis, may provide helpful critiques of the central role accorded to natural selection in neo-Darwinism. For an excellent overview, see Ian G Barbour, 'Five Models of God and Evolution', in Robert John Russell, William R Stoeger and Francisco J Ayala (eds), *Evolutionary and Molecular Biology: Scientific Perspectives on Divine Action* (Vatican City State: Vatican Observatory Publications; Berkeley, CA: CTNS, 1998), 419–42. Still, even if our understanding of what drives evolution 'evolves', the facticity of natural evil remains to be dealt with one way or another theologically, and no glib appeal to

This paper is an elaboration of one theme—natural theodicy—in a previous paper presented and discussed in Adelaide in 2002.[4] Both are sections of a large-scale research and writing program.[5] My overall argument is that diverse areas in contemporary theology drive us to construct an eschatology that entails the transformation of the universe into a 'new creation' and addresses the challenges of both natural evil *and* big-bang cosmology. This paper spells out in more detail the ways in which natural theodicy compels us to respond with such a robust eschatology.

At the outset, I want to underscore the *apophatic* context of theology. What little light we have to shed on theological issues is surrounded by the overwhelming mystery of God, which we confess through faith. That there is such inevitable mystery should not be an excuse for sloppy thinking; instead, the acknowledgment of mystery should drive us to pursue theology's fundamental task of reflecting self-critically on our encounter with God. This is particularly important for the task of theodicy: We should never seek to 'solve' the problem of evil. As the book of Job discloses, our fundamental response to evil must be faith in God and not rational argument. Karl Rahner writes that the deepest answer to the incomprehensibility of suffering is 'the incomprehensibility of God in his [*sic*] freedom and nothing else'.[6] This paper is written with the hope that the *kataphatic* affirmation of God's ultimate goodness might have a place within the *apophatic* mystery of the world as God's creation, including its trenchant and stunningly excessive moral and natural evil.

the challenges to neo-Darwinism will nullify the problem of evolutionary theodicy.

4.   See Robert John Russell, 'Sin, Salvation, and Scientific Cosmology: Is Christian Eschatology Credible Today?', in Duncan Reid and Mark Worthing (eds), *Sin and Salvation*, TTT III (Adelaide: ATF Press, 2003), 130–54.

5.   Sponsored in part by a grant (# 357) from the Philadelphia Center for Science and Religion.

6.   Karl Rahner, 'Why Does God Allow Us to Suffer?' in his *Theological Investigations* (New York: Crossroad, 1983), 206–8.

2. Evolution in theological perspective: Two challenges and responses

2.1 Challenge 1: Evolution and chance—atheism or theism?

Before turning to theodicy, it is important to recall that evolutionary biology has been used repeatedly by atheists to challenge Christian faith and to support a dysteleological metaphysics of nature. The typical charge is that 'blind chance' in evolution makes God's purposeful action as the Creator of life impossible, or more simply that evolution leads inevitably to atheism—or at most to a pale deism.[7] In the well-known words of Jacques Monod, '. . . chance *alone* is at the source of every innovation, of all creation in the biosphere. Pure chance, absolutely free but blind, [lies] at the very root of the stupendous edifice of evolution. . .' He concludes that 'the ancient covenant is in pieces; man [*sic*] at last knows that he is alone in the unfeeling immensity of the universe out of which he emerged only by chance'.[8]

The enormous cultural impact of Monod's views was stressed by David Bartholomew in 1984: 'The devastating attack on belief in a purposeful God made by Jacques Monod . . . is the most penetrating and damaging that has been launched in the name of science.' Were Monod correct, it 'would be sufficient to demolish Christianity and most of the other higher religions'.[9] Theists such as Donald MacKay and Mary Hesse quickly responded to Monod, but in his 1979 Bampton Lectures Arthur Peacocke[10] gave what Bartholomew called

---

7. Chance in the context of biological evolution occurs at and between many levels of biological complexity. There is random variation at the level of genes, including genetic mutation, crossing over and its dissimilation through sexual reproduction. There are random changes in the environment of biological populations. Finally, there is a random relation between these changes in the environment and the phenotypic characteristics expressed by individuals in the population.

8. Jacques Monod, *Chance and Necessity: An Essay on the Natural Philosophy of Modern Biology*, translated by A Wainhouse (New York: Vintage Books, 1972), 112, 180.

9. DJ Bartholomew, *God of Chance* (London: SCM Press, 1984), 16. Bartholomew's book provides an excellent survey of theistic responses before the mid-1980s.

10. Arthur R Peacocke, *Creation and the World of Science: The Bampton Lectures, 1979* (Oxford: Clarendon Press, 1979). See, for example, the discussion on pages 90 and following where Peacocke specifically refers to the two kinds of chance.

'the most extensive and convincing reply to Monod'.[11] According to Peacocke, the initial potentialities built into the universe by God are actualised in time through chance. Peacocke developed this idea into an elaborate theology of God's continuous creation (*creatio continua*): In creating the world *ex nihilo*, God bequeathed it both lawfulness and chance, and God works continuously in time and immanently 'in, with, under and through' the processes of nature. This view, which has been termed 'theistic evolution', contends that evolution is 'how God creates life'.

2.1.1 Initial response: Theistic evolution—but is it more than 'statistical deism'?

Today, theistic evolution is widely advocated in the literature in theology and science. It represents a common starting point for a variety of distinctive and more fully developed positions about what it means to say that God acts immanently within nature. An enduring problem for this approach is that without such further development, it could amount to little more than what I have termed 'statistical deism': If 'chance' refers to epistemic ignorance, namely, our lack of knowledge of the underlying natural causes that deterministically produce apparently chance events, then the phrase 'chance and law' really amounts to '(unknown) law and (known) law', and God's action amounts to little more than the realisation in time of potentials and possibilities written into the universe at its creation. Thus without further development, theistic evolution reverts to the deism of which Christians have been accused, even by Monod! Meanwhile, even deism is on shaky grounds from recent challenges that undercut the claim that there was a beginning to the universe, denoted by 't = 0'.[12] This coup for atheism is reflected with relish in Carl Sagan's caustic remark that Stephen Hawking has given us 'a universe with no edge in space, no beginning or end in time, and nothing for a Creator to do'.[13]

---

11.   Bartholomew, *God of Chance*, 34.

12.   See, for example, Robert John Russell, 'Finite Creation without a Beginning: The Spiritual and Theological Significance of Stephen Hawking's Quantum Cosmology', *The Way: Review of Contemporary Christian Spirituality* 32/4 (October 1992): 268–81.

13.   Carl Sagan, 'Introduction' to Stephen W Hawking, *A Brief History of Time: From the Big Bang to Black Holes* (New York: Bantam Books, 1988), xi. For a

2.1.2 Developed response: 'Full-strength' theistic evolution via noninter-
ventionist objective divine action (NIODA)

What is needed if theistic evolution is to flourish is an underlying
account of God's *ongoing* action within the processes of nature that
meets three stringent criteria: (1) God's acts are objective and specific;
without such action things would have turned out differently. (Claims
about divine action involve 'counterfactuals'.) (2) God's acts are hidden
to science; science sees strictly random events. This entails that divine
causality can not be reduced to secondary or natural causality, the
subject of scientific inquiry. (3) God's action is noninterventionist, and
both epistemic and ontological 'gaps' arguments are rejected.[14]

Such an account of divine action combines commitment to objective
divine action as found in conservative Christianity (but at the expense
of interventionism) and noninterventionist divine action as found in
liberal Christianity (but at the expense of its being merely our
subjective, religious interpretation of regular natural causes). It has
thus been labelled 'noninterventionist objective divine action'
('NIODA').[15] NIODA offers to deliver on the 'promissory note' of

---

response to Hawking and an extended discussion of the changing role of t = 0 in
big-bang, inflation and quantum cosmology in relation to creation *ex nihilo*, see
Robert John Russell, 'Finite Creation without a Beginning: The Doctrine of
Creation in Relation to Big Bang and Quantum Cosmologies', in Robert J
Russell, Nancey C Murphy and Chris J Isham (eds), *Quantum Cosmology and the
Laws of Nature: Scientific Perspectives on Divine Action* (Vatican City State:
Vatican Observatory Publications; Berkeley, CA: CTNS, 1993); Robert John
Russell, 'T = 0: Is It Theologically Significant?' in W Mark Richardson and
Wesley J Wildman (eds), *Religion and Science: History, Method, Dialogue* (New
York: Routledge, 1996), 201–226.

14. A noninterventionist account would depict God's regular action and God's special
     action as two modes of a single, coherent form of divine action. See Robert John
     Russell, 'Divine Action and Quantum Mechanics: A Fresh Assessment', in
     Robert John Russell and others (eds), *Quantum Mechanics: Scientific
     Perspectives on Divine Action* (Vatican City State: Vatican Observatory
     Publications; Berkeley, CA: CTNS, 2001), section 2.

15. For an overview, see Robert John Russell, 'Does "The God Who Acts" Really
     Act? New Approaches to Divine Action in Light of Science', *Theology Today*
     54/1 (April 1997): 43–65. The CTNS/VO series includes: Robert John Russell,
     Nancey C Murphy and Chris J Isham (eds), *Quantum Cosmology and the Laws of
     Nature: Scientific Perspectives on Divine Action* (Vatican City State: Vatican
     Observatory Publications; Berkeley, CA: CTNS, 1993); Robert John Russell,
     Nancey C Murphy and Arthur R Peacocke (eds), *Chaos and Complexity:*

theistic evolution and, in the process, to undercut further the atheistic attempt to co-opt evolution.[16]

Scientific Perspectives on Divine Action (Vatican City State: Vatican Observatory Publications; Berkeley, CA: CTNS, 1995); Robert John Russell, William R Stoeger, SJ, and Francisco J Ayala (eds), *Evolutionary and Molecular Biology: Scientific Perspectives on Divine Action* (Vatican City State: Vatican Observatory Publications; Berkeley, CA: CTNS, 1998); Robert John Russell and others (eds), *Neuroscience and the Person: Scientific Perspectives on Divine Action* (Vatican City State: Vatican Observatory Publications; Berkeley, CA: CTNS, 1999); Robert John Russell and others (eds), *Quantum Mechanics: Scientific Perspectives on Divine Action* (Vatican City State: Vatican Observatory Publications; Berkeley, CA: CTNS, 2001). For a brief description of these approaches, see the Introductions to Russell, Murphy and Peacocke (eds), *Chaos and Complexity*, section 3.4, and Russell and others (eds), *Quantum Mechanics*, section 2.1. Summaries can be found at www.ctns.org/books.html

16.   There are at least four options that scholars are currently exploring in relation to causality between different levels of complexity: (1) top-down causality involving God's action on the universe-as-a-whole and its effects on the macroscopic world; (2) bottom-up causality involving God's action at the quantum level and its effects on the macroscopic world; (3) causality within a single level of complexity (lateral amplification), including God's relation to chaotic processes in the macroscopic world; and (4) a process philosophy-based discussion of divine action at every level in nature. In my view, bottom-up causality, relying on quantum indeterminism, could hold for God's action throughout the entire history of the universe, including the evolution of life through genetic mutation and natural selection. Top-down causality in the form of divine action within the context of the mind/brain problem could be appropriated by God once the evolution of creatures capable of primitive sentience has occurred. Lateral amplification refers to processes in the ordinary, everyday world described by classical physics. The problem is that the very early universe was characterised entirely by quantum processes; there was no 'ordinary, everyday world' for millions of years after the Big Bang. Hence if God's action was restricted to lateral amplification processes, God could not have been actively involved in the earliest epochs of the universe. If instead God's action takes place at the quantum level, God could have been active from the beginning of the universe, and such action might have been one of the factors in making it possible for the ordinary, everyday world to arise over time from the strictly quantum world. In addition, unless chaotic processes in the ordinary world can be shown to point to ontological indeterminism, God's action in the ordinary, everyday world would have to be interventionist, which is what all of us are trying to avoid. Divine causality as viewed by process theology also applies

2.2 Challenge 2: Evolution and suffering—theism or atheism revisited
An even more compelling argument for an atheistic interpretation of
evolution than the appeal to 'blind chance' is God's apparent creation
of, complicity in or at least permission given to suffering in nature.
From Charles Darwin to Richard Dawkins, the sheer horror so frequent
in the biological world has seemed to make Christianity unintelligible
and even offensive. As Darwin wrote in a letter to Asa Gray, 'I cannot
persuade myself that a beneficent and omnipotent God would have
designedly created the Ichneumonidae with the express intention of
their feeding within the living bodies of Caterpillars.'[17] More recently,
Dawkins has pointed to the predator/prey cycle of cheetahs and
antelopes to conclude, not that God is evil but that there simply is no
God at all: 'The universe we observe has precisely the properties we
should expect if there is, at bottom, no design, no purpose, no evil and
no good, nothing but blind, pitiless indifference.'[18]

The bulk of this paper is devoted to precisely this challenge, that is,
the challenge of 'natural evil' and thus an evolutionary-based theodicy.
What I acknowledge and underscore at the outset is that NIODA
intensifies the problem of theodicy beyond what it would have been in
earlier 'statistical deistic' versions of theistic evolution. If one chooses
to move forward along the trajectory of theistic evolution by the
strategy of NIODA, there is simply no way to avoid this problem.

3. 'Theodicy lite': Natural evil is not really evil

We will first look at two important variations on the view that since
what we call natural evil is just a normal part of biological evolution,
'evolutionary theodicy' is a non-issue. I call this view 'theodicy lite'
because it represents one of three ways to undercut the paradox of
theodicy: the denial (or at least de-escalation) of the reality of evil. (The
other ways are to deny or to reinterpret God's goodness or power.)

3.1 Natural theodicy is irrelevant
The most elementary response is to view natural evil as theologically
irrelevant. Natural evil is 'just natural' and it is therefore inappropriate

---

throughout the entire history of the universe. Hopefully all forms of divine action
can be integrated into one picture.

17.   The quotation is taken from a letter written by Darwin to Asa Gray, 22 May 1860.
     References can be found in Dawkins, *River out of Eden*, 95.
18.   Dawkins, *River out of Eden*, 133.

to call it 'evil'. What we take, erroneously, to be evil is in fact *a constitutive factor of life*; it is no more in need of theological attention or explanation than other biological features that reflect the way evolution works. Pain and suffering go hand in hand with sentience, and the death of organisms and the extinction of species are built into, and necessary for, the processes by which life evolves. In his illuminating article on theodicy, Christopher Southgate calls this response 'The Problem Dismissed'.[19]

One finds this view in much of the literature on theology and science. According to Peacocke, 'evolution can operate only through the death of individuals—"new life (arises) only through the death of the old."'[20] Similarly, Denis Edwards writes that '. . . natural selection is simply the differential reproductive success that is built into nature. When a theologian, biologist, or anyone else describes natural selection as "selfish", or nature as "cruel", that is an anthropomorphic way of speaking'.[21] Of course, theologians such as Peacocke and Edwards move on to robust theodicies, but more attention is then given to suffering and God's response to it without returning to the point about the irrelevance of biological death.

3.2 Natural theodicy is marginally relevant
The previous response can be given a minimal theological gloss in two ways. Each focuses on the crucial scientific insight that natural evil is constitutive of life.

3.2.1 The first argument is that because natural evil is *constitutive of life*, it cannot be viewed as a *consequence* of an historical event, 'the Fall' from paradise. Liberal Protestant theology from Friedrich Schleiermacher onwards has taken this more or less for granted: Natural evil is not a consequence of human sin or of a prehistorical cosmic drama (the

---

19.   Christopher Southgate, 'God and Evolutionary Evil: Theodicy in the Light of Darwinism', *Zygon: Journal of Religion and Science* 37/4 (December 2002): 803–824, especially 808–9.

20.   Arthur Peacocke, *Theology for a Scientific Age: Being and Becoming—Natural, Divine and Human*, enlarged ed (Minneapolis: Augsburg Fortress, 1993), 63, 221.

21.   Edwards, *The God of Evolution*, 38.

fall of the angels), as the traditional Augustinian 'Fall' depicted it. Quoting Peacocke again,

> Biological death can no longer be regarded as in any way the *consequence* of anything human beings might have been supposed to have done in the past, for evolutionary history shows it to be the very *means* whereby they appear and so, for the theist, are created by God.[22]

3.2.2 The second argument is that even God had 'no choice' but to opt for Darwinian evolution if God was to create life by acting immanently through the processes of nature rather than by intervening in them. This means that adaptation by natural selection is unavoidable and that the resulting 'natural evil' is an unavoidable consequence of God's action in creating life, which even God could not eliminate. The 'no choice' argument aims at lessening the intensity of natural theodicy by letting God 'off the hook'—slightly. In an interesting move, Michael Ruse offers the 'no choice' argument in defence of Christianity against one of its most vocal critics, Richard Dawkins, by citing Dawkins's own reference to it: 'Dawkins . . . argues strenuously that selection and only selection can do the job. No one—and presumably this includes God—could have got adaptive complexity without going the route of natural selection.'[23]

3.3 Critique and implications of 'theodicy lite'
Contrary to *3.1*, I do not think that the constitutive nature of natural evil implies that natural evil is theologically irrelevant. The NT narratives of the ministry of Jesus combine both physical healing and the raising of the dead with the forgiveness of sins.[24] They thus link the realm of natural evil (disease and death) with the realm of moral

---

22.   Peacocke, *Theology for a Scientific Age*, 222.
23.   Michael Ruse, *Can a Darwinian Be a Christian? The Relationship between Science and Religion* (Cambridge: Cambridge University Press, 2001), 136. Here Ruse cites Richard Dawkins, 'Universal Darwinism', in DS Bendall (ed), *Molecules to Men* (Cambridge: Cambridge University Press, 1983), 403–425. Ruse gives a thoughtful and promising account of what he believes is really at stake in the Christianity/ evolution controversy.
24.   Ron Cole-Turner makes a similar point in *The New Genesis: Theology and the Genetic Revolution* (Louisville: Westminster John Knox Press, 1993).

evil (sin), and the salvation offered by the ministry and resurrection of Jesus applies to both realms, although the latter only emerges with humanity. It would thus be impossible to affirm the theological significance of moral evil while dismissing the theological significance of natural evil. Thus, while rejecting the biblical framework in which natural evil is the result of moral evil (ie the Fall), we must not reject the theological question raised by natural evil, both in the context of humanity and now in the context of all living creatures. The way forward, then, will take us along a more complex path than the dismissal of the relevance of natural evil *per se*.

In response to *3.2.1*, I would suggest two points. First, I agree that natural evil is not the consequence of the 'Fall', but this in itself is of tremendous theological significance because it sharply distinguishes liberal versus conservative interpretations of and responses to sin and evil. Second, the rejection of the Fall does not imply that traditional theologies which accept it have nothing to offer towards constructing an evolutionary natural theodicy, as we shall see when we turn to the Augustinian theodicy. Nor does it imply that modern theology prior to Darwin, in which the Fall is rejected, has nothing to offer, as we shall see in turning to Schleiermacher.

In response to *3.2.2*, I would point out that the 'no choice' argument is based on a crucial assumption usually overlooked in these discussions—the assumption that the laws of physics underlying cosmology, astrophysics, geology, chemistry, molecular and evolutionary biology, etc, are a 'given'. Admittedly, were God to create life by natural processes *and* if laws of physics governing these processes are taken for granted, then God may have had 'no choice' other than neo-Darwinian evolution. This approach to theodicy 'eases the burden' of accounting for God's action in evolution, as Ruse points out. But if we push it one step further, we see that this argument does not really help with theodicy because the question of whether God had a 'choice' returns at a more fundamental level in what I call *cosmic theodicy*. Since God created our universe *ex nihilo*, including the laws of physics and constants of nature, why did God choose to create *this* universe with *these* laws and constants, knowing they would then make neo-Darwinian evolution unavoidable and with it the sweep of natural evil? Thus the Ruse/Dawkins argument does not rescue God from blame, but places blame at a more foundational level, leading to the Leibnizian challenge: Is this the best of all possible *universes* that God could have created with the intention of the evolution of life, or could there be another kind of universe in which life evolved without natural evil? In the end, we must accept an 'agnostic cosmic theodicy', in which the problem of evil simply cannot be answered, or we must continue to press for a more adequate response to the problem of theodicy that evolution and NIODA together raise. In sum, 'Theodicy lite' is ultimately fruitless and we must turn to more complex responses to natural evil.

4. Robust theodicies: Traditional forms

I propose that any robust theodicy must meet at least three criteria: first, it must ward off Manichean tendencies to 'blame God' for creating natural evil or to view nature as unambiguously evil; second, it must ward off Pelagian tendencies to undercut the universality of moral evil; and third, it must take fully on board Darwinian evolution, and in particular the constitutive character of natural evil to life.

Christian theology includes a variety of theodicies that meet these criteria. For the purposes of this paper, I will employ John Hick's analysis of this variety as falling within two broad types—the Augustinian and Irenaean. The task will be to reformulate these theodicies so that they meet all three criteria and then to deploy them to the task of evolutionary natural theodicy.

4.1 Augustinian theodicy: The free-will defence

Historical Christianity provided a framework that met the first two criteria via the Augustinian theodicy, drawn in large measure from NT, especially Pauline, texts and the dominant context of neoplatonism. Augustine's theodicy had a profound influence upon Aquinas, Calvin and Luther, as well as such contemporary theologians as Barth and Rahner.

According to Augustine,[25] both moral and natural evil are ultimately the result of free rational beings who sin; they wilfully turn from God as the highest good toward a lesser good. Augustine avoided Manicheism by affirming the goodness of all that God creates. Sin began with the premundane, cosmic fall of angels and continued with Adam and Eve who, though created 'very good' by God, did of

25.   See, for example, St Augustine, *Confessions*, trans. Henry Chadwick (Oxford: Oxford University Press, 1991), and *The City of God*, trans. Henry Bettenson (London: Penguin Books, 1984).

their own free will choose creaturely goods over God. The resulting corruption or bondage of the will is transmitted sexually from generation to generation to all humanity from the common human origin in Adam and Eve. On the one hand, then, human beings still have the power of free will and are thus responsible for, and deserve punishment for, their actions by God. On the other hand, although in Eden it had been possible not to sin (*posse non peccare*), in human history free will is corrupt and without God's predestination of grace it is not possible not to sin (*non posse non peccare*). Augustine embedded his 'free-will defence' in a neoplatonic understanding of the plenitude of creation, in which evil is a privation of being, and in an overarching aesthetic, in which God sees all things ultimately as 'very good', including sin and its punishment.

4.2 Schleiermacher's theodicy: The moral growth argument

Liberal Protestant theology in the nineteenth century and much of Catholic and Protestant theology in the twentieth century has worked within an alternative framework provided by Friedrich Schleiermacher. The roots of Schleiermacher's theology lie in the eighteenth-century Enlightenment's rejection of biblical history and traditional theology as mythological. In the early nineteenth century, Schleiermacher's *Speeches* and *The Christian Faith* provided a massive reformulation of original perfection and original sin in a developmental or proto-evolutionary framework.[26] Briefly, the *original perfection of the world*, according to Schleiermacher, consists in the world being such that God's purposes can be achieved in and through natural processes. In particular, the world is such that our experience of our relative dependence on the world leads to our experience of our absolute dependence on God as the source of all that is. The *original righteousness of humankind* consists in our capacity for religious experience, both as the personal experience of individuals and as

---

26.   Friedrich Schleiermacher, *On Religion: Speeches to Its Cultured Despisers*, trans. John Oman (New York: Harper & Row [Harper Torchbooks], 1958), and *The Christian Faith*, edited by HR Mackintosh and JS Stewart (Edinburgh: T&T Clark, 1968). Most references in what follows can be found in Schleiermacher, *The Christian Faith*, sections 58–89.

communicated through culture.[27] *Sin* consists in the obstruction of our awareness of God due to our dependence on the world. It is virtually inevitable because we are 'sentient animals' embedded in the world as physical and biological creatures, and because in our individual lives our physical character precedes the development of our individual cognitive and spiritual capacities. Yet sin is not necessary, since in Jesus the development of his consciousness of God was unobstructed; he was 'sinless'. Thus, we are still personally responsible for our sins. *Original sin* is both individual and societal in character,[28] leading to Schleiermacher's distinctive aphorism, 'sin is in each the work of all, and in all the work of each'. Finally, *natural evil* does not arise from sin. Nevertheless, because of our sinfulness we experience natural evils as genuine evil, and thus natural evil can be considered a penalty of sin. Clearly, Schleiermacher's pivotal reformulation of original perfection and original sin in a time-independent, developmental/proto-evolutionary framework meets our three criteria for an evolutionary natural theodicy.

5. Retrieving and extending the Augustinian theodicy to physics and cosmology: Insights and failures

At first glance, it might seem that Schleiermacher's theodicy would be more compatible with our project of an evolutionary natural theodicy than Augustine's. The latter is grounded in the framework of the Fall, which in many ways Schleiermacher overcame, and Schleiermacher's approach, particularly through the lens of John Hick's revisions, has been influential in the 'theology and science' community. However, there are resources in Augustine's theodicy that should not be overlooked.

---

27. The term 'original' designates a timeless character of the world and of humankind, not a state in the past (Eden) from which we have 'fallen'. Schleiermacher rejected the Fall unequivocally.

28. The original sinfulness of the individual ('congenital sin') is grounded in our developmental phenomenology prior to any specific action or 'acts of sin'; we are born this way, and yet we are personally responsible for our specific acts of sin. The original sinfulness of society ('conditioning sin') is the distorted character of society into which each individual is born, which influences each individual's life and to which each individual contributes by his or her own acts of sin.

5.1 Retrieval: Reinhold Niebuhr

The first task is to divest the Augustinian theodicy of its 'creation/fall' framework by uncovering its underlying philosophical argument, and then reinterpret this argument in an evolutionary perspective. To do so I have turned, in previous writings, to Reinhold Niebuhr's immensely influential Gifford lectures.[29] Here Niebuhr presented the underlying argument of the Augustinian theodicy stripped of its mythological language. Niebuhr showed that Augustine rejected the Manichean view, which ontologises evil; instead he argued that 'all that is is good'. Thus sin has no ontological status, and humans are not sinful because of their created nature. Augustine also argued against the Pelagian view that sin could be overcome by human will alone. Instead, redemption is due to God's grace, and this applies to all of humanity through Augustine's theory of the biological inheritance of sin and of the participation of all people in Adam. Finally, against neoplatonism, Augustine located sin within the human will as corrupted by original sin.

Niebuhr then rendered the underlying logic of the Augustinian theodicy as asserting that sin is *unnecessary but inevitable*.[30] This phrase captures Augustine's argument without tying it to the Fall. It expresses in stark terms what Niebuhr called the 'absurd paradox' of the Christian free-will defence. Augustinian theodicy rephrased through Niebuhr's formulation now meets our three criteria for an evolutionary natural theodicy.

5.2 Preconditions in physics that underlie the free-will defence

We are now in a position to extend the free-will defence to evolution and, in what I believe is more useful here, to the underlying laws of physics that shape the character of neo-Darwinism, as I pointed out previously in reference to Ruse and Dawkins. What, in particular, must physics be like for the reformulated Augustinian/Niebuhrian free-will

---

29. Reinhold Niebuhr, *The Nature and Destiny of Man, volume I. Human Nature* (New York: Charles Scribner's Sons, 1941 [1964]).
30. Niebuhr, *The Nature and Destiny of Man, volume I. Human Nature*, 242: 'Original sin, which is by definition an inherited corruption, or at least an inevitable one, is nevertheless not to be regarded as belonging to his essential nature and therefore is not outside the realm of his responsibility. Sin is natural for man in the sense that it is universal but not in the sense that it is necessary.'

defence to hold? Here we will explore two responses. The first is the
diachronic method, which entails the search for those areas of physics
and cosmology that underlie and make possible biological evolution.
What, if anything, reflects the Niebuhrian logic of 'unnecessary but
inevitable' at the level of physics? The second is the *synchronic method*,
that is, the search for the conditions in physics such that free will can
be enacted physically.

5.2.1 Diachronic method involving thermodynamics

We must first reformulate Niebuhr's claim that 'sin is unnecessary but
inevitable' such that it can be more readily discussed at the level of
physics. In previous publications, I have suggested that the underlying
logical structure of Niebuhr's claim can be described by the term
'universal contingent': that which is ontologically contingent but which
holds in all cases.[31] The task, then, is to search for examples of a
'universal contingent' in physics.

A prime example is found in non-linear, non-equilibrium thermodynamics, with its concepts of 'entropy' and 'order out of chaos'. In
brief, the entropy of all 'closed' systems increases inevitably to a
maximum according to the second law. But as Ilya Prigogine and
many others have shown, when a closed system contains 'open'
subsystems, they can spontaneously move to greater degrees of order
by exhausting entropy to their environment, the closed system which
contains them. In the process, the total entropy of the closed system
increases, obeying the second law, even though its open subsystems
may decrease in entropy and increase. This simple fact underlies the
homeostasis of life on earth through a thermodynamic 'heat exchange'
between the sun and the earth. It also underlies the processes of
biological evolution in which vast increases in complexity over time
are driven by the thermodynamics of the sun/earth system. Without
thermodynamics, which applies *universally* to all physical and thus all
biological systems, the evolution of life on earth would have been
impossible.

Yet although thermodynamics applies to all physical systems, we
cannot predict whether a given system will spontaneously fluctuate
towards more complexity or dissipate and decay; both paths are
possible by the laws of non-linear, non-equilibrium thermodynamics,

---

31. Robert John Russell, 'The Thermodynamics of "Natural Evil"', *CTNS Bulletin*
    10/2 (Spring 1990): 20–5.

but the details depend on other areas of physics such as kinetic theory. Thus the advancement to increased complexity in such systems, including biological ones, is entirely *contingent* on factors and processes beyond the limitations of these systems. Non-linear, non-equilibrium thermodynamics thus carries both of the characteristics underlying Augustine's argument about the nature of sin: universality and contingency.

5.2.2 Synchronic method involving thermodynamics

A central theme of the NIODA project is that the enactment of (voluntarist/incompatibilist) free will requires ontological indeterminism at some level in physics. I believe a similar argument can be made that the enactment of human freedom and moral evil require something like thermodynamics in physics.

In a previous article I explored a metaphorical relation between entropy and evil that stressed both similarities and dissimilarities.[32] Here I followed Paul Ricoeur's understanding of metaphor as including a negative as well as a positive analogy, both an 'is' and an 'is not', Ian Barbour's insight that metaphors are extendable to new contexts and Sallie McFague's development of these resources into what she termed 'metaphorical theology'.[33] To summarise the idea briefly, we typically find beauty and goodness in the patterns of emergent complexity and creative novelty characteristic of life, while tragedy and sorrow play themselves out in terms of the dissipation and destruction associated with decay, disease and death. Curiously, thermodynamics underlies and is entailed by all of these phenomena. The second law thus plays a *dual* role; it makes possible the physical and biological consequences of our moral action both for good and for ill. This metaphorical argument then led to a more pointed claim that thermodynamics is needed if moral evil is to be actualised in the

---

32.   Robert John Russell, 'Entropy and Evil', *Zygon: Journal of Religion and Science* 19/4 (December 1984): 449–68. I am grateful for the appreciative inclusion of these insights by Mark W Worthing in his *God, Creation, and Contemporary Physics*, Theology and the Sciences Series (Minneapolis: Augsburg Fortress, 1996), chap 4, 'The Problem of Evil' and 'Summary'.

33.   Ian G Barbour, *Myths, Models and Paradigms: A Comparative Study in Science and Religion* (New York: Harper & Row, 1974); Sallie McFague, *Metaphorical Theology: Models of God in Religious Language* (Philadelphia: Fortress Press, 1982).

world. As I wrote almost two decades ago, 'if evil is real in nature, entropy is what one would expect to find at the level of physical processes'.[34] So thermodynamics provides an example at the level of physics of what is needed if the consequences of sinful acts are to be expressed physically, including dissipation and disruption, as well as the consequences of virtuous acts, including acts of beauty and goodness.

5.3 Extending the Augustinian/Niebuhrian free-will theodicy to cosmology
There are several ways to extend the Augustinian/Niebuhrian free-will theodicy to cosmology. Here I will touch on one of them by returning briefly to the Ruse/Dawkins 'lite theodicy'. According to their argument, even God had 'no choice' but to opt for Darwinian evolution if God was to create life by acting immanently through the processes of nature rather than by intervening in them. But in responding above, I pointed out that the question of whether God had a 'choice' returns at a more fundamental level in what I called *cosmic theodicy*.

Now, in light of what has just been said about the logic of 'universal contingent' and the complex relation between 'entropy and evil' in thermodynamics, the problem of 'cosmic theodicy' appears to be far more serious than it may have sounded initially. It now becomes: Why did God choose to create *this* universe with *these* laws of physics, knowing that they would not only make neo-Darwinian evolution unavoidable, and with it the sweep of natural evil in the biological realm, but also that they would contribute to *natural evil at the level of physics*—and thus to natural evil *throughout the universe* and not just within biological phenomena? Alternatively, if God intended

---

34. Russell, 'Entropy and Evil', 465. I compared Augustine's understanding of evil as privation of being with entropy in physics: Entropy does not refer to something physical (eg matter) or even a property of something physical (like mass, which is a property of matter). Instead, it is a measure of the loss of available energy or the increase in disorder. Hence neither evil nor entropy are 'ontological'; both are dependent on being, lacking independent existence. In that paper (see pp 457–9), I compared entropy in physics to evil in Paul Tillich's theology. For Tillich, evil has 'no independent standing in the whole of reality, but . . . is dependent on the structure of that in and upon which it acts destructively'. Note, too, his memorable phrase that the form of evil is the 'structure of destruction'. Thus evil '"aims" at chaos', and when chaos is attained 'both structure and destruction have vanished'.

to create life through the processes of neo-Darwinian evolution, then not only is biological natural evil an unavoidable consequence, as Ruse/Dawkins argue, but *so is physical natural evil*—and *it occurs throughout the universe even where there is no possibility of life.*

With this in mind, I have suggested renaming the 'anthropic principle' the 'thermodynamic anthropic principle' to underscore the irreducible but often overlooked role of thermodynamics in arguments about the anthropic principle in relation to the evolution of moral agents (eg, the Murphy/Ellis thesis)[35] and to stress its implications for cosmic theodicy.

5.4 Implications for eschatology and for contemporary physics

The Augustinian/Niebuhrian theodicy ultimately fails, not because it is tied to a mythical 'fall', which it clearly is not, nor because it views death as a consequence of sin instead of as constitutive of life, which it clearly does not, but because, like 'Theodicy Lite', it leads to the recognition that underlying moral evil is natural evil that, in an implicitly Manichean way, characterises the universe as a whole. I believe this fundamental problem points at last to the impossibility of articulating an adequate response to theodicy in terms of the universe as it presently exists and thus in the theological context of the doctrine of creation. Instead, it forces us to relocate the response to the context of eschatology and its portrayal of the 'new creation'.

But this failure brings with it an exceptional gift: It gives us a crucial insight into what eschatology must include if it is to address the failure of theodicy to account for natural evil. The insight is that if in the new creation it will be impossible to commit moral evil because we will be liberated from the bondage of the will into true freedom (Augustine: *non posse peccare*), then the new creation will not include natural evil either. This claim could be taken in two ways. First, in its simplest form it might mean that the new creation will not include thermodynamics because it contributes to natural evil. Second, in a

---

35.   Nancey Murphy and George FR Ellis, *On the Moral Nature of the Universe: Theology, Cosmology, and Ethics*, Theology and the Sciences Series (Minneapolis: Augsburg Fortress, 1996). For my response, see Robert John Russell, 'The Theological Consequences of the Thermodynamics of a Moral Universe: An Appreciative Critique and Extension of the Murphy/Ellis Project', *CTNS Bulletin* 19/4 (Fall 1998): 19–24.

slightly more complex form it might mean that the new creation will
not include thermodynamics to the extent that it produces natural
evils, though it might include it to the extent that it produces natural
goods. I am reminded by the apostle Paul that '. . . the whole creation
has been groaning in travail until now. . . [T]he creation itself will be
set free from its bondage to decay and obtain the glorious liberty of the
children of God' (Rom 8:22, 21). As I asked in an earlier paper, 'Are we
somehow to be freed from the tyranny of entropy, and is the universe
to shine forever as the respondent creation of God—a *new* heaven and
earth?' As a Christian I answer, 'Yes!'

What is even more interesting is the way this insight works
'backwards' from eschatology to the universe as we now know it via
the doctrine of creation. It implies that thermodynamics, as a 'universal
contingent' characterising this universe, is itself 'contingent' since it
will not characterise the new creation. This in turn carries *implications
for current physics*. One question that has been discussed extensively is
whether thermodynamics is a 'fundamental' theory comparable to
dynamics (quantum mechanics, quantum field theory, etc). The
implication here is that it is not a fundamental theory because it will
not be part of the eschatological destiny of the universe, at least not in
the way in which it contributes to natural evil. If that is so, it could
suggest interesting questions for future research in the foundations of
physics regarding the relation of thermodynamics to fundamental
physical theories.

6. Retrieving and extending Schleiermacher's theodicy to evolution and cosmology

6.1 Retrieval: John Hick
The legacy of Schleiermacher's theodicy can be found in John Hick's
profound treatment.[36] In turn, Hick's theodicy has been widely
influential among scholars in theology and science. His development
of Schleiermacher's theodicy is 'regarded generally as the first clearly
defined alternative to the Augustinian-Thomistic perspective'.[37] Hick
names this type of theodicy after Irenaeus (*c* 130–202 CE), who first
brought together themes found in the subapostolic Eastern church,
such as the distinction between the image and likeness of God in

---

36. John Hick, *Evil and the God of Love*, rev ed (New York: Harper & Row, 1978).
37. Barry L Whitney, *What Are They Saying about God and Evil?* (New York: Paulist Press, 1989), 38.

humanity, the understanding of our earthly life as one of gradual
spiritual growth from image to likeness, sin as due to weakness and
immaturity, and the world as a mingling of good and evil appointed
by God for our growth towards perfection.[38] In the nineteenth
century, Schleiermacher developed and systematised themes such as
these into the rich framework we have touched upon.[39]

Hick provides a helpful comparison of the theodicies of Augustine
and Schleiermacher.[40] Whereas the Augustinian theodicy looks to a
created paradise in the past, focuses crucial importance on the fall of
angels and humankind, and looks to a future last judgment that
includes eternal punishment for the damned, the Irenaean theodicy
accepts evil as an inevitable factor in a world suited for moral
development. It does not deny the fall, but it rejects the ideas of lost
righteousness and inherited sinfulness. It also views an eternal hell as
'rendering a Christian theodicy impossible'. The key difference, as I
read Hick, is that the Augustinian theodicy seeks to protect God from
responsibility for the existence of evil by stressing the fall, while the
Irenaean theodicy accepts God's ultimate responsibility for evil by
showing how a world that includes evil is justifiable and inevitable.

Despite these contrasts, there are areas of agreement that reflect
'certain basic necessities of Christian thought concerning the problem
of evil'. Both affirm the aesthetic conception of the perfection of
creation. For the Augustinian theodicy, the world is 'very good' as it is
now, even including sin and evil. For the Irenaean theodicy, the
perfection of the world lies in an eschatological future in which the
end, the kingdom of God, will justify the means of its achievement, the
ambiguous historical process. Both theodicies attribute ultimate
responsibility for the existence of evil to God, although the
Augustinian theodicy does so only implicitly through the doctrine of
predestination. Both affirm that the world is valuable to God
independent of its fitness for humankind and that God may be at work
elsewhere in the world to achieve divine purposes. Both affirm the *O
felix culpa* theme: The Augustinian theodicy admits that bringing good

38.   Hick, *Evil and the God of Love*, 211–18.
39.   Hick notes that there is no evidence that Schleiermacher was directly influenced
      by Irenaeus or the early church, leading Hick to refer to this form of theodicy as a
      'type', not a 'tradition'. See Hick, *Evil and the God of Love*, 219.
40.   Hick, *Evil and the God of Love*, 236–40.

out of evil is better than not permitting evil to exist, but such 'greater good' or 'means-end' arguments play a minor role in its overall structure, while the Irenaean theodicy treats it as central and stresses the eschatological context of the 'greater good'.

6.2 Hick's contribution: The crucial role of eschatology

Hick develops his own Irenaean theodicy through an extraordinarily careful, detailed and judicious exploration of multiple problems involving moral and natural evil. In the second edition of his *Evil and the God of Love*, he engages with a variety of issues and objections raised by his most severe critics and offers relatively persuasive logical responses to the question of why God does not act to remove or diminish suffering in nature. These include the impossibility of our doing the necessary 'means/end calculation', limitations on the perspective needed for a 'greatest good' argument and the relativity of the 'worst evil', which Tom Tracy has explored in detail.[41] The arguments 'do not seek to demonstrate that Christianity is true, but that the fact of evil does not show it to be false. . .'[42] They do not constitute a theodicy as much as clear the way for one to receive a fair hearing.

Central to Hick's robust theodicy is the argument that 'pain and suffering are a necessary feature of a world that is to be the scene of a process of soul-making'. Even their 'haphazard and unjust distribution' and excess are ultimately beneficial, since 'the right must be done for its own sake rather than a reward'. Closely related is Hick's claim that 'epistemic distance' is required if humans are to be capable of moral growth. 'God must be a hidden deity, veiled by His [*sic*] creation' so that, unlike our physical surroundings, God's presence is not coercively imposed on us. The world must be *etsi deus non daretur* ('as if there were no God') because in such a world we have the necessary 'cognitive freedom' by which faith and moral growth are possible. A great virtue of this claim is that it goes a long way to accounting for moral evil, since the hiddenness of God makes evil a 'virtually inevitable result' of the actions of a free agent.[43]

---

41. See Thomas F Tracy, 'Evolution, Divine Action, and the Problem of Evil', in Russell, Stoeger and Ayala (eds), *Evolutionary and Molecular Biology*, 511–30.

42. Hick, *Evil and the God of Love*, viii.

43. Hick, *Evil and the God of Love*, 281–82, 353.

The gravest challenge, according to Hick, is excessive suffering and the attempt to justify it by a 'means-end' argument. Can Christian theodicy respond to a world of 'extreme and crushing evils . . . so severe as to be self-defeating when considered as soul-making influences . . . [a world] which seems at best to be utterly indifferent and at worst implacably malevolent. . .'?[44] To underscore this challenge, Hick concludes the second edition of his *Evil and the God of Love* with the agonising quotation from Dostoievski's *The Brothers Karamazov*.[45] His response is that eschatology provides the only context for addressing these challenges: '[W]e cannot hope to state a Christian theodicy without taking seriously the doctrine of a life beyond the grave.'[46] Such hope is for a 'future of infinite goodness'. He connects this view of eschatology to a rejection of hell, an affirmation of universal salvation and an understanding of heaven as an endless opportunity for continued spiritual growth. Hick ends with the *O felix culpa*: it lies 'at the heart of Christian theodicy' and expresses the central paradox that while present-day evil is really evil, it will eschatologically 'be defeated and made to serve God's good purposes'.[47]

7. Expanding the Schleiermacher/Hick theodicy in a wider theological context: *Kenosis and* eschatology

My goal will now be to appropriate the Schleiermachian theodicy through its reformulation by Hick, to expand and strengthen it theologically and then to apply it to our evolutionary problematic. By adding the concept of *kenosis*—the self-emptying of Christ in taking on human life and, in turn, the suffering of God with humanity—to Hick's theodicy, many scholars in theology and science have strengthened the connection between the suffering of creatures and God's suffering with creatures. Now, by grounding Hick's theodicy in combination with *kenosis* in an eschatology explicitly in the Easter event, the bodily resurrection of Jesus, I believe we can offer an eschatology appropriate to Hick's 'means/end' argument. To start the process here, I will suggest criteria that such an eschatological theodicy must meet. It

---

44.   Hick, *Evil and the God of Love*, 327–31.

45.   Hick, *Evil and the God of Love*, 385.

46.   Hick, *Evil and the God of Love*, 339–40.

47.   Hick, *Evil and the God of Love*, 364.

could later be extended to the question of life in the universe ('ET') and a 'cosmic Christ'. The challenge from the far future of the universe, however, is much more severe than the challenge of evolution. I will touch on it in setting out these criteria, but I will leave the details to future work (and to initial probing in previous writings).

7.1 Background: Kenosis and the suffering of God

> If you can accept the Christianity, then you can certainly accept the Darwinism. Conversely, if you are a Darwinian looking for religious meaning, then Christianity is a religion which speaks to you. Right at its center there is a suffering god, Jesus on the Cross.[48]

> The way of nature is the way of the cross; *via naturae est via crucis*.[49]

Overviews of *kenosis* are readily available.[50] In a study focused on *kenosis* in 'theology and science', Sarah Coakley notes that exegetical, christological and trinitarian reflections on *kenosis* are often left out. She implies, however, that these should be 'in some sense normatively binding',[51] a view I share. Here I will highlight portions of Coakley's overview.

7.1.1 Exegetical issues
In Paul's letter to the Philippians, the Greek verb ωππωω occurs in the phrase, 'he emptied himself' (Phil 2:7). The full text of Philippians 2:5–8 reads:

---

48.   Ruse, *Can a Darwinian Be a Christian?* 134.

49.   Holmes Rolston, III, *Science and Religion: A Critical Survey* (New York: Random House, 1987), 146.

50.   See the following three studies in John Polkinghorne (ed), *The Work of Love: Creation as Kenosis* (Grand Rapids, MI: Eerdmans, 2001): Sarah Coakley, 'Kenosis: Theological Meanings and Gender Connotations', 192–210; Jürgen Moltmann, 'God's Kenosis in the Creation and Consummation of the World', 137–51; and Keith Ward, 'Cosmos and Kenosis', 152–66.

51.   Coakley, 'Kenosis: Theological Meanings and Gender Connotations', 203.

> Have this mind among yourselves, which is yours in Christ Jesus, who, though he was in the form of God, did not count equality with God a thing to be grasped, but *emptied himself*, taking the form of a servant, being born in the likeness of [people]. And being found in human form he humbled himself and became obedient unto death, even death on a cross (RSV).

But what does 'emptied' refer to? According to Coakley,[52] there are two distinct interpretations. The first is incarnation. Philippians 2:6 provides the hermeneutical key to 2:7; 'in the form of God' refers to Christ's divine pre-existence, and 'emptying' refers to the humility of Christ in becoming human. The second interpretation is the cross. Phil 2:8 offers the meaning of 2:7; 'emptying' means 'he humbled himself' through death on the cross. Here the phrase, 'in the form of God', refers to the humanity of Jesus, which bears the *imago dei*. In short, the first, incarnational, reading leads to metaphysical issues in christology, while the second reading stresses the moral significance of self-sacrifice.

7.1.2 Kenosis *as a christological issue*

The first reading became the dominant view of the patristics, who presupposed the immutability of God and understood the incarnation to mean that Christ 'became flesh' without a loss of his divine nature. The Chalcedonian formula, 'one person in two natures' (451 CE), was used to affirm that Jesus suffered in his human nature while his divine nature remained impassible. Debates concerning the relations between his two natures, in particular, the 'communication of idioms' (*communicatio idiomatum*), continued through the Protestant reformation and into the modern period. Ted Peters argues that Luther understood *kenosis* as referring to '[Jesus'] willingness to allow the pangs and pains of human despair to have an impact on his divine nature'.[53] The resulting view was *theopassianism*: God suffers in and

---

52. Coakley, 'Kenosis: Theological Meanings and Gender Connotations', 193–4.

53. Ted Peters, *God—The World's Future: Systematic Theology for a New Era*, 2nd ed (Minneapolis: Augsburg Fortress, 2000), 206–7.

through the life of Jesus, but this did not entail that God as Father suffers (*patripassianism*).

7.1.3 Kenosis *as a trinitarian issue*

With divine passibility a broadly accepted concept in the twentieth century, contemporary trinitarian theologians such as Jürgen Moltmann, Paul Fiddes, Hans Urs von Balthasar and Denis Edwards have extended the idea of kenosis beyond christology to all three persons of the Trinity. Moltmann describes his own work as transforming the metaphysical attribute of divine impassibility into the biblical conception of the faithfulness of God such that we can now affirm that God not only loves but also suffers with the world.[54] Finally, with *kenosis* now situated in a trinitarian context, kenotic self-surrender is seen to affect all of God's acts *ad extra*, including the trinitarian creation of the world.

7.2 *Sketching an eschatology which, when combined with* kenosis, *will lead to a robust evolutionary natural theodicy*

Many scholars in theology and science have appropriated a *kenosis*-based theodicy influenced by Hick's contributions and have extended it to evolution in response to natural evil; just as God suffers with the experiences of people, God embraces the history of life on earth and suffers with it. If God enters into the physical and biological processes of the world through the incarnation, it is through the crucifixion of Jesus that God experiences the suffering of all life and offers it the possibility of redemption. Some, in turn, combine a kenotic theodicy with a minimalist or ambiguous eschatology. Few have begun to develop it with attention to the challenge, not only of evolution but also of the far future of the universe ('freeze or fry').

The task, then, is to construct an eschatology that meets both of these challenges and to connect it with *kenosis*. This task lies beyond the scope of this paper, but I will list some key criteria by which we can assess any proffered eschatology in light of what has already been said about natural evil. Then I will briefly assess how some of the existing proposals address (or fail to address) these criteria.

---

54. Moltmann, 'God's Kenosis in the Creation and Consummation of the World', 142, especially n5.

7.3 Criteria for assessing eschatology in light of evolutionary natural evil and cosmology

7.3.1 It must be modelled on the *bodily* resurrection of Jesus at Easter as a new act of God and as a proleptic instantiation of the *new creation* of God through a transformation of the present creation (universe).[55]

7.3.2 It must include a transformation of the human person as a whole, including those aspects that are bodily (material, physical) as well as those that are mental and spiritual.

7.3.3 It must include not only humanity but also all the species and individual creatures in the history of life on earth.

7.3.4 It must include them in terms of the concrete details of their own lives and in light of their own capacities and characteristics, not somehow included through the human experience of redemption. In particular, every moment of the time of evolution, not just the 'end' of historical time, must be taken up and transformed eschatologically by God into eternal life. Thus the 'means/end' form of this theodicy must be such that *every means is also an end in itself.* I call this a 'nested means/end argument' (an 'every sparrow that falls' theodicy).

7.3.5 It must address the problem of continuity of identity between death and the *parousia.* Thus, even if a concept of immortality is used to address the problem of continuity between death and the general resurrection (eg immortal soul, memory of God), it must be connected with such a general resurrection at the eschatological transformation of the universe and thus reintegrate all aspects of the human person (and, in turn, of all creatures).

7.3.6 Perspectives on the new creation should be shaped by all of the fundamental resources in the Christian tradition: the new Jerusalem descending, nature redeemed as symbolised by a return to the garden

---

55.   For discussions of the 'bodily' resurrection and its eschatological implications, see Robert John Russell, 'Eschatology and Physical Cosmology: A Preliminary Reflection', in George FR Ellis (ed), *The Far Future: Eschatology from a Cosmic Perspective* (Philadelphia: Templeton Foundation Press, 2002); Robert John Russell, 'Bodily Resurrection, Eschatology and Scientific Cosmology: The Mutual Interaction of Christian Theology and Science', in Ted Peters, Robert John Russell and Michael Welker (eds), *Resurrection: Theological and Scientific Assessments* (Grand Rapids, MI: Eerdmans, 2002); and Russell, 'Sin, Salvation, and Scientific Cosmology: Is Christian Eschatology Credible Today?'

of Eden, the worship of God in community and the inner, personal vision of God (the *viseo dei*).[56]

7.3.7 In sum, a 'greater-good' argument must place this 'good' within an eschatological context because only such a context can offer a goodness sufficient to address the extent of evil in the history of the universe (*The Brothers Karamazov* problem).

7.3.8 Both kenotic theodicy and eschatology must be structured in accordance with a trinitarian doctrine of God because it is the trinitarian God who will act to bring this about, as we know based on the revelation of the cross and resurrection of Jesus. A kenotic theodicy (that God suffers voluntarily with the world) in and of itself is not redemptive. What is also required is an eschatology in which the Father who suffers the death of the Son acts anew at Easter to raise Jesus from the dead. In turn, the involuntary suffering of all of nature—each species and each individual creature—must be taken up into the voluntary suffering of Christ on the cross (*theopassionism*) and through it the voluntary suffering of the Father (*patripassionism*).

7.4 Brief assessment of existing proposals against these criteria (6.3)

Most natural theodicies have in common a 'greater-good' argument frequently drawn from Hick and coupled with the kenotic suffering of God with the whole of creation and some reference to eschatology. Each should be assessed in detail against the preceding criteria, but here I can only do so briefly.

7.4.1 Holmes Rolston provides a moving kenotic account of nature as 'cruciform', the 'passion play of God'. However, he does not connect this with a developed eschatology, nor does he clarify whether his view of redemption includes all creatures or just some individuals or species.[57]

7.4.2 Arthur Peacocke's eschatology is based on an understanding of the resurrection of Jesus that does not necessarily include materiality or physicality. This leads to a highly anthropocentric and 'disembodied' eschatology; the *viseo dei* may await individual believers, but

---

56. See, for example, Peters, *God—The World's Future*, 2nd edition, 330–5.
57. Rolston, *Science and Religion*, 144–6, 289–92. See also Holmes Rolston III, 'Does Nature Need to Be Redeemed?', *Zygon: Journal of Religion and Science* 29/2 (June 1994): 227, and 'Kenosis and Nature', in Polkinghorne (ed), *The Work of Love*, 58–65.

resurrection in the 'bodily' sense and, in turn, the redemption of nature and its transformation into the new creation are set aside.[58]

7.4.3 Process theology offers a striking way to affirm the redemption of every creature in the history of evolution; it builds into its metaphysics the crucial feature that God prehends every actual occasion during its concrescence so that every actual occasion is remembered forever in God's consequent nature. Moreover, some process theologians such as Ian Barbour and Marjorie Suchocki include the continuance of our subjectivity in God's memory. However, although Suchocki argues that process theology does include bodily resurrection—and, in a creative argument, even justice and redress of evil—I am persuaded that process theology does not offer a concept for the resurrection of the body (*pace* Suchocki) that leads to a transformation of the universe into a new creation.

7.4.4 John Haught draws on both Roman Catholic and process theology to insist that redemption should include all of life and not just humanity. Unfortunately, he offers three contrasting views of redemption: the first is clearly based on process theology's notion of objective immortality; the second is based on the power of nature; and the third is grounded in the bodily resurrection of Christ and the future transformation of the universe. In my opinion, the second view might be nested within either the first or third, but the first and third cannot be reconciled. In discussing the first view, Haught argues that cosmology and the far future of the universe is irrelevant to God's prehension of actual occasions, and potential conflicts with science are dismissed. In the third view, however, he admits that cosmology poses a crucial challenge to his resurrection-based eschatology.[59]

7.4.5 Christopher Southgate notes the need for an eschatology and is critical of Moltmann, who in his view draws us away from the challenge of science. His thought is promising though under-developed.[60]

---

58.   See Peacocke, *Theology for a Scientific Age*, 126–8, especially n72. See also Arthur Peacocke, 'The Cost of New Life', in Polkinghorne (ed), *The Work of Love*, 21–42. Cf Russell, 'Bodily Resurrection, Eschatology and Scientific Cosmology', 13–14.

59.   John F Haught, *God after Darwin: A Theology of Evolution* (Boulder, Colorado: Westview Press, 2000), 43, 109–15, 160–4.

60.   Southgate, 'God and Evolutionary Evil: Theodicy in the Light of Darwinism'.

7.4.6 Denis Edwards offers a strikingly clear and robust trinitarian approach to theodicy, and he recognises the challenge posed by cosmology to a resurrection-based eschatology. He stresses the crucial importance of redeeming 'every sparrow that falls' and not just humanity.[61]

7.4.7 John Polkinghorne is admirably clear about the challenge posed by cosmology to eschatology. He proposes that the future of creation is a new creation arising *ex vetere* out of the present world, and he articulates this in full awareness of the challenges raised by science. Our first taste and ground for hope in this new creation is the bodily resurrection of Jesus at Easter. The crucial feature that amplifies the challenge from science is the 'embodied' character of Jesus' resurrection and the empty tomb.[62] I strongly endorse this approach and am developing a detailed response to eschatology and cosmology along similar lines.

My concern is with Polkinghorne's kenotic response to theodicy. His 'free-process defence' advocates divine self-limitation instead of divine coercion with regard to human freedom and the integrity of nature.[63] This view is widely shared in the theology and science community. However, I do not think that human freedom depends on limiting God's power, whether by self-limitation or metaphysical limitation. Instead, I believe that God's grace is the condition for our true freedom from the bondage of sin. Many of these scholars make *additional* connections between *kenosis* as divine limitation and the

---

61.   Edwards, *The God of Evolution*, 39–44. See also Denis Edwards, 'Every Sparrow that Falls to the Ground: The Cost of Evolution and the Christ-Event', forthcoming in *Ecotheology: The Journal of Religion, Nature and the Environment.*

62.   See John C Polkinghorne, *The Faith of a Physicist: Reflections of a Bottom-up Thinker* (New Jersey: Princeton University Press, 1994), chap 9; 'Eschatology: Some Questions and Some Insights from Science', in Polkinghorne and Welker (eds), *The End of the World and the Ends of God*, 29–41; and 'Eschatological Credibility: Emergent and Teleological Processes', in Peters, Russell and Welker (eds), *Resurrection*, 43–55.

63.   Polkinghorne, *The Faith of a Physicist*, 83 ff. See also John C Polkinghorne, *Science and Providence: God's Interaction with the World*, 1st Shambhala ed (Boston: Shambhala Publications, 1989), 63–4, and 'Kenotic Creation and Divine Action', in Polkinghorne (ed), *The Work of Love*, 102–5.

theology of creation, which I also find questionable.[64] I expect that progress will be made when we begin to maintain the crucial distinctions between three separate but related topics: (a) free will and physical determinism; (b) grace and free will; and (c) God's action and physical determinism.[65] I simply state here that I distinguish the problem of free will and its somatic enactment, on which I also take an incompatibilist view, from both the problem of divine and human will and the problem of divine will and natural causality.[66] The latter two problems require considerable discussion and are not simply analogous to the first problem.

8. Conclusions: The failure of evolutionary natural theodicy and the need for a robust eschatology of new creation

> Does Darwinism make Christianity impossible?
> Dawkins, Yes; Ruse, No.[67]

64. Peacocke, *Theology for a Scientific Age*, 123; Polkinghorne, *Science and Providence*, 66–8. See also Polkinghorne, *The Faith of a Physicist*, 83–5; Ian G Barbour, *Religion in an Age of Science*, Gifford Lectures 1989–90 (San Francisco: Harper & Row, 1990), 241; Haught, *God after Darwin*, 111–12; and Murphy and Ellis, *On the Moral Nature of the Universe*. Murphy and Ellis add to the problem by using the term 'noninterventionist' in two different ways—to refer both to noninterventionist divine action, as in the NIODA project (p 215) and to God's self-restraint in the face of violence (p 247). The former suggests that God *does* act in the world but in such a way that it does not violate the laws of nature. The latter suggests that God does *not* act in the world, even when God's action might seem highly desirable, because that would be an 'intervention' and such interventions might, in turn, undercut their arguments for pacifism.

65. These distinctions have also been made by Kirk Wegter-McNelly, 'Reflections on the CTNS/VO Series, "Scientific Perspectives on Divine Action"', to be published by the Vatican Observatory and CTNS in the Capstone conference volume (2004). He refers to them as 'anthropo-physical in/compatibilism', 'anthropo-theological in/compatibilism' and 'theo-physical in/compatibilism', respectively.

66. See Coakley's remarks on 'incompatibilism' in her 'Kenosis: Theological Meanings and Gender Connotations', 203.

67. Adapted from the CTNS Spring Forum by Michael Ruse, in which he gave what he takes to be Dawkins's answer and then his own.

> [W]e cannot hope to state a Christian theodicy
> without taking seriously the doctrine of a life beyond
> the grave.[68]

How, then, do we respond to the problem of natural theodicy? My response is to recognise that the problem is generated in part by the fact that natural evil has been discussed in the context of the theology of creation. I believe, however, that we *cannot* address the challenge of theodicy if the framework is creation, that is, the universe as we know it and the laws that science has discovered, through either an Augustinian/Niebuhrian or Irenaean/Hickian approach alone. Given science, we see ever more clearly and ominously the *scale* of the problem of natural evil; it extends back before and down under biology, even to the physics of thermodynamics and outwards endlessly to cosmology as the scientific description of the universe as a whole. More ominously, we see that the *challenge* is immense; we have been forced to recognise 'natural evil' as *constitutive of life* and *not just a consequence* of an historical event now understood as mythological.

Hence I propose that the only possibility for an adequate response to natural theodicy is to relocate the problem of sin and evil beyond a theology of creation into a theology of redemption—the kenotic suffering of God with the world together with the eschatological transformation of the universe in the new creation beginning proleptically with God's new act at Easter in the bodily resurrection of Jesus. This combined *kenosis* and eschatology might respond in a more helpful way to natural evil as well as moral evil than previous approaches. In doing so, the implications we have identified should serve to help in constructing such an eschatology, and the criteria should help to assess its value. Conversely, such a nuanced eschatology might shed light on contemporary physics, cosmology and evolutionary biology as suggested by the methodology of creative mutual interaction.

---

68.   Hick, *Evil and the God of Love*, 339–40.

'(I Can't Get No) Satisfaction'[1]: Eschatology, Theodicy and Our Sacred Power

Heather Thomson

> We do not yet have a moral theology that teaches us the awe-ful, awe-some truth that we have the power through acts of love or lovelessness literally to create one another . . . Because we do not understand love as the power to act-each-other-into-well-being we also do not understand the depth of our power to thwart life and to maim each other.[2]

> [Paul's] own zeal and the Law he served had murdered an innocent man. Having drawn that conclusion he went over to the side of the victim. Instead of continuing the crucifixion he joined the crucified. The revelation of the significance of the Cross uncovered the sacred violence in the institutions of this world.[3]

In relation to the central question of theodicy, Tillich argued that 'All theological statements are existential; they imply the [one] who makes the statement or who asks the question.'[4] I have never been too troubled by the question of theodicy, in the sense of getting to a point where my faith is at stake as I wrestle over the alleged goodness and

---

1. *Rolling Stones* song by Jagger/Richards, on their album, *Big Hits (High Tide and Green Grass)*, 1966.
2. Beverly W Harrison, 'The Power of Anger in the Work of Love', in A Loades (ed), *Feminist Theology: A Reader* (London: SPCK, 1990), 203.
3. Robert G Hamerton-Kelly, *Sacred Violence: Paul's Hermeneutic of the Cross* (Minneapolis: Augsburg Fortress, 1992), 82.
4. Paul Tillich, *Systematic Theology*, volume 1 (London: Nisbet & Co, 1953), 299.

love of God in a world of suffering and violence. I sometimes wonder why it has not been a problem. In part it may be a testimony to a relatively comfortable, middle-class life; I simply have not experienced the horrors that others have. However, I also do not make the same theological move as others do when faced with evil or suffering. Rather than asking, 'Where is God in this?' or 'How can I believe in a just and loving God when this is allowed to happen?', I find myself convicted even more of the evil of evil and the goodness of good, and resolve again with which side I will cast my lot. I see it as a 'choose you this day' situation (Deut 30:15), in which we have set before us life and good, death and evil. I don't tend to put God on trial but am instead thankful that there is goodness in the world.

In my view, much of the blame for suffering and violence that has been sent God-ward has been misdirected and has served as an excuse for humans to shirk our responsibility for the world. We have failed to take into account the depth of our power in relation to each other—to love each other into being or to thwart life and maim each other.

This response to theodicy has led me into theological anthropology and the question of our sacred power, our God-given interrelatedness and responsibility for making (and not breaking) each other. What it means to reflect God in the world, or to treat each other in a God-like manner, is the question, but that question pushes us back to theology, to God. What is God like, that we might be and act like God? Along with orthodox Christian theology, I take the measure of God-likeness to be found in Jesus Christ, the true image of God and the victim of *human* violence.

In this paper I take a theological anthropology line on the question of eschatology and theodicy. These two doctrines are tied together on the question of hope and salvation: How is it that God has saved us and given us new life and hope? How we answer that will be our theodicy, our justification of God. In taking this line of argument, I am focusing on a specific question. In this violent and war-mongering world, in what may I hope? The question of violence sits at the heart of the problem of theodicy. For if God wrought our salvation through an act of violence, through the necessity of having Jesus Christ die for our sins so that we (who really deserved it) might be pardoned, then we end up with a violent God. We have a God who requires satisfaction, one way or another, for being wronged, and that satisfaction includes blood, sacrifice and death. What makes God any different from humans who require vengeance when wronged, except that God took it upon Godself to die the death required? While vengeance resides in God, we do not have a satisfactory answer for theodicy—not one that gives hope for peace in a violent world nor one that undoes human vengeance to make way for new being and a new creation. With this kind of theology, 'I can't get no satisfaction'.

1. Atonement and theodicy

The interpretation of Jesus' violent death is crucial to our understanding of God and the questions theodicy raises. It is interesting that the symbol of the cross has been raised in current discussions on violence in society, where people are searching for what they can name or blame as causes for violence. The film documentary, *Bowling for Columbine*, addresses this question, in particular, what led to the fatal shootings, then suicides, by two boys at Columbine High? One target of blame was Marilyn Manson because the boys had been listening to his music before the killings.

Marilyn Manson made a reply both in the film and also in *Rolling Stone*. He pointed out that 'the first few people on earth needed no books, movies, games or music to inspire cold-blooded murder. The day that Cain bashed his brother Abel's brains in, the only motivation he needed was his own human disposition to violence'.[5] Further, and more to our point, Manson turns the gaze to Christians who oppose his music. He wonders about the basis on which they criticise him when they worship an icon of violence and death—the cross:

> Christianity has given us an image of death and sexuality that we have based our culture around. A half-naked dead man hangs in most homes and around our necks, and we have just taken that for granted all our lives. Is it a symbol of hope or hopelessness? The world's most famous murder-suicide was also the birth of the death icon.[6]

In our violent world, is the cross a symbol of hope or hopelessness? This is an existential question arising from the life of the one who has

---

5.   Marilyn Manson, 'Columbine: Whose Fault Is It?', *Rolling Stone*, Issue 564 (August 1999): 19.

6.   Manson, 'Columbine', 19.

asked it. I still live in the shadow of a fearful God. As a child I was led to believe that I belonged on death row because of my sin. Jesus, in his mercy, took my place. My appropriate response should have been one of gratitude, which I am sure I had, but I could not help wondering, even at that younger age, whether I was really *that* bad. And I could not help feeling that behind God the loving Father was God the angry Father who would have killed me if Jesus had not stepped into the breach.

As an adult, I see this teaching to children as misdirected, and further, as a particular kind of theology that does not necessarily have to be the 'word of the cross' (1 Cor 1:18). Yet I am surprised at how common and tenacious this interpretation of the cross and of salvation is. That Marilyn Manson could see it this way is one thing; that Karl Barth could is another.

When Barth addressed the question of theodicy in his *Church Dogmatics*, he consistently argued that the wrath of God required satisfaction:

> We can only be overlooking or misunderstanding the biblical message if for one reason or another we try to be spared having to take quite seriously the fact that God is the God who for the sake of His righteousness is wrathful and condemns and punishes. He is not only this but he is also this.[7]

For Barth, Good Friday was God's 'No' to human sin, and Easter Sunday was the 'Yes' of God's vindicating and rewarding righteousness. Nevertheless, in speaking of the salvation brought about in the Easter event, Barth put it in terms of Jesus Christ bearing God's wrath in our stead. If Jesus had not done this, God's 'avenging and smiting wrath' would have annihilated us.[8] But in falling on Jesus instead of us, God's wrath, which we merited by offending God's righteousness, 'was really revealed and satisfied'.[9] Barth reiterated this point when he spoke of 'the cross of Calvary where satisfaction was done to the righteousness of God in condemnation and punishment'.[10]

7. Karl Barth, *Church Dogmatics* II/1 (Edinburgh: T&T Clark, 1957), 394.
8. Barth, *CD* II/1, 396.
9. Barth, *CD* II/1, 396.
10. Barth, *CD* II/1, 405.

Barth spoke of the death of Christ, taking the righteousness of God upon himself, as foreordained. Christ is the 'Lamb slain from the foundation of the world'.[11] God's justification consisted in having taken responsibility for God's creation and bearing its sin, in justice and mercy. The theodicy question was clearly answered when Barth maintained that in the cross of Christ and his death for us, God's righteousness and mercy were both satisfied. God was thus justified in relation to the world as being a God who is both righteous and merciful without conflict, that is, without allowing one aspect of God's being to be satisfied without the other. God could do no other than to satisfy both.[12]

There is little here about God's wrath that is different from an abusive father—both loving and violently punitive at the same time. Why is there a necessary relation in Barth's thinking (and the whole line of thinking that preceded and followed him in this) between righteousness and violence? If righteousness is offended, why is a violent action necessarily needed for 'satisfaction'? In this theology, 'I can't get no satisfaction'. We know the satisfaction of vengeance to be common in human experience. However, I hope for something better in God.

To repudiate Barth's violent theology of the cross, an alternative, nonviolent theology needs to be offered that deals adequately with human sin and evil, and the grace of God to which the NT gives testimony, precisely in the death and resurrection of Jesus Christ.[13] How is this Easter event a sign of hope without also being a sign of the requirements of a violent God? To answer this I turn to the interpretation of the cross provided by Robert Hamerton-Kelly, who makes use of the hermeneutical theory of René Girard.[14] From this perspective, the cross of Christ is an epiphany of violence—human violence—and what it reveals is that God never wanted violence and

---

11.   Barth, *CD* II/2, 123.

12.   Barth, *CD* II/1, 504.

13.   Thorwald Lorenzen, 'The Meaning of the Death of Christ', *American Baptist Quarterly* 4/1 (1985): 3–34. Lorenzen examines various models used to interpret the death of Christ and argues that any adequate model must take account of both the depth and destructive quality of sin and the initiative and grace of God in saving humanity.

14.   Robert G Hamerton-Kelly, *Sacred Violence: Paul's Hermeneutic of the Cross* (Minneapolis: Augsburg Fortress, 1992).

sacrifice. How, when seen from this perspective, the cross is a saving event will become apparent. First, however, some introductory remarks about René Girard.

There is nothing new in arguing for a nonviolent theology of the cross. Liberation and feminist theologians have done so for some time. They see Jesus' death as a consequence of the life he lived, as a result of his identification with the poor and marginalised and those held in low esteem. Jesus was thus a subversive force in his society and, given his influence, was a threat to the political and religious power structures of his day. So they got rid of him. What is revealed in this is the side that God is on—the side of the poor and powerless. I remain sympathetic to this basically political reading, but wish to flesh it out using Girard's hermeneutic. What Girard offers is an explanatory theory for both the persistent presence of violence in human culture and the religious sanctioning of that violence. The close connection between social order built on victims and scapegoats and the transference of this violence on to God (or the gods), who then appears to require it in the form of sacrifice, is the focus of Girard's theory. Until we are enabled to see the hidden patterns and consequences of the violence at the basis of our cultures, we cannot renounce it and live in alternative nonviolent cultures as new beings, or the new creation, to use theological terms. Girard's is thus an illuminating theory when applied to the question of atonement, of what was revealed or disclosed in the cross that made it a saving event. It is also illuminative on the question of power, of what is God-like power in relation to others. In this, the category of desire is important, and Girard's is a theory about desire.

2. The Girardian challenge

Hamerton-Kelly applies Girard's theory to Paul's hermeneutic of the cross. In his introduction, Hamerton-Kelly declares his interest in this subject as follows. In our time, violence and the threat of violence have become overwhelming. Theological thought must take place in the light of such violence—'the burning children of Auschwitz' (Irving Greenberg).[15] Girard's cultural theories help us to understand both the structures that generate violence (especially those sanctioned by religions) and ways in which a culture may be generated (a 'new creation') on a foundation of nonviolence.

---

15.   Hamerton-Kelly, *Sacred Violence*, 15.

A study of Paul using a Girardian hermeneutic discloses Paul's conversion as transference from identification with persecutors, that is, perpetrators of violence, to identification with the victim of that violence (Jesus). This was a genuine *metanoia*, a change of heart that came from Paul's realisation of the sacred violence contained in his religion (a form of Judaism in his time).

It is important to understand that the sacred violence Paul discovered is present (in actuality or as potential) in all religions and is certainly found in the Christian tradition. Girard's theory indicts all religions, and all institutions and structures of 'this age'. Although Paul's issue was with the Law (Torah), he did not reject the authority of the Law as such but only a particular Jewish interpretation of it. His argument with Judaism centred on how to interpret the Law. For Paul, Law must be read through the hermeneutic of the cross. Therefore he concentrated on the Jewish role in the killing of Jesus. How did this religion end up killing the son of its God? What might we learn from this about the way religions have a propensity to generate and sanction violence?

Hamerton-Kelly develops Girard's theory of sacred violence, showing its significance for interpreting the atonement. A Girardian hermeneutic gives atonement theories a social and ethical dimension, often overshadowed by the 'vertical' concern for what God has done for humanity.[16] The two dimensions belong together. Three Girardian themes in particular will be discussed here. The first concerns the question of desire, the second considers the causes of violence, and the third looks at the relation of violence to religion.

2.1 *Girard on desire*
Girard is situated in the line of Hegel, Freud and Sartre in being interested in the nature of *desire*. Since Girard is a literary critic rather than a philosopher, his theory derives from literary texts and human sciences of culture. He is therefore allied with Durkheim in considering desire from the perspective of social theory, rather than from Freud's

---

16.   I was alerted to the importance of keeping the balance between the ethical and social implications of the cross and its more strictly theological (vertical) concerns, as well as Girard's positive contribution in this, by an article by George Hunsinger, 'The Politics of the Non-Violent God: Reflections on René Girard and Karl Barth', *SJT* 51/1 (1998): 61.

psychological view. Girard's interest is in the way desire is imitative (triangular) and how this plays a role in the hominisation process (the creation of human society). By 'triangular', Girard means that desire is more than something each of us has as part of our psychological and physical makeup. Desire is socially constructed, pictured as a triangle between two people and the desired object. We want what others have, and we want it because others have or want it, whether this is a physical object or more intangible 'goods' such as prestige or fashion. Imitative desire puts us into rivalry and conflict with each other, which leads to violence.

Imitative desire leads to mimetic rivalry and the 'deformation of desire'. The antidote to this is a culture (a new creation) founded on the good mimesis of *agape* (non-acquisitive love). As Hamerton-Kelly puts it,

> The triangularity of desire means that the human being is structured with reference to transcendence; desire is structured through mediation from without, not from within. Human being is constituted relationally—that is, transcendentally—and the state of mimetic rivalry is the pathology of a . . . desire that should be aroused from a truly transcendent source but instead is aroused by the immanent neighbor. The biblical name for this is idolatry; its antidote is faith in the unseen God. Its ethical expression is eros, whose antidote is agape. So when we describe desire as deformed, we make a theological judgment in the light of the grace of agape.[17]

2.2 Causes of violence

Violence is aroused by mimetic desire and threatens the social system. To maintain order and peace, violence is deflected onto a victim or scapegoat. A key category for Girard is *surrogate victimage*, where rivals converge, no longer on the object that unites them but on the victim that unites them; that is, the victim is seen as the cause of their violence and unites them in a common desire to destroy it.[18] Another key category is that of *double transference* relating to the surrogate victim.

---

17.   Hamerton-Kelly, *Sacred Violence*, 21.
18.   Hamerton-Kelly, *Sacred Violence*, 25.

What is transferred to the victim is the assumption that (1) they were the problem, the cause of the violence, and (2) through their death there will be peace (they are the cause of peace). 'Violence was not repressed and cast off into the unconscious, but was detached and transformed into culture by being transferred to the victim.'[19] Hamerton-Kelly puts this in theological language:

> we make the victim bear both our sins and the sin of making the victim bear our sins. It is not we who threaten vengeance and demand victims; it is the victim! Thus the double transference is the foundational lie of culture and the original act of bad faith.[20]

The *interpretation* of victims is therefore the issue at the heart of cultures. The order of the Sacred, in Girardian terms (that is, religion arising from culture), is founded on surrogate victimage and on the prohibitions, myths and rituals that attempt to keep violence in check, through the fear of the vengeance of the god. But the order of the Sacred is a lie.[21]

Victimage is hidden from view, the violence covered up. Yet the role of victims is foundational for culture. In the beginning was the murder.[22] Hence Girardian theory takes an opposite view to Barth on interpreting the 'Lamb slain from the foundation of the world', with Girard seeing it as a disclosure or revelation in the Christian scriptures of the original victim at the foundation of culture and a call to live as new people in a new culture without the need for victims.[23] For Barth, the Lamb was fore-ordained as a victim to take God's wrath, thereby

---

19. Hamerton-Kelly, *Sacred Violence*, 27.
20. Hamerton-Kelly, *Sacred Violence*, 27.
21. Hamerton-Kelly, *Sacred Violence*, 28–30.
22. For an application of Girardian theory to the Cain and Abel story, see James G Williams, *The Bible, Violence, and the Sacred: Liberation from the Myth of Sanctioned Violence*, Foreword by René Girard (HarperSanFrancisco, 1991), chapter 2: 'Enemy Brothers'.
23. See René Girard, *Things Hidden since the Foundation of the World* (Stanford: Stanford University Press, 1987).

deflecting it from humanity. In this reading, Barth is blind to the system of sacred violence.[24]

2.3 The relation of violence to religion

Girard sees the sacrificial system in a religion as a ritual way of controlling vengeance (by appeasing the god and re-enacting the original sacrifice of the victim that made order possible). The law is the rational way of controlling vengeance (through prohibitions against mimetic rivalry). Both law and sacrifice assume a vengeful god.[25]

Girard maintains that the biblical texts in general, and the NT in particular, expose the lie of the surrogate victim and demythify the process of double transference by telling the story from the point of view of the victim. Hamerton-Kelly applies Girard's hermeneutic to Paul's conversion; he sees Paul's conversion as a transference of allegiance from the Sacred system in the name of its vengeful God to the one who saw through this system, its victim, Jesus Christ, Son of God. From then on Paul preached only Christ crucified.

Since the interpretation of the cross as a propitiatory sacrifice is a strong tradition in Christian theology, founded on certain biblical texts, it is interesting to see the alternative interpretation that Hamerton-Kelly gives using a Girardian hermeneutic. A central question concerns the meaning of righteousness or, more particularly, whether in Christian theology righteousness includes satisfaction through vengeance for a wrong done. It may seem a strange question, but that is the logic behind the Barthian argument for the justice of God and theodicy—that the justice of God needed to be satisfied, so God is justified in being seen as just. Of course, the answer to the question of righteousness has implications for how we should act towards each other, as icons of God.

3. Reinterpreting 'righteousness'

In seeking to reinterpret righteousness, I am moving from Barth to Girard. This is in contrast to George Hunsinger, who begins with Girard, then turns to Barth to fill in some of Girard's 'theological

---

24.   It is interesting in this regard to read Luke 11:49–50, where Jesus speaks of 'the blood of all the prophets, shed from the foundation of the world'. This is easily read in Girardian terms as the revelation of the violence upon which culture and religion had been built.

25.   Hamerton-Kelly, *Sacred Violence*, 30ff.

deficiencies'.[26] Hunsinger argues that Girard, although 'rich, intriguing and suggestive', offers 'an essentially "Pelagian" solution to an inherently "Augustinian" problem'.[27] I shall return to this issue in section 4. below. For now, I will outline Hamerton-Kelly's reinterpretation of righteousness that deconstructs the sacred violence associated with it, first in relation to Abraham and Phineas as fathers of the faith, then with respect to the interpretation of Romans 8:32, and finally with regard to the cross and sacrifice.

3.1 Abraham and Phineas

Hamerton-Kelly contends that in Galatians 3:6–18, Paul was engaged in a discussion with his opponents about the question of righteousness, which Paul interpreted in light of the crucified Christ.[28] In a midrash on Numbers 25:1–13 (on Phineas), Paul's opponents linked Abraham and Phineas because both were understood to have righteousness reckoned to them. Psalm 106:30–31 says that Phineas, by killing offenders in the camp and stopping the plague, had this deed 'reckoned to him as righteousness' (cf Sirach 45:23; 1 Macc 2:54). Phineas was the archetypal zealot, jealous for God's Law, who kept the peace by killing those who did not keep the strict boundaries of the Law (Num 25:10–13). For the Jewish Christians who were Paul's opponents, Phineas was linked with Abraham because Abraham also had righteousness reckoned to him (Gen 15:6). 1 Maccabees 2:50–54 also links them as ancestors who showed zeal for the Law.

Paul wanted to dissociate Abraham from Phineas. Abraham's righteousness was reckoned to him through an act of faith and trust in God. It concerned belief in God's promise for a child (Gen 15:6). It was faith before the Law was even given, not faith in or through the Law or its zealous defence (as in the case of Phineas). Under the Law, all are cursed (Gal 3:10), since the Law itself curses those who cannot or do not keep it. Christ died under the Law, put to death by those who zealously defended it, like those 'hanging in the sun before the Lord' in the story of Phineas (Num 25:4). Paul seemed astounded that the Jewish Christians in Galatia appeared blind to this scapegoating in the name of righteousness: 'You foolish Galatians! Who has bewitched

---

26.   Hunsinger, 'The Politics of the Non-Violent God', 71.

27.   Hunsinger, 'The Politics of the Non-Violent God', 61, 69.

28.   Hamerton-Kelly, *Sacred Violence*, 74–75.

you? It was before your eyes that Jesus Christ was publicly exhibited as crucified!' (Gal 3:1, NRSV).

Paul therefore claimed Abraham as 'the father of us all' (Rom 4:16) because his righteousness was reckoned to him as a result of faith, not because of works of the Law. This is in contrast to 1 Maccabees 2:54: 'Phineas our father, because he was deeply zealous, received the covenant of everlasting priesthood.' For Paul, when righteousness is interpreted in light of the cross of Christ, violence in defence of religious beliefs and practices cannot be justified. 'Thus Paul reverses the valences of the paradigmatic zealot story and shows up the lie of sacred violence, which deals with violence by means of violence, purchasing order by means of victims'.[29]

3.2 Interpreting Romans 8:32, 'He who did not withhold his own Son, but gave him up for all of us, will he not with him also give us everything else?'
Hamerton-Kelly's interpretation of Romans 8:32 also perceives in this verse a disclosure of human (not divine) violence and vengeance in the cross. Paul's statement, 'He who did not spare his own Son, but gave him up for us all', has usually been interpreted in the light of Abraham's willingness to sacrifice Isaac (the Akedah, Genesis 22). It is usually taken to mean that although Isaac was saved, God did not spare his own Son but was willing to sacrifice him for us. However, following Daniel Schwartz, Hamerton-Kelly suggests reading Romans 8:32 in light of 2 Samuel 21:1–14, the hanging of the sons of Saul.[30]

In the Isaac story, Isaac was not said to be 'given'; he did not die; his near sacrifice was on an altar, not a cross; and had he died, his death would not have been 'for' anyone. In Pauline theology, Christ's death was 'for us all'. By contrast, 2 Samuel 21:1–14 has closer textual and theological parallels with Romans 8:32 than does Genesis 22.

In 2 Samuel 21:1, there is famine in the land, and David is told by God that it is because there is 'bloodguilt on Saul and on his house, because he put the Gibeonites to death'. The people of Israel had sworn to spare the Gibeonites, but 'Saul had sought to slay them in his zeal for the people of Israel and Judah' (21:2). David approached the Gibeonites seeking reconciliation and asked them what they wanted.

29.   Hamerton-Kelly, *Sacred Violence*, 75.
30.   Hamerton-Kelly, *Sacred Violence*, 78. Cf Daniel R Schwartz, 'Two Pauline Allusions to the Redemptive Mechanism of the Crucifixion', *JBL* 102 (1983): 259–68.

They did not want silver or gold, but asked for seven sons of Saul to hang (21:4–6). David 'gave' them over but 'spared' Mephibosheth, son of Jonathan, son of Saul. This act stopped the cycle of vengeance (21:14). David spared someone else's son; God did not spare his own son. In the light of this story, Romans 8:32 speaks of human vengeance that needed appeasing, not God's. According to Hamerton-Kelly,

> This Pauline midrash on 2 Samuel 21:1–14, in which God gives God's own son to stop the cycle of vengeance and does not demand anything in return, but rather because of this, 'cannot fail to give us everything' (Rom 8:32b), is intended to show that God does not need to be appeased like the Gibeonites. Thus we have another inversion of sacrificial violence; we are told that God does not take vengeance, but rather suffers it.[31]

3.3 The cross and sacrifice

The third question to be considered here is the interpretation of the cross as sacrifice. In Girardian theory, sacrificial religions assume a vengeful god who requires appeasement (having transferred to god human vengeance). This justifies the violent defence of the Law, since not keeping the Law had terrible consequences. The prophetic tradition unmasks the sacred violence behind these assumptions and calls for steadfast love and mercy, not sacrifice (Hos 6:6; Mic 6:6-8; cf Matt 9:13; 12:7).

Hamerton-Kelly argues that Paul used the metaphor of ransom (rather than sacrifice) as his basic understanding of the cross, and that when he used sacrificial categories he inverted them to show that it is God offering Christ as a sacrifice to us, not a human offering to God. In a footnote he writes,

> Paul probably inherited the general tendency to redefine sacrifice from Jewish Christianity but responded to it more radically. While they were content to argue as in the Epistle to the Hebrews that Christ's death is the perfect sacrifice that renders the

---

31.　Hamerton-Kelly, *Sacred Violence*, 79.

system passé, he argues that Christ's death shows the
system always to have been a grotesque error that in
fact caused the death of Christ.[32]

For Paul, Christ's death ransomed us from slavery to the spirits of
this world (Gal 4:1–10) and the curse of the Law (Gal 3:13), purchasing
our freedom so that we might become free children of God (Gal 3:21ff;
Gal 5:1). He did this by being born of a woman and by being born
under the Law (Gal 4:4). For Hamerton-Kelly,

> The imagery behind this passage is the image of the
> scapegoat that is sent out to redeem, but the direction
> of the scapegoat's movement is reversed; . . . normally
> the scapegoat is sent out from the sacred precinct,
> whereas Christ was sent into it, 'born under the Law'.
> Therefore Paul is inverting the scapegoat ritual, as
> part of the disclosure of sacred violence; he is telling
> us that scapegoating is itself a fantasy of religious
> violence and that chaos reigns in the sacred precinct
> as much as in the wilderness.[33]

Further, the category of propitiatory sacrifice used in Romans
3:21–26 shows God to be the offerer and humanity to be the recipient.
The spatial categories are also reversed. Normally the offerer of a
propitiatory sacrifice goes from profane to sacred space. But God in
Christ moves from sacred space into profane, being put forward or set
forth there (Rom 3:25). 'These inversions of the normal order of
sacrifice mean that it is not God who needs to be propitiated, but
humanity, and not in the recesses of the Sacred, but in the full light of
day.'[34] For Paul, then,

> . . . the primary saving effect of the Cross is as a
> disclosure of religious violence, not as a sacrificial
> transaction that appeases the divine wrath. When we
> see the effect of religious exclusiveness in the Cross

---

32.   Hamerton-Kelly, *Sacred Violence*, 80, n38.
33.   Hamerton-Kelly, *Sacred Violence*, 78.
34.   Hamerton-Kelly, *Sacred Violence*, 80. (Cf Gal 3:1, where Jesus' crucifixion is
      not something hidden, but he is 'publicly exhibited as crucified'.)

we can withdraw credibility from the religious system (Gal 6:14) and receive 'the blessing of Abraham in Christ Jesus' (Gal 3:14).[35]

4. A 'Pelagian' solution for an 'Augustinian' problem?

Having viewed the atonement as an unmasking or revelation of sacred violence (deformed desire) and the disclosing of God's grace in buying us back (redeeming us) into righteousness (right relations or transformed desire), let us return to the question posed by Hunsinger resulting from his comparison of Barth and Girard. Does Girard offer an essentially 'Pelagian' solution to an inherently 'Augustinian' problem? Hunsinger elaborates this further:

> All that is needed if mimetic desire and its murderous consequences are to be dispelled, [Girard] claims, is for the victimage mechanism to be revealed for what it is . . . Once we see things clearly, no more is needed, apparently, than simple renunciation . . . Illumination is thus thought to be sufficient to annul the disorders of the heart.[36]

I have two responses to this criticism. The first is to defend 'illumination' and to suggest that it can genuinely contribute to the annulment of the 'disorders of the heart'. I agree with Hunsinger that Girard tends to make his theory say too much or to overstate his case in somewhat absolute terms.[37] However, as an explanatory theory for human relations that gives an account of violence in society and religion, it is illuminating, and Hunsinger himself accepts that when applied to the biblical texts, 'the results are astonishing'.[38] In defence of illumination, this is closely aligned with the biblical concept of revelation and with the metaphor of light—Christ as the light of the world, bringing light into the darkness and giving sight to the blind. It may be that for Hunsinger illumination *per se* is not the problem, but rather whether 'seeing' is enough. Perhaps behind Hunsinger's critique

---

35. Hamerton-Kelly, *Sacred Violence*, 79.

36. Hunsinger, 'The Politics of the Non-Violent God', 69–70.

37. Hunsinger, 'The Politics of the Non-Violent God', 66–70.

38. Hunsinger, 'The Politics of the Non-Violent God', 65.

is the distinction between Greek philosophy, which assumed that if one only knew the good one would do it, and Christian theology, which knows that one can know the good and still not do it. The doctrine of sin makes the difference. Christian theology, in knowing our slavery to sin, knows a deeper truth about the 'disorders of the heart'.

Yes, but this is precisely the value of an explanatory theory such as Girard's. It seeks to name what might have changed Paul's heart, what turned him around from one who breathed threats and murder against the church (Acts 9:1) to one who preached Christ crucified. There was something about his encounter on the road to Damascus that was a visionary experience—but also more than that. It led him to see his life and faith differently. It was not merely illumination; it was a *metanoia*.[39] On this point, Hunsinger's critique of Girard is unfair.

My second response to Hunsinger is that Augustine's doctrine of atonement is actually closer to Girard than to Barth. Augustine repudiated a substitutionary atonement theory and spoke instead of ransom. He argued that the fall into sin comes from willing or loving the wrong thing; thus our power or capacity to be God-like is warped. In Girardian terms, sin comes from desire formed through our relation to others (mimetic rivalry) rather than through our relation to God as the primary relation that constitutes the self and community. 'For man's true honor is God's image and likeness in him, but it can only be preserved when facing him from whom its impression is received.'[40]

Since Augustine named pride and the desire for personal power as being at the root of our sin, it is significant for him that the incarnation of Christ reveals to us God's humility and grace, thus confuting and curing our pride.[41] However, it is in the death of Christ that the most profound drama is played out between God and the devil, who had held humanity in its grip since the Fall. What Augustine saw as being revealed in this encounter is the moral emptiness and the destructiveness of power that is not preceded by justice and goodwill.

---

39.   Hamerton-Kelly, *Sacred Violence*, 66, addresses this point, arguing in reference to Paul's Damascus experience: 'Vision is an extraordinary experience and the validity of the gospel does not depend on it. The validity of the gospel rests rather on the more general basis of its power to illumine the human condition and to convince the mind and will (Rom 12:1–3).'

40.   Augustine, *The Trinity*, XII. 3. 16, in JE Rotelle (ed), *The Works of Saint Augustine*, volume 5 (New York: New City Press, 1991).

41.   Augustine, *The Trinity*, XIII. 5. 22.

Naming 'the devil' as the symbol of the type of power that is ungodly, Augustine showed its demonic capacities in that the devil put to death an innocent man. In contrast, in this battle between good and evil, God puts justice before power:

> But the devil would have to be overcome not by God's power but by his justice. What, after all, could be more powerful than the all-powerful, or what creature's power could compare with the creator's? The essential flaw of the devil's perversion made him a lover of power and a deserter and assailant of justice, which means that men imitate him all the more they neglect or even detest justice and studiously devote themselves to power, rejoicing at the possession of it or inflamed with the desire for it. So it pleased God to deliver man from the devil's authority by beating him at the justice game, not the power game, so that men too might imitate Christ by seeking to beat the devil at the justice game, not the power game. Not that power is to be shunned as something bad, but that the right order must be preserved which puts justice first.[42]

For Augustine, illumination is what does take place in the gospel and particularly in the cross. Yet that very illumination is saving in that by being shown to be morally bankrupt, we are released from being in its thrall. We can 'withdraw credibility' from that exercise of power.[43] Our human concepts of power are judged by Christ's humility and justice. Jesus Christ reveals to us what God-like power is, and it is *not* the kind of power that puts innocent people to death.

Hunsinger offers Barth, and his doctrine of 'enemy love', to balance Girard's 'deficiencies'. I have great respect for Barth and often turn to his theology for wisdom and inspiration. However, on this point, 'I can't get no satisfaction'. For all that can be said of God's grace and mercy, in Barth's theology God remains one who would annihilate us. As he wrote regarding sin,

---

42. Augustine, *The Trinity*, XIII. 4. 17.
43. As quoted earlier from Hamerton-Kelly, *Sacred Violence*, 79.

It consists in an alienation from God, a rebellion against him, which ought to be punished in a way which involves our total destruction, and which apart from our annihilation can be punished only by God Himself taking our place . . . This is what it costs God to be righteous without annihilating us.[44]

The meaning of righteousness and God-like power is still at stake. If God took violence upon Godself instead of inflicting it on us, merciful as that is, where is the illumination of human violence and vengeance that will bring us up short and cause a *metanoia* of our hearts and minds? If God is breathing threats of murder against us for being wronged, what is there, finally, in the Christian gospel to deconstruct violence and vengeance as God-like desires?

I propose that for a more satisfactory theodicy we use Girard (and Hamerton-Kelly's reading of him) to modify Barth, rather than the other way around. In contemporary theology we have come to understand both the significance of the cultural and communal aspect of being human and the importance of moving beyond an individual-before-God mode of thinking. This is something to which Barth made a significant contribution. Beverly Harrison, a former pupil of Barth's, expresses this relationality well, as quoted at the beginning of this paper. She draws our attention to the awe-ful and awe-some truth that we have the power of life and death over each other, the power to bring each other into wellbeing, or to thwart and maim each other.

Our power in relation to each other is illuminated, in my view, by Girard's work, particularly in relation to desire. Somewhere along the way, *metanoia* needs to involve the process of moving from deformed desires (being conformed to this world) to transformed desire (righteousness, or in humility putting love first, then justice and power). We are enabled in this by looking into the mirror of Jesus, who disclosed the powers of this world to be morally bankrupt—the mirror of the victim and scapegoat. 'We are not most godlike in our human power when we take the view from the top, the view of rulers, or of empires, or the view of patriarchs'.[45] In taking the view of the victim,

---

44. Barth, *CD* II/1, 399, cited in Hunsinger, 'The Politics of the Non-Violent God', 79.

45. Beverly Harrison, 'The Power of Anger in the Work of Love', in A Loades (ed), *Feminist Theology: A Reader* (London: SPCK, 1990), 203.

and explicating the social construction of desire that creates rivals and victims, Girard contributes to Christian theology and ecclesiology.[46] When our desires are transformed in Christ, our hunger and thirst is for righteousness, right relations founded on 'the word of the cross'. Is this not what Jesus taught?

> Blessed are those who hunger and thirst after righteousness, for they shall be satisfied (Matt 5:6).

---

46.   Hamerton-Kelly, *Sacred Violence*, 83–7, draws out some implications of a Girardian reading of Paul for the church, 'The Community of the Cross'.

Creation and Eschatology

Roland Chia

In a recent study of the doctrine of creation Colin Gunton reminds us that 'when we seek to speak of the eschatological dimension of creation theology, we should be careful to define what it is that we mean theologically'.[1] This reminder is timely because of the appearance, in recent years, of a number of secular eschatologies, many of which are influenced by scientific theories about the end of the universe. But this reminder is pertinent even to those who wish to essay a Christian doctrine of creation because of certain tendencies in modern theology. One approach—characteristic of eschatologies of a processive or evolutionary kind—is to read the present of creation into the future, while another is simply to project the end into the future. These various approaches have to do with the different ways in which creation and eschatology are understood and how they are related. Theologians like Moltmann and Pannenberg, in pointing out the weaknesses of some of these approaches, have attributed the loss of eschatology to the inadequate understanding of eschatology in theology, and not primarily because of secular culture. This essay is an attempt to reflect on the relationship between creation and eschatology in the wake of some of these concerns. In order to do this, we will address, albeit in very broad brush-strokes, some significant and relevant theological themes—faith and creation, sin and the Fall, creation and covenant, and creation and new creation—and their inter-relationships.

1. The meaning and promise of creation

In volume III of his magisterial *Church Dogmatics*, Karl Barth maintains that the doctrine of creation is an article of faith like the rest of the content of the Creed. Epistemologically this is significant: since the doctrine is accessible only by faith, it is knowledge which 'no man has

---

1.   Colin Gunton, *The Triune Creator* (Grand Rapids: Eerdmans, 1998), 213.

procured for himself or ever will'. This is because human beings have no 'organ' or 'ability' to attain this knowledge 'by way of observation and logical thinking'.[2] Emil Brunner concurs with this judgment, and argues that knowledge of creation is made possible only by divine revelation.[3] Brunner further maintains that creation is not an idea that is 'posited' by faith, but by God: it is not something that we can grasp, or an idea that gradually emerges from human experience. The doctrine of creation therefore does not begin with an empirical observation of the world; it is not arrived at by a 'natural theology'. Rather the doctrine is located in the doctrine of God: it receives its form and meaning from the Triune Creator. This means that the doctrine of creation is a thoroughly religious-theological affirmation. '"Creation"', as Philip Hefner wrote, 'is a word that refers to the whole of the world when viewed as belonging to God, and the doctrine of creation is an elaboration of how we understand the world when we permit our understanding of God to permeate and dominate our thinking'.[4]

The distinctive feature of the doctrine of creation is the concept of *creatio ex nihilo*. God created the world out of his unlimited freedom, without depending on some pre-existing matter. This concept has played a significant role in the church's understanding of the relationship between God and the world, particularly in the wake of the church's battle against the metaphysical errors of the Gnostics. The concept of creation out of nothing insists on the ontological difference between God and the world. The world is ontologically distinct from God and did not emanate from God's being. The concept further points to the fact that God is the originator of all that there is, that he determines all things while he himself is not determined by anything. The concept also emphasises that the world is not eternal, that it has a beginning. 'Nothing' is not to be interpreted in the Barthian sense of 'nothingness', an opposition and resistance against which God asserts his will.[5] Neither does 'nothing' refer to the space in which God creates and allows his creatures to be, as in Moltmann's conception.[6]

---

2.   Karl Barth, *Church Dogmatics* III/1: 3.

3.   Emil Brunner, *The Christian Doctrine of Creation and Redemption*. Dogmatics II:11–12.

4.   Philip Hefner, 'The Creation of the World', in *Church Dogmatics*, volume 1. Edited by Robert Jensen and Carl Braaten (Philadeplhia: Fortress Press, 1984), 298.

5.   Karl Barth, *CD III/1*:351.

6.   Jurgen Moltmann, *God in Creation* (San Francisco: 1985), 86–8.

Creation out of nothing simply asserts that before God created the world, there was no-thing, only God and his Word. Needless to say, creation out of nothing is beyond the grasp of the natural sciences and human imagination. This concept 'expresses something which is utterly beyond all human understanding. What we know as creation is never *creatio ex nihilo*, it is always the shaping of some given material'.[7]

Some modern theologians have rejected the concept of creation out of nothing and favoured the notion of continuing creation. This is especially common among theologians and philosophers who integrate versions of Whiteheadian process philosophy and the theory of evolution to their understanding of creation. Ian Barbour, for instance, rejects the traditional conception of creation out of nothing, and favours the notion of continuing creation. As a result Barbour rejects the idea of the initial beginning of the universe. In agreement with the process theologians he admires, Barbour argues that one must dispense with the idea of *creatio ex nihilo* as 'an initial act of absolute origination' and that 'God's priority in status can be maintained apart from proximity in time'.[8] The idea of continuing creation is favoured because it implies that 'creation occurs throughout time',[9] and this concurs with current evolutionary science. This account, however, fails to do justice to the traditional understanding of *creatio ex nihilo* and *creatio continua*. It betrays a misunderstanding of the two concepts that resulted in the mistaken view that they are antithetical to each other.

The early Fathers of the church maintain that the creation of the world was completed at the outset, on the sixth day, in accordance to Genesis 1:1 – 2:3. They, however, also taught that God continues to work, even on the seventh day, although this work is different from that of the original creation. The Fathers therefore make the important distinction between creation and preservation. The term *creatio continua* was introduced in the Middle Ages to refer to the divine work of preservation. Continuing creation therefore is not a new act of God by which he brings into being new creatures but the continuation of that original work of creation out of nothing. This was the way in which Thomas Aquinas understood and used the term. Continuing creation,

7. Brunner, *Creation and Redemption* II:12.
8. Ian Barbour, *Issues in Science and Religion* (New York: Harper & Row, 1966), 458.
9. Barbour, *Issues in Science and Religion*, 348.

unlike the original creation, implies a temporal distinction, that of beginning and continuance. Unlike *creatio ex nihilo*, *creatio continua* or preservation is always an act in time. And unlike the original creation, *creatio continua* is not 'creation out of nothing' because preservation presupposes that which already is in existence. Process theology's attempt to privilege continuing creation over creation out of nothing suffers from one fundamental weakness. It fails to appreciate the distinction between the original creation from preservation, and as a consequence historicises the event of creation.

What is the purpose of the creation? There is a sense in which one can simply say that because the creation has no other foundation than the fact that it is willed by God, God's will is the *ratio sufficiens* of the creation.[10] But the creation is not just the work of the divine omnipotence; it is also the work of divine Love. To say this is not to countenance the argument that God needs the creation in order to love. The triune God does not need this 'other' in order to love, for in the eternal communion of Father, Son and Holy Spirit, there is perfect love and reciprocity. Here divine love, as the reason for creation, must be understood in light of the divine freedom. In his sovereign freedom, God wishes to express his love towards something 'over against' himself, and to give of himself to *an*-other. The love of God is the *causa finalis* of the creation. The same argument may be forwarded in regard to the self-glorification of God. If God's self-glorification consists in God's self-glory, why is there a need to create the world through which God may be glorified? Here, as previously, the distinction between God's essential nature and his will is important.[11] Although God remains satisfied in himself and with the impassable glory and blessedness in his own inner life, he *chose* to create another for his own glory. Medieval scholasticism and Protestant theology have advanced the thesis that God himself is the final goal of his action. But a sound doctrine of creation must also take into account the creation's independence that is the result of the divine will. That is to say, although the creation is dependent upon God for its existence and would slip into nothingness once God removes his preserving grace from it, God has nonetheless created the world to be an entity distinct from him. The world has its own integrity, and is in this sense independent from the Creator. God does not only create the creature so

---

10. Brunner, *The Christian Doctrine of Redemption and Creation*, 13.
11. Moltmann, *The Coming of God*, 325.

that he may receive glory from it. His creative act is oriented to creatures, and allows the creature to be itself. Herein, too, lies the glory of the Father, who is glorified by the Son and the Spirit in the creation.[12]

2. Sin and curse

The second theme that must be explored in a discussion on creation and eschatology is the disruption to the created order that resulted from the Fall. At the outset, however, we must state that it is impossible to answer questions regarding the *when* and the *how* of the Fall from the standpoint of human history.[13] It is impossible to trace the origin of the fallen condition of human beings even though we may be aware of sin as something that is indissolubly connected with our present existence and constitution. What is of moment is that sin cannot be understood as the beginning, but rather a turning away from the beginning. Sin is not the origin, but a breaking away from that which was the original divine intention for humankind. Furthermore, the reality and nature of sin cannot be gleaned from our empirical observation of the world but must be christologically defined. In the incarnation, Jesus Christ declares in his being and action the true anthropology promised in creation. From this standpoint, sin is 'whatever falls short of, whatever denies, whatever misses the way of faithfulness to God's rule embodied in Jesus Christ'.[14]

Sin, scripture tells us, is rebellion against God. Bonhoeffer describes the Fall as man's desire to live out his life out of his own resources, to create his own life, and thus to become his own creator.[15] He maintains that sinful humanity, which is now *sicut deus*, has eliminated and destroyed its creatureliness: 'Losing the *limit* Adam has lost *creatureliness*'.[16] In similar vein, Brunner defines sin fundamentally as apostasy. The story of the Fall tells us that man wants to be like God, and seeks to be independent from his Creator. The 'deepest root of sin

12.   Pannenberg, *Systematic Theology* II: 57.

13.   Brunner, *Creation and Redemption*, 100.

14.   James Wm McClendon Jr *Systematic Theology: Doctrine* II (Nashville: Abingdon Press, 1994), 124.

15.   Dietrich Bonhoeffer, *Creation and Fall: A Theological Exposition of Genesis 1–3*. Dietrich Bonhoeffer Works, vol 3 (Minneapolis: Fortress Press, 1997), 115.

16.   Bonhoeffer, *Creation and Fall*, 115.

therefore is not the senses—they are, at most, occasions of sin—but the spiritual defiance of one who understands freedom as independence, and thus only regards himself as free when he "feels that he owes his existence to himself alone" (Marx)'.[17] Sin has caused man to lose his 'creatureliness', not in the sense that he ceases to be a creature, but in the sense that he is no longer a creature who acknowledges and obeys his Creator. However problematic the doctrine of original sin may be, it points to some of these important theological insights regarding the nature of sin. It points firstly to the fact that sin is not the original intention, but rather its contradiction. It points further to the fact that sin and human sinfulness is a mystery, and that sin is personal, intrinsically and profoundly bound up with who we are and what we do. Finally, the doctrine of original sin implies the universality of sin and thus human solidarity.

How does the Fall affect human beings and the non-human creation? With this question, we come to the heart of what this section hopes to address. Here, the relationship between sin and death must be explored. Modern theology since Schleiermacher has rejected the traditional teaching that death is the consequence of sin. Schleiermacher argued that neither Genesis 2:17 nor Romans 5:12 'compel us to hold that man was created immortal, or that, with alteration in his nature, the whole arrangement of the earth relative to him was altered as well'.[18] Death *per se*, according to Schleiermacher, is neither evil nor the punishment of sin. The latter rather has to do with the fear of death.[19] Karl Barth, following Schleiermacher, categorically asserts that 'finitude means mortality'.[20] Modern theologians have enthusiastically welcomed this view because it appears to be in agreement with modern biological science. In response, we argue that the logical link between sin and death arises from the theological presupposition that all life comes from God. Since sin is a turning away from God, sinners do not only reject the will of God but they also sever themselves from the source of life. Death is not just a punishment that is imposed externally, but is intrinsic to sin's nature and its conesquence. Death comes as the result of sin, but death must be understood

---

17.   Brunner, *Creation and Redemption*, 93.
18.   Friedrich Schleiermacher, *The Christian Faith* (Edinburgh: T&T Clark, 1928), 244.
19.   Schleiermacher, *The Christian Faith*, 316.
20.   Karl Barth, *CD* III/2:625-6.

more profoundly as separation from God, and not just mortality.[21] The modern idea of death as a consequence of finitude espoused by Barth must be called to question. This idea must be challenged from the standpoint of christology and eschatology. The raising of Jesus Christ from the dead and hope in the resurrection show that the Christian eschatological hope knows of a finite creaturely existence without death. Thus in the face of all difficulties, we must say that 'as distinct from the finitude of creaturely existence, death is part of God's creation only in connection with sin'.[22]

If sin has brought death to humankind, it has also caused disruption to the non-human creation. We return once again to the story of the Fall in Genesis 3. There we are told that God cursed the ground because of Adam's disobedience (Gen 3: 17–19). How are we to understand this? The cursed land is the antithesis of Eden, the land which is well-watered and fertile because it is blessed by God (see Deut 33:13–16; cf Gen 2:8–14). Thus the human being who is *sicut deus* must live in a *sicut deus* world, a world that has been cursed.[23]

> With the fall of humankind, however, they themselves, as creatures made subject to humankind, fall into dividedness as well; they become nature without a master and thus in rebellion and despair, nature under the curse, accursed ground. That is our earth. Cursed, it is cast out of the glory of its created state, out of the unambiguity of utter strangeness and enigma. The trees and the animals which once immediately represented God's word as the Creator, now in often grotesque ways point instead as though to the incomprehensibility and arbitrariness of a despot who is hidden in darkness.[24]

In his epistle to the Romans, Paul maintains that the world is presently subjected to futility (Rom 8:20). The context seems to suggest that Paul is referring to the solidarity between human sinfulness and

---

21.   Wolfhart Pannenberg, *Systematic Theology*. II: 266.
22.   Pannenberg, *Systematic Theology* II: 274.
23.   Bonhoeffer, *Creation and Fall*, 132.
24.   Bonhoeffer, *Creation and Fall*, 134.

the chaos and decay that the world is subjected to. Paul establishes this connection more clearly than does Western theology, which tends to confine the consequences of sin to human nature.[25] The 'bondage' and 'decay' that Paul speaks of has to do with the frustration of the non-human creation because it is unable to achieve its proper *telos*, the true purpose of its existence. Creation is so subjected, not due to its own choice, 'but by the will of the one who subjected it' (Rom 20b). This refers to Adam whose transgression has thrown the material creation into disorder.[26] As Fitzmyer has pointed out, Paul here alludes to Genesis 3:17–19 and 5:29, which speak of the divine curse upon the earth due to Adam's sin. But Paul was here also thinking of the 'new heavens and the new earth', that is, the apocalyptic promises of Trito-Isaiah (Isa 65:17; 66:22).[27] Paul further makes the profound connection between the redemption of human beings and the liberation of the non-human creation. Fitzmyer states that 'in such groaning and travail Paul sees the eschatological expectation of material creation, awaiting the glory of Christian humanity'.[28] While Paul sees 'all things condemned to a repetitious and wearisome routine, and ends on a note of unrelieved gloom',[29] he also sees the light at the end and God's purpose being finally fulfilled in humankind and in the non-human creation.

3. Creation and redemption

Human rebellion and the resultant disruption in the created order imply that the eschatology of creation must be understood in the context of a doctrine of redemption. Our attempt to articulate the relationship between creation and redemption shall follow the lead of two theologians, the one modern and the other ancient. In his discussion on the doctrine of creation, Karl Barth relates creation with redemption by conceiving the former in light of the covenant. Barth begins by arguing that the creation is the external basis of the covenant. By this assertion, Barth wishes to show the utter dependence of the creature on its Creator, the fact that the creature is not self-

---

25.   George Henry, *Theology of Nature* (Philadelphia: Westminster Press, 1980), 189–190.

26.   Joseph Fitzmyer, *Romans* (New York: Doubleday, 1992), 508.

27.   Fitzmyer, *Romans*, 505.

28.   Fitzmyer, *Romans*, 509.

29.   Henry, *Theology of Nature*, 192.

existent, and that its goal and purpose are not self-determined but determined by the Creator.[30] Thus the creation is inextricably bound to the divine will, and any attempt to establish the independence of the creature from the Creator is rejected by Barth as utterly impossible. 'By its very creation, and therefore its being as a creature, all such views are shown, like this illusion, to be basically impossible, and thus disclosed as falsehoods.'[31]

Because the existence and destiny of the creation are profoundly established in the divine will, the goal of creation becomes clear. 'Because God loves the creature, its creation and continuance and preservation point beyond themselves to an exercise and fulfilment of his love which do not take place merely with the fact that the creature is posited as such and receives its existence and being alongside and outside the being and existence of God, but to which creation in all its glory looks and moves, and of which creation is the presupposition.'[32] According to Barth, apart from this covenant, there is really no basis for the existence of the creature. To be sure, the creation itself is not the covenant, for 'the existence and being of the one loved are not identical with the fact that it is loved'.[33] As distinct from the creation, the covenant may be said to be the creature's true goal: 'the covenant is the goal of the creation and creation is the goal of the covenant'.[34]

If the creation is the external basis of the covenant, the covenant, Barth maintains, is the internal basis of the creation. To say this is to repeat the point that was made earlier that the creature does not merely exist causally, but meaningfully. To say that the covenant is the internal basis of the creation is to emphasise the fact that the creature came into being because God wills it. And if God does not exist causally but in the 'power of his own divine meaning and his own divine necessity', the creature which exists because of him must serve as a revelation of the divine glory.[35] Creation must travel the road that leads to the covenant, for creation, not being itself that covenant, is promise, pointing to and also moving towards what God has intended

---

30. *CD* III/1: 94.
31. *CD* III/1: 95.
32. *CD* III/1: 95–6.
33. *CD* III/1: 97.
34. *CD* III/1: 97.
35. *CD* III/1: 230.

for it, thus participating in the history of the covenant. Creation is expectation and prophecy of the purpose and plan that God will bring to completion through the giving of his Son. The creation therefore cannot be said to be the internal basis of the covenant, but rather it is the covenant's external power and basis. This is because 'for its fulfilment the latter (ie the covenant) depends wholly on the fact that the creature is in no position to act alone as the partner of God'.[36]

However one may wish to understand the independence of creation, one must make this important qualification: that the independence of the created order, its freedom to be 'creation', is itself made possible by the divine grace, which upholds it and which brings it to fulfilment. Undergirding all this is christology, for as Barth has pointed out Christ is not only the goal of creation, he is also beginning—better, Christ is the beginning because he is creation's goal.[37] Although some have rightly criticised Barth's formulation for subordinating the creation to the covenant,[38] his contribution is nonetheless important because it relates creation with the divine intentionality christologically, thus providing a proper framework within which the relationship between creation, redemption and eschatology can be understood.

This christological focus is found in an exemplary fashion in the theology of Irenaeus, who in his battle against the Gnostics sought to bring together the material content of salvation and the eschatological orientation of the creation in Jesus Christ. Gnosticism not only presents an absolute dualism of creation and salvation but it also postulates that the two are antithetical to each other since according to the Gnostics the higher deity is concerned with spirit and not with matter. Irenaeus surmounts this antithesis christologically and with his eschatological vision of creation. But Irenaeus's approach also addresses the tendency to treat creation as having to do only with the beginning. If the doctrine of creation has to do only with beginnings, the teleological dynamic of creation that the New Testament alludes to is lost. Salvation is thereby severed from creation because it is understood as signalling a new beginning. What Irenaeus has shown is that creation is not only through Christ, but also *to* Christ. Salvation (*in* Christ)

---

36.   *CD* III/1: 231.
37.   *CD* III/1: 232.
38.   Gunton, *Christ and Creation*, 94–5.

'takes place within the created and material order with an eye to the perfection of that which was begun'.[39]

Central to Irenaeus's thought are the doctrine of the incarnation and the concept of recapitulation. For Irenaeus, the incarnation is the key to the whole salvation history. The incarnation is the convergence of Man's approach to God and God's reaching out to Man. But this convergence Irenaeus saw as having taken place right at the beginning, for it was the Word who created Man in the image of God, and that Word continues to be with him.[40] Even after Man had rebelled against God this Word continues to be present and did not abandon mankind. It was the Word 'who ascended and descended for the salvation of the afflicted, in order to deliver us from all idolatry'.[41] Following Justin, Irenaeus argues that the Word was present with the patriarchs of the Old Testament. There is therefore continuity between the earlier presence of the Word among human beings and the incarnation.[42] By this emphasis Irenaeus refuted the theology of Marcion which postulates progress as consisting of passing from the Old Testament God to the God of the New Testament. There is only one God, only one divine plan, and this God is at work in Abraham as well as in the Apostles.[43]

The heart and the climax of salvation history, for Irenaeus, is the incarnation. The incarnation does not imply a new creation, but rather the recovery of the old. For this reason Ireaneus resisted all forms of docetic Christology, emphasising instead that 'if the Lord had become incarnate in accordance with some different dispensation, and had taken flesh of another substance, he would not have recapitulated Man in himself'.[44] As Gunton has put it, the Word took upon himself fallen human flesh simply because there is no other flesh to take. More importantly, the incarnation points to the fact that the creation is the work of the same Word and that redemption is not the negation of the material creation—as the Gnostics had taught—but its restoration and perfection.

---

39.   Gunton, *Christ and Creation*, 97.
40.   *Adv Haer* IV, 20, 1.
41.   Irenaeus, *Demonstratio*, 45.
42.   *Adv Haer*, IV, 12, 4.
43.   *Adv Haer* III, 9, 1; IV, 7, 3; IV, 11, 1.
44.   *Adv Haer*. V, 14, 2.

It is thus from this theology of the incarnation that Irenaeus developed his concept of 'recapitulation' which establishes the profound relationship between creation and redemption. Harnack explains: '. . . this work of Christ can be conceived as *recapitulatio* because God the Redeemer is identical with God the Creator; and Christ consequently brings about a final condition which existed from the beginning in God's plans, but could not be immediately realised in consequence of the entrance of sin'.[45] Christ is the fulfilment of everything that has gone before, the consummation of the human nature in its concrete reality, the perfection of the creation.[46] Irenaeus grounds his understanding of the relationship between creation and salvation not on the creation itself but on christology. 'There is therefore one God and Father, as we have shown, and one Christ Jesus our Lord, who came by a universal plan, and recapitulated all things in himself (Eph 1:10).'[47] According to Irenaeus, such a recapitulation is possible because 'the Word has summed up in himself Man, formed by God, that, in virtue of the power which belongs to him, he who is already head of the whole creation now becomes in a new sense head of the human race, drawing everything to himself, and in himself concentrating all the generations of mankind'.[48] The recapitulation of all things in Christ is not only the recapitulation of human beings, but also of the entire cosmos.

Gunton provides an eloquent and succinct summary to the discussion in this section:

> Jesus Christ is the one through whom all things take
> their shape and to whom the Spirit directs them.
> When the Spirit shapes him a body from the flesh of
> Mary, what we see is not just the working out of
> election—though we do see that—but the renewing
> of the whole of creation, the redirecting of the world
> to its end. Only through his cross is the creation
> 'redeemed from its fault and shame' so that it may
> be perfected in praise of its creator and redeemer.
> Some such account, it seems to me, can take into

---

45.   Adolph Harnack, *History of Dogma*, volumes II & III (New York: Dover Publications, 1961), 242.

46.   *Adv. Haer.* III, 11, 8.

47.   *Adv Haer.* III, 16, 6.

48.   Jean Danileou, *A History of Early Christian Doctrine*, volume Two: Gospel Message and Hellenistic Culture (London: DLT, 1973), 176.

itself the strengths of Barth's placing of the covenant at the very heart of God without the danger of appearing to incorporate everything into Christ in advance, and without the tendency to an anthropocentric exclusion of the non-human creation from the process. The teleology of the whole creation, past, present and to come is shaped through Christ: begun through him, reordered to its end through his self-emptying, and directed to him as its end.[49]

4. Continuities and discontinuities

The preceding discussion has enabled us now to turn to our final theme, the relation between this world and the new creation. The discussion in the previous section is an attempt to answer the question: What is the relationship between creation and redemption? Should creation be understood in the light of redemption, or should redemption be understood in the light of creation? The Western tradition has favoured the second approach. The original creation, according to this view, is finished, complete and perfect. Adam enjoyed the *status integritatis* before the Fall—a state of virgin purity. The disobedience of Adam has resulted in the lost of the *iustitia et sanctas originalis*, his original status of righteousness and holiness. As a consequence, Adam was driven from the perfect primal condition of Eden. According to this view, then, redemption and eschatology have to do with the *restitutio in integrum*, the restoration of the original state and the return to a pristine beginning. In the previous section we saw in our discussion of Barth that the basis of creation is the covenant (not redemption as such). And from the insights of Irenaeus, we concluded that redemption has to do not just with the return to the beginning. Rather, the Irenaean doctrine of recapitulation maintains that the restoration of man and the cosmos in Christ allows them to achieve their true destiny.

Creation and eschatology are profoundly related because only in the eschatological consummation will the destiny of the creature be fulfilled. To the creature, however, creation and eschatology are not

---

49. Gunton, *Christ and Creation*, 97–8.

directly identical. The human creature sees the future as open and uncertain. Yet, despite the ambiguities of the future, human beings in their self-awareness open themselves to the future and see it as a dimension in which they may find fulfilment. Both Barth and Irenaeus in their different ways have pointed to the fact that the relationship between creation and eschatology is to be found in God and in the unity of his divine action in Christ. The relationship between creation and eschatology can only be understood from the premise that God is the First and the Last (Isa 44:6; 48:12; Rev 1:8; cf 21:6; 22:13). 'He is not restricted to being the First, nor is he only the Last (ie as a result of the cosmic process). He stands above the alternative of beginning and end and is Lord of both.'[50] But although creation and eschatology are related, they must be distinguished from each other. Because the consummation of creation is its fulfilment, the eschatological future of the coming kingdom of God must be the standpoint from which we understand the cosmos. It is also from this standpoint that we must view the beginning. The beginning cannot be seen as that which provides the unity for the whole process. It is the eschatological vision of the consummation of the creation that should inform our understanding of the meaning of its beginning. Barth helps us to see this when he posits the covenant, which cannot be understood in any other way except eschatologically, as the internal basis of creation.

How are we to conceive of the consummation of the world? How is the new creation, the new heavens and earth, similar to and different from our present world? Western theology has provided two different answers to this question. Lutheran orthodoxy postulates the annihilation of the world, its complete end.[51] 2 Peter 3:12 is often cited as the biblical evidence which supports this view. This view conforms to a kind of mysticism that pictures the eschatological perfection of human beings as the image of God in such a way that they no longer require the created environments of heaven and earth. This view therefore introduces a disjunction between human beings and the non-human creation. God, according to this account, is the eschatological salvation of believers. Believers at the consummation of the kingdom will be in God: God himself will be their 'environment'. The created order is seen here as a mere scaffolding which will become redundant and therefore destroyed once believers have attained the state of

---

50.   Pannenberg, *Systematic Theology* II: 140.
51.   See Paul Althaus, *Die letzten Dinge*, first edition (Gütersloh, 1922), 350.

blessedness or the beatific vision. Arguing for the reversal of the *creatio ex nihilo* at the end, the theologians of Lutheran orthodoxy maintain that the world as we know it will be reduced to nothing (*reductio in nihilum*) at the close of the age and the consummation of the kingdom of God.

Lutheran theologian Jürgen Moltmann has strongly criticised the annihilationism of Lutheran orthodoxy. The soteriological theocentrism, he says, should not be allowed to slide into an anthropocentricism that cannot allow the existence of world or body in the eschaton. This would mean that God has ceased to be Creator. Care must be exercised when interpreting the meaning of 'the form of this world' which certain biblical texts say will pass away (1 Cor 7:31). Moltmann rightly insists that this phrase does not mean that the created order will be no more. Rather, the '"form of this world" which is destined to pass away is the God-contraverting form of the creation in which in itself is destined for correspondence with God'.[52] The final, most glaring criticism of the annihilationist vision is that if the future of human existence is conceived as the blissful beatific vision of a disembodied soul, 'the resurrection of the body' is lost completely. Moltmann reflects on the consequences of this: ' . . . if that [the resurrection of the body] is surrendered, the Christian faith becomes a world-denying, world-despising gnosticism. Anyone who teaches the annihilation of the world eschatologically, would like to call off creation, and would seem to be more fascinated by nothingness than by existence'.[53]

The second view postulates the transformation of the world at the consummation of the kingdom of God. Various versions of this view have been presented throughout the history of theology. Calvinist or Reformed theology speaks of the transfiguration of the bodily and the material, a *transfiguratio mundi*. The end of the world therefore does not refer to its total annihilation and a new creation. Rather it refers to the transformation of the world from out of transience to eternity. Thus the 'theology of the Cross' in the Reformed tradition does not compel it to speak of the annihilation of the world. Rather, the cross of Christ has brought about the salvation of the world, and this is understood in terms of its restoration and renewal. Calvin writes:

---

52. Moltmann, *The Coming of God*, 270.
53. Moltmann, *The Coming of God*, 270.

> For in the cross of Christ, as in a splendid theatre, the
> incomparable goodness of God is set before the whole
> world. The glory of God shines, indeed, in all
> creatures on high and below, but never more brightly
> than in the cross, in which there was a wonderful
> change of things—the condemnation of all men was
> manifested, sin blotted out, salvation restored to men;
> in short, the whole world was renewed and all things
> restored to order.[54]

Consequently for Calvin 'judgment' does not refer to condemnation but 'reformation', the complete restoration of the world.[55] In his *Reformed Dogmatics*, Anthony Hoeksema maintains that 'from scripture it is abundantly evident that the whole cosmos shall partake of the glorious liberty of the children of God . . . taken in the proper sense of the term, in the final regeneration in eternal glory'. This is clearly taught in Romans 8:19–22, where 'the creature that with uplifted head expects the glorious liberty of the children of God, and itself looks for the redemption from the bondage of corruption, certainly refers to the brute creation'.[56]

The continuities and discontinuities with the present creation that obtains in the 'new heavens and the new earth' can be gleaned from the relationship between time and eternity. The gospels announce the in-breaking of the coming kingdom in the appearance of Jesus Christ the enfleshed Word. The eschatological future that the world awaits is already present in the incarnate one. Put differently, the future is already here in the present, and this future gives the present its hidden meaning.[57] Paul brings this out with his statements regarding the 'already' and 'not yet' of the kingdom of God and of salvation. Through baptism, the believer is buried with Christ in his death (Rom 6:3), and is free from sin (Rom 6:7). Believers share in the Spirit of the new life (8:11) although they continue on the path towards death, and their resurrection is still future (Rom 6:5). This urges us to look at eschatology rather differently. Pannenberg explains: 'If the future is already in hidden form the present, we have an answer here to the

54. John Calvin, *Commentary on John*, 13:31.
55. Calvin, *Commentary on John*, 12:31.
56. Anthony Hoeksema, *Reformed Dogmatics* (Grand Rapids: Reformed Free Publishing Association, 1966), 862.
57. Pannenberg, *Systematic Theology* III: 604.

question of the identity of what is present with the future of its consummation'.[58] From this basic insight, Pannenberg extrapolates:

> In this regard the relation of the essential reality of things to their present appearance is mediated by the relation between eternity and time, for the essence of things is the totality of their manifestation in the form of simultaneity but purged of all the heterogeneous admixtures, perversions and woundings of their earthly existence, not of traces of the cross, but of traces and consequences of evil in achieving of independence from God by creatures.[59]

This is seen profoundly in the doctrine of the bodily resurrection of the dead. What does resurrection mean and what does it entail? How does one understand eternal life in regard to the doctrine of resurrection? Is eternal life 'another life' different from the previous one? If this is the case, then the term 'raised' is a misnomer, and death will bring about another life, a new birthday. This, however, is not the case, since from Paul we learn that resurrection means that 'this mortal life will put on immortality' (1 Cor 15:54). But what does this mean? To be sure, it points to the fact that resurrection does not mean the negation of the earthly life but its 'immortalising'. Resurrection therefore means the transformation and the transfiguration of this life. There is continuity in that it is *this* person who has died who will be raised. Nothing is lost to God in the resurrection; everything, the person's entire history, his lived *Gestalt*, is present. But because resurrection is transformation, and not merely resuscitation, the *I* is raised as one whose history is reconciled, rectified and healed. This is how Paul's statement regarding the negation of our present condition is to be understood (1 Cor 15:42–54). In the spiritual body (*soma pneumatikon*), the perishable will be replaced with the imperishable, dishonour with glory, the physical with the spiritual, and weakness with power. But, as we have seen, because humankind and nature cannot be separated, the resurrection reaches beyond the human being. 'It applies to all the living, so that in that future world the creation that

58.   Pannenberg, *Systematic Theology* III: 605.
59.   Pannenberg, *Systematic Theology* III: 606.

"groans" under transcience (Rom 8:19–21) will also be delivered, because there will be no more death.'[60]

For Christian eschatology, therefore, the end of time and history does not entail annihilation. God—not nothing—is at the end of time. The end of time and of the temporal therefore refers to the transition into eternity, the encompassing of the finite by the infinite. This must be understood as participation in the eternal life of God. To be sure, this event includes judgment insofar as eternity may be understood as the antithesis of fallen time. But Christian eschatology also maintains that at the eschaton, at the consummation of God's kingdom, 'eternity will no longer have to be an antithesis of time but must be thought of as including time or leaving a place for what is distinct in time'.[61] To say that God's eternity includes time is to say that God's eternity is the basis of time, and that time is a creature of God. Furthermore, it is to acknowledge the fact that time is a gift from God and its fullness is to be seen in its participation in God's eternity. Such a view of the relationship between time and eternity is a requisite of a truly incarnational christology which takes the humanity of Christ in the resurrection and ascension seriously. It is from the standpoint of creation's participation of God in Christ (*participatio Christi*) that the relationship between creation and eschatology can be properly understood. And it is from the standpoint of eschatology that the purpose of creation is fully revealed.

> Only in the light of the eschatological consummation
> is the verdict justified that in the first creation story
> the Creator pronounced at the end of the sixth day
> when he had created the first human pair: 'And God
> saw everything that he had made, and behold, it was
> very good' (Gen 1:31). Only in the light of the escha-
> tological consummation may this be said of our
> world as it is in all its confusion and pain. But those
> who may say it in spite of the suffering of the world
> honour and praise God as their Creator. The verdict
> 'very good' does not apply simply to the world of
> creation in its state at any given time. It is true
> rather, of the whole course of history in which God

60.   Moltmann, *The Coming of God*, 70.
61.   Pannenberg, *Systematic Theology* III: 595.

is present with his creatures in incursions of love that will finally lead it through the hazards and sufferings of finitude to participation in his glory.[62]

---

62. Pannenberg, *Systematic Theology* III: 645.

Theodicy and Eschatology:
A Fundamental Orthodox Viewpoint

Archbishop Stylianos

In order to identify from the outset the significance that by definition both of the above theological terms have in the topic that we are called to examine, we must immediately state unreservedly that the main objective is expressed by the first term, 'theodicy', which has come to mean the relationship between God and 'evil' in the world generally.

The second and more inclusive term, namely 'eschatology', forms —as we shall see below—the appropriate 'framework' or, more accurately, the 'conditions' under which the whole question of theodicy should be explored. For eschatology is indeed the only legitimate and proper basis for resolving this question as it deserves. Any other approach in dealing with this topic might be **psychological**, **sociological**, **philosophical** or whatever else, but it would not be **theological**, since God is the Alpha and the Omega, the Beginning and the End, the First and the Last.

Now in order to view the topic in all its implications, it is not sufficient simply to affirm the **eschatological horizon** as the main point of orientation. What is of special significance is also of course the point in time (within the whole course of the divine economy) at which the issue of theodicy arises with sufficient clarity in the human conscience. This is regardless of how it is subsequently experienced as a 'problem' or even as a 'scandal', according to the personal or general historical context of each era.

In our attempt to determine—even by approximation—the historical starting point of theological engagement with 'theodicy', we notice that this has primarily been considered the life of the righteous Job, with his exceptionally provocative suffering. Alternatively, even if rarely cited, the starting point for the problem of theodicy has been thought to be the general pessimism expressed in the book of Ecclesiastes.

Without overlooking that both these books of the Old Testament are indeed highly characteristic instances giving rise to the question of 'theodicy', we believe that there is rather another text in Biblical literature that could be underlined. This describes another earlier phase of human life and self-consciousness, being more comprehensive—and for this reason more crucial—in the broader relationship between God and human beings. We refer to the passage of Genesis 3:23, in which the problem of theodicy is truly presented more **radically**, and undoubtedly more **generally**. Here, for the first time, the 'fallen' state of humankind is described with such fullness of self-awareness, immediately after the expulsion from Paradise.

In this biblical passage of Genesis we can recognise today the clearest, almost 'atavistic', root of the highly inclusive language established by existential philosophy of recent times, with the well-known general term 'human condition'. And it is obvious that such a foundation excludes every **detached**, ie **partial**, evaluation of the problem of **theodicy** for two reasons:

First, because it refers to the common ancestor of the entire human race, and second, because it does not relate only to one specific misfortune, but rather to the now general forfeiture of 'Paradise', which is the collective, and at the same time the only visible and communicable 'place' of **presence** and **participation** in God.

If we look more closely at this universal deprivation of Paradise, we shall see that this does not mean a final and objective **loss**. The sense of absolute orphanhood and abandonment, as presented, for example, in poetry ('Paradise Lost') almost borders upon simplification when compared with the much deeper grief of 'Paradise' being still **visible to**, yet no longer **approachable** by, 'exiled' man. The pathos of this loss is that it is still visible. And precisely this causes the grief to be unbearable. Here we see for the first time that Adam only realises the value of 'Paradise' when he is 'homeless'.

Pain, therefore, and evil in the world do not constitute a self-contained and objective reality. Rather, they have a direct relationship with the **presence**, and indeed the **experience**, of God. This very point is also the 'Copernican Revolution', so to speak, of the entire problematic concerning 'theodicy', as this has been developed in modern times.

From the very moment that the discussion about theodicy takes seriously into consideration the most fundamental biblical doctrine, namely the creation of the world 'out of nothing' (*ex nihilo*), then we will have necessarily ensured the truly theological **hierarchy** of persons, on the one hand (God-human), and the ethical ties between them, and on the other (sin-reconciliation), both of which are by definition involved in the mystery of **existence** and **salvation**.

However, we shall properly appreciate the significance of the doctrine of the creation of the world 'out of nothing' for the topic at hand—not only at the **outset**, but also in its **individual aspects**—only when we recall the following basic truths which derive from that doctrine:

a) That God created the world 'out of nothing' means that absolutely nothing pre-existed—not even the 'formless chaos' which philosophers of ontological dualism have speculated about since time immemorial. And since nothing pre-existed in order to 'oblige', or at least provoke, the creative energy of God outwards (*ad extra*), this means that God created the world in absolute **freedom**. Yet creation in absolute freedom signifies an act of absolute **love**. Therefore God's only motivation to create was his **goodness** which, on account of being totally without **presuppositions**, and which cannot possibly be repaid in any way, is called '**grace**'.

   Thus it is clear that the world made in absolute **freedom** and absolute **grace** could not have been created without being in accordance with the **omnipotence** and **wisdom** of God. That all **good** energies of the uncreated divine essence worked effectively together in this creation is apparent from the 'evaluation' that God himself makes concerning the 'quality' of the created world, in characterising all things as 'very good' (Gen 1:31).

b) From these presuppositions, it can be seen that it would not be possible to consider 'evil' in the world as having an **objective** existence. For this reason, many Fathers and theologians of the early church spoke not so much about the **existence of evil**, but rather about the **absence of good** (*privatio boni*).

Yet in spite of this, no one could deny that the ancestral **Fall** disturbed that which Leibniz would later call 'pre-established harmony', and so an attempt was made to identify more clearly the nature of the **damage**, or at least of the **change**, brought about by the Fall. In this attempt it was immediately recognised that there was no change in **organic structure** in the form of 'mutilation' within Creation. That is, the material destruction which can cause physical deformation does not necessarily influence the eternal and moral integrity of the person. Rather, the harmony of **relationships** and **functions** of the physical world have been altered to the point of complete perversion, such that what was previously 'in accordance with nature' became 'contrary to nature'.

Accordingly, 'use' was degraded to the level of 'abuse' through relationships. And when we speak of disturbance or disharmony in relationships, we of course mean above all the relations between God and the human person, and, by extension, relationships between humans and all other created beings. For, according to the well-known statement of the Apostle Paul, 'the whole of the creation groans and labours with birth pangs together until now' (Rom 8:22).

This general and initially somewhat vague factor of deregulation of the good relationships between God and human beings, or between humans and other beings, having subsequently assumed a more precise classification in human thought and consciousness, is described as either '**moral**' or '**natural**' evil. Certain philosophers and theologians spoke of a third category also, namely '**metaphysical**' evil.

What became gradually clearer in time, however, with regard to this issue was that 'evil' had no 'substantiated' objective reality. Rather, it is an intention which can have decisive significance in both the use and abuse of the goodness of God which is spread throughout creation.

It is appropriate to mention at this point a second biblical doctrine which axiomatically determines as a prelude the relationships between God and man. On that basis, we can appreciate the degree to which these relationships can be 'tested', given any kind of 'evil' in nature or history. This is the doctrine concerning the creation of man 'in the image' of God (Gen 1:26), for the sole purpose of achieving God's 'likeness' by grace.

As the human person knows from the very beginning that he possesses a power that transcends the merely human realm (according to nature), he is justified and at the same time obliged to continually look ahead with the greatest possible optimism. This has to do not only with the **destination** of being in the likeness of God by grace, but also with the handling of the **trials** and **temptations** that are encountered along the way.

Human life in the present world means constant **vigilance** and *askesis* for self-transcendence, assisted permanently by grace from above, since God **knows** and **wishes** and is **able** to 'heal that which is weak and supplement that which is deficient'. In this regard, the words of St Paul are very characteristic: 'God is faithful, who will not allow you to be tempted beyond what you are able, but with the temptation will also make the way of escape, that you may be able to bear it' (1 Cor 10:13).

Precisely this **dynamism** of human life, from which we know that even the incarnate Son of God was not exempt during his earthly life (Luke 4:1–13), is what enables the 'synergy' between God and the human person, so that **salvation** follows as an almost natural **consequence** and verification of our being made in 'the image' of God.

The mystical and liturgical theologian of the fourteenth century, Nicholas Cabasilas, viewed synergy leading to salvation mainly on the basis of sacramental and liturgical life. And in so doing, he was not simply expressing his optimism in terms of the desirable outcome. He was in fact expressing his absolute certainty that, since man was made in the image of God, he possesses not only the inclination and potential, but indeed the explicit command, to become 'god by grace'. According to Cabasilas, we have all 'received an order to become gods'!

If sacramental life in the church is the 'positive' and sanctifying power which directly edifies the faithful, the *catharsis* or purification achieved through ascetical endeavour is the 'negative' and indirect path, which likewise leads to salvation. For this reason, **sufferings** are **blessings** nonetheless. Moreover, the Neptic Fathers of the church go even further, with the categorically repeated ascetic axiom 'take away temptation, and none would be saved'!

To clarify the meaning of 'temptation', however, we must admit that it is a very broad term. It is not limited only to those **trials** which are apparently allowed from above for our edification, but also any other kind of **evil** in the world, from natural disasters right through to intricate personal adventures, or illnesses of body and soul. Indeed, the sensitivity and gratitude of the faithful servant of God for all the undeserved gifts received from birth reaches the point of considering not only the **sorrowful** and **painful** moments of life to be unsearchable 'temptations', but sometimes even the **bright** and **joyful** aspects as well, such as physical health and wellbeing.

In the lives of the great saints and ascetics, there is frequent mention of visions of angels and other good spirits which the saints themselves took to be 'Satan in disguise', as they considered themselves unworthy to see such visions.

From a position of such infinite indebtedness, how is it now possible for one to expect even God to give an enlightening 'account' of any natural or moral evil in the world? This is a question which only psychiatry could answer.

Is it not the same **unacceptable** 'accountability' that even the faithful demand, when they expect to put God on 'trial'—and even 'accusing' him—for **evil** in the world, with so-called theodicy?

If we take into consideration the basic biblical doctrines mentioned above, while analysing their basic **dogmatic** and **ethical** implications, there is no doubt that the truly unprejudiced person (ie a just and healthy mind) would be obliged to reverse the question, that is to see the degree of **human** responsibility, rather than **God's** responsibility. So we then evidently have a problem of '**anthropodicy**' instead of '**theodicy**'!

For it is certainly only natural to search for responsibility in this regard from '**changeable**' human beings, rather than from an immutable and **unchanging** God.

The mutability and instability of human **nature** and **will** was in any case recognised most insightfully by Gregory of Nyssa, from the very manner in which people are born, coming as they do through a transition from **non-existence** to a state of **being** and **existing** (*Catechetical Oration* 6).

Consequent upon all of the above, one can easily guess what the Orthodox viewpoint would be concerning the relationship between the All-good, All-wise and All-powerful Creator on the one hand, and 'evil' in nature and history on the other.

Instead of **conjecturing** irresponsibly and impiously concerning the **reasons**, **purposes** and **responsibilities** in the interaction between the visible and invisible universe, it is sufficient for the theologian to simply recall vital and highly indicative coordinates in terms of **revelation**, **creation** and **history**. And there is no doubt that these coordinates commonly bear witness to the **mysterious complexity** of life in the present world of continual fluidity and instability.

It is this fluidity, expressed as **indeterminancy**, that defines the character of Orthodox theology in general which, as is known, is more **apophatic** than **cataphatic**.

We therefore remind ourselves of the following by way of summary:

First, not only the **doctrinal** texts of the church, but also the research of related **sciences** regarding the structure and course of the world, testify to and converge on a universally acknowledged confirmation that neither nature nor history are a 'closed system' of accomplished values and procedures. Thus the axiom of Heraclitus that **'all things are in a state of flux'** maintains at all times universal validity, which obliges man to have appropriate **modesty** but also **reverence**, since he is only able to know a very limited amount about the **present**, and much less about **expected events** and **likely outcomes**.

Second, this **fluidity** and **uncertainty** is due both to the **object of our knowledge** *per se*, but also to the **finite nature** of the (human) subject. This is not only stated—and indeed categorically—by the Pauline 'we know in part and we prophesy in part' (1 Cor 13:9), but also the description of us 'seeing in a mirror, dimly' (1 Cor 13:12) indicates that even what we know 'in part' is itself enigmatic.

Third, on the basis of this data, it would not only be **absurd**, but also impious, for the faithful to dare to make a **final** verdict about any **substance** and **condition** of created things. This would undoubtedly constitute an impermissible, premature and merely supposed experience of the 'fullness' that is promised for the **end times** (*eschata*), since the entire plan of the divine economy for humankind and the world is still continuing towards 'perfection' and completion. More specifically concerning the **moral** evaluation of **things, situations** or **actions**, it is impossible for one to know the extent to which something that is usually taken to be 'evil' is truly 'evil', and whose responsibility this is first of all.

It would be useful to recall at this point a recent statement of a distinguished Athonite spiritual father, the now late Father Paisios, who is considered by Orthodox not only within Greece, but also around the world, to be a saint. While almost the whole of humanity today is afraid of the disease of **cancer** and calls it 'cursed', that venerable elder, who himself suffered a painful form of cancer for many years without complaining, always stated categorically: 'In the twentieth century, cancer has sent many people to heaven'!

Finally, it is indicative that Leibnitz, who we know was the first to introduce the term 'theodicy', had a very strange view of the **universe**. He considered the present world to be the 'best of all possible worlds'! Yet, such a viewpoint does not only limit the freedom of the **All-powerful** God. It rejects at the same time the dynamism of the world, rendered by the Creator himself. More importantly, it also rejects the gradual **moral perfection** of the human person who, as we have seen, is already placed before various temptations in life, so that the 'image' within can be fulfilled in the 'likeness' of God through the process of **synergy**.

From all the above, it arises as a final conclusion that any explanation of evil or imperfection in the present world will not be sufficient until we reach, in the life to come, the *eschaton* in all its fullness.

Afterword: Theodicy, Eschatology and Postmodernity

Bruce Barber

For more than a decade I have been interested in what has come to be known as the Chicago/Yale conversation concerning the appropriate theological response to the increasing crisis attached to the human experiment we call modernity. A convenient summary of the focus for this response has been to use the language of *inter*textuality (the method proposed by Chicago) versus that of *intra*textuality (the method proposed by Yale). It is no secret to many theological colleagues in Melbourne that I have been an advocate for what I believe to be the sophistication of the intratextual agenda—a sophistication regrettably concealed by the sorts of superficial slogans which all too easily attach themselves to each and every theological enterprise.

I found it encouraging, and in a real sense confirming, to see in the categories being employed during the conference what I take to be the strength of the postliberal enterprise. That these thoughts appear here is due to what I now see to be an injudicious disclosure of them to a friend at the conference.

Those who took part in the conference may well see here and there allusions, indeed even the language, employed over the four days. But they remain an individual construction. I hope that their fragmentary and condensed style may not conceal significant nuances where the claims might have something to them, but above all, I welcome necessary corrections that need to be made, but to which from my partial vantage point I am blind. In order to assist understanding of what I have written, or perhaps better, to reduce the likelihood of misunderstanding, I have taken the course of italicising key words or contrasts in developing the theses.

I would like to record my gratitude for the way the conference has encouraged me to think new thoughts and to make connections hitherto unrecognised.

1. The legacy of modernity

Thesis : *There appears to be theological consensus that the questions posed by theodicy are unable to be answered in the context of creation, much less in the 'hope-less' static categories of a purported 'all powerful' and 'all loving' deity proposed by Enlightenment theologies in the face of the various manifestations of 'evil' identified therein.*

1. The problem of theodicy first arose in the Old Testament in relation to the *specific* problems posed by the *history* of Israel as it attempted to live out the mandates of its covenantal faith in Jahweh. Eschatology, an ingredient in the very *identification* of Jahweh (Exod 3:14), came lately to provide a problematic 'solution' to Israel's experience. It did so by reconfiguring the *theodicy* question ('When will the unequivocal righteousness of God be revealed?') into the *anthropodicy* question ('When and how will the human dilemma of obedience to God be concluded?').

2. This question was answered in the Old Testament by offering to the theodicy/anthropodicy question (i) an *eschatological* 'solution' ('In that day') and (ii) a double destination for human life, one destination for the righteous, and another for the unrighteous (eg Dan 12:2–3). Only in an expanded sense of an anthropodicy can this expectatation be called theodicy, since now with this answer it is revealed that it is *God* who, in the future, will take responsibility for solving the problem of the hidden working out of the righteousness of God in creation. That is to say, in the beginning, we have to recognise that the question of theodicy/anthropodicy was the *exposition* of eschatology, not its *presupposition*.

3. The New Testament, first of all with Paul, accepted this framework for the articulation of Christian faith in the conviction that 'the God of Abraham, Isaac and Jacob' has *already* begun to solve the eschatological problem of anthropodicy. Paul achieved this outcome through a monumental reformulation of this problem in two ways. First, he pushed the eschatological moment *back* into the history of the cross of Jesus of Nazareth, and second, he insisted that in that event there was offered a *single* destination for life for all in the face of the evil which that death represented. For Paul, the justification of God (theodicy) is *at the same time* the justification of the human (anthropodicy) in the God/human, Jesus Christ. The tradition spoke of this reality as *atonement*, in which the unity of God and the human is mediated to the creation on the cross of the new Adam.

4. This christological universal was suppressed by the power of the 'unbaptised' ontotheological God of developing Christendom (the God of the philosophers), which ultimately received its sometimes grotesque theistic and atheistic characterisations in modernity, for example in the phenomenon known as deism. The Enlightenment determined to replace atonement by a second reformulation of theodicy, namely now of a non-christological appeal to the question that human beings 'come of age' must address to their independently constructed ontotheological God. This God it was, and still is, concluded is a God who, in the face of the human estimation of 'evil', is purportedly 'all powerful', or 'all loving' and finally, in one or both of these incarnations, impotent. But at the same time as this restatement of the theodicy question emerges, the centre of gravity shifted from history to nature. The paradigm of history (for which in modernity we human beings are responsible rather than God, and which thereby makes the traditional categories of theodicy/ anthropodicy anachronistic) was required to be replaced by the paradigm of nature, the powers of which still largely elude us. In this modern paradigm, evil is assumed to be a 'problem', such that we must ask 'God' to justify himself/itself to us. In the light of the cross of Christ, this question mus*t always* be regarded as a blasphemous question.

5. As an aside, from the tradition of theological orthodoxy, a possible refutation of the rationalistic Enlightenment concept of evil fuelling the theodicy question could go as follows:

(i) Evil cannot, as modernity demanded, be 'explained', since if it could be so explained it would in principle not come within the radical theological definition of evil. Why is this so?

(ii) An explanation is a continuity. How can one explain a discontinuity, which is what evil ultimately is, by a continuity?

(iii) Therefore, from our side evil always remains, and must continue to remain, the insoluble mystery. Theologically speaking, evil is an 'impossible possibility' (Gen 2:16–17), and it is this which is *revealed* by the cross of the God/man.

2. Theodicy, eschatology and postmodernity

Thesis: *Modernity privileged the 'one' over the 'many'. Some see post-modernity as the inverse, namely the privileging of the many over the one, with the concomitant rejection of the foundationalist[1] quest which was the hallmark of modernity. In the same way, most postmodern theologies accept the postmodern rejection of the Enlightenment view of objectivity, but they continue the modern correlation with human experience, now not as objective and neutral, but as deeply pluralistic. The issue is whether, in the final analysis, this formulation is only modernity in disguise. Whatever be the conclusion, it seems clear that such theologies regard (approved) 'texts' as Christian* visions *of God, inviting* our *quest for their completion. Is this what is meant by 'eschatology'? Is this the identification of* God *as the theos of theology and theodicy? The answer must presumably be: no.*

6. Can the rejection of a 'foundation' be a permanent condition, or is not the implicit, if not explicit, necessity of some 'universal', freed from its hitherto metaphysical pretensions in both premodernity and modernity, sooner or later inevitable? It is, indeed, doubtful whether some form of metaphysics can be dispensed with. But what is under-stood by 'metaphysics'? The conventional understanding of meta-physics is the utilisation of a *foundation* for the projection of an ideal world behind or above the one in which we live. As such, the foundation and the projection essentially function as a 'rationalised mythology'. Whatever power such postulations might once have possessed, they have increasingly become unreal in postmodernity. Although postmodernity in principle rejects the claim of metaphysics, most human beings will inevitably seek to understand the mystery *of* the world and, whether negatively or positively, to live that under-standing. This is in itself the engagement with metaphysics.

7. The *form* of metaphysics offered by Christian faith is that of eschatology, but not that of apocalyptic. Eschatology functions as messianic promise *for* the world, not *above* the world. The difference between apocalyptic and eschatology is that the former offers a *determinate content* to particular messianic promises. Apocalyptic thus

---

1.   Foundationalism may be described as the doctrine that knowledge constitutes a structure the foundations of which support all the rest but themselves need no support. Classic illustrations of foundationalism in modern philosophy may be seen in the concept of 'duty' for Kant and *'geist'* for Hegel. In modern theology, the clearest manifestation is that of *'gefuhl'* (absolute dependence) in Schleiermacher.

functions as a horizon, in contrast to eschatology, which is not *in itself* a horizon but is always the *instrument of disruption* for discerning a horizon.

8. By means of eschatology, Christian faith offers to postmodernity a recovery of the universal by the fundamental structure of what might be called a 'mediating' eschatology. The heart of the Christian faith is the mediating eschatology of the incarnation. The incarnation of the second person of the Trinity (the 'Word made flesh') is the particularisation of the theological universal in such a way that it might be encountered precisely as a universal. Traditional metaphysics concealed the radical expression of this universal by a covert form of Platonism in an effort to *compensate* for the particularity of Christian revelation. Postmodernity has erroneously but understandably come to equate this received non-eschatological covert form of Platonism as the true identity of Christian faith.

9. In contrast, trinitarian mediating eschatology understands that the particularity of Jesus Christ is of universal significance in that *particular* men and women find their fulfilment and completion in him (1 Cor 3:11,12). In the creature, God communicates his own divine nature and makes it a constitutive element in the fulfilment of the creature (divinisation, *theosis*). God is thus both the *origin* and the *end* of this Christian universal, which is why eschatology cannot be identified with *any one particular expression of it*, as might be assumed, for example, by modern physics assuming that God is an alternative to its own speculations about 'the beginning' or 'the end'. Far less may this eschatological foundation function as any identification with the status quo, or some intellectually exhaustive metaphysical entity. This 'founded' hope (a non-foundational foundation?) is expressed communally and liturgically by anticipatory symbols (eg the Lord's Prayer, the sacraments, the sermon), and replaces the modern credo of a resentful anthropocentric requirement of God to justify himself.

10. Neither religious nor non-religious ideologies can finally satisfactorily answer the theodicy question in the way that that question has already been answered in the eschatological foundation of Christian orthodoxy.

Index

God's commands, 13

God's creation, 123, 157, 179

God's creativity, 40

God's deliverance, 6, 24, 35

God's design, 113

God's existence, 1, 116

God's grace, 88

God's judgment, 33

God's justice, 9, 91, 115

God's kingdom, 24, 190

God's love, 6, 71, 99

God's omnipotence, 90, 100, 102

God's patience, 79

God's power, 16, 25, 26, 102, 150, 169

God's purpose, 11, 13, 14, 15, 17, 61, 180

God's sovereignty, 23, 25

God's vindication, 21,

God's way of working in the world, 26, 30, 40

God's wrath, 3, 4, 82, 156, 157, 161

kingdom of God, 23, 24, 29, 35, 141, 186, 187, 188

Son of God, 39, 46, 47, 53, 59, 61, 72, 162, 197

triune God, the 60, 106, 107, 110, 176

goodness, 2, 11, 17, 23, 44, 46, 47, 54, 71, 82, 94, 100, 116, 122, 123,

128, 133, 137, 143, 148, 153, 188, 195, 196

Gospel:

Fourth Gospel, 43-65

of Mark, 19–41, 55, 68, 92, 123, 126, 137

of Matthew, 21, 76

of Philip, 69, 70, 74

of Thomas, 70, 72, 74

grace, 78, 88, 89, 90, 91, 92, 93, 94, 133, 135, 150, 157, 160, 167, 168, 169, 176, 182, 195, 196, 197

Greenberg, I, 99

Gregory of Nazianzus, 52

Hamerton-Kelly, R, 153, 157, 158, 159, 160, 161, 162, 163, 164, 165, 166, 168, 169, 170

Hauerwas, S, 106

Haught, J, 149, 151

Hawking, S, 125

Hays, R, 40, 41

Hesse,M, 124

Hick, J, 76, 82, 98, 101, 132, 135, 140, 141, 142, 143, 146, 148, 152

Holy Spirit, the 37, 48, 56, 57, 58, 59, 72, 75, 76, 79, 81, 93, 107, 109, 110, 116, 176, 184, 188

hope, 1, 14, 16, 17, 20, 24, 25, 26, 36, 40, 67, 81, 84, 89, 91, 93, 106, 110, 111, 112, 114, 116, 117, 118, 119, 120, 121, 123, 143, 150, 152, 154, 155, 157, 179, 202, 206